The Closest
of Enemies

The Closest of Enemies

A PERSONAL

AND DIPLOMATIC ACCOUNT

OF

U.S.–CUBAN RELATIONS

SINCE 1957

Wayne S. Smith

W · W · NORTON & COMPANY
New York · London

Published simultaneously in Canada by Penguin Books Canada Ltd.,
2801 John Street, Markham, Ontario L3R 1B4.
Printed in the United States of America.

The text of this book is composed in Janson, with display type set in Janson.
Composition and manufacturing by The Haddon Craftsmen, Inc.
Book design by Jacques Chazaud.

First published as a Norton paperback 1988

Library of Congress Cataloging in Publication Data

Smith, Wayne S. The closest of enemies.

Includes index. 1. United States—Foreign relations—Cuba. 2. Cuba—Foreign
relations—United States. 3. Castro, Fidel, 1927–   . 4. Cuba—Politics and
government—1959–   . I. Title. E183.8.C9S64   1987   327.7307291   86-12567

ISBN 0-393-30530-9

W. W. Norton & Company, Inc., 500 Fifth Avenue, New York, N. Y. 10110
W. W. Norton & Company Ltd., 37 Great Russell Street, London WC1B 3NU

2 3 4 5 6 7 8 9 0

For Roxanna
and all the others
in the interests-section family
who were in Havana
during that trying spring
and summer of 1980

Contents

Acknowledgments

───────◆───────

The Carnegie Endowment for International Peace gave me temporary shelter immediately after I left the Foreign Service and made it
possible for me to begin this book. For that I am most grateful.

I also wish to thank William Attwood, Bill Bowdler, John Hugh
Crimmins, David Newsom, Larry Pezzullo, Robert Stevenson, Peter
Tarnoff, Pete Vaky, and Bill Wieland for having read all or parts of
the manuscript and for their helpful comments. Any remaining errors and all conclusions and interpretations are of course my own.

The Closest
of Enemies

I

Early Days
1957–1959

Cuba. *Mi Cubita bella*, its people call it—"my beautiful little Cuba." An island of soft beauty, rolling green hills, and graceful royal palms; an island of haunting music and sad legends; an island that has always had a certain fascination for Americans—and since 1959 has frustrated and bedeviled them. Cuba.

I carry with me a vivid memory of a brilliantly clear midnight in 1980 when I was returning to Cuba by air from Miami. As the plane lined up high over the center of the island to begin its westward descent, I could see the lights of Havana directly ahead, and to the north, just over the right wing, the lanterns of fishermen putting out to sea from the inlet at Cojimar, Santiago's village home in Hemingway's *The Old Man and the Sea*. Farther out, the Straits of Florida shimmered in the moonlight, and beyond, in the ethereal distance, the lights of the Florida Keys curved like a string of fireflies off to the northeast.

The image of those two sets of lights etched itself into my mind. How close they were. Only minutes before, I had sat watching the late-night news in the lounge of the Miami airport. In a few more minutes, I would be back in Havana. But as the plane descended and the lights of Key West dropped below the horizon, the fleeting sense of nearness was gone. Gliding down to touch the Cuban land mass, I reentered a world far removed from the United States. The nearness had been an illusion. Only minutes apart and on a clear night visible to the same eye, the United States and Cuba were nonetheless separated by an immense gulf.

A good many years of my life have been devoted to bridging that gulf, and, yes, in earlier years I may have played some small part in creating it. As a junior officer in the U.S. embassy in Havana, I saw Castro's triumphal entry into the city. I was still there two years later when we broke relations and boarded up the windows of the embassy. I was political officer on the Cuban Desk in 1964 when we rejected an overture from Castro that might have been worth exploring. In 1977, I was back in Cuba to take the boards off the embassy windows, having returned with the first group of American diplomats back into the country. Subsequently, I became chief of the U.S. interests section we had set up in 1977. Perhaps I closed a circle by returning. In any event, as Havana had been my first overseas post in the Foreign Service, so would it be my last. In August 1982, in profound disagreement with the Reagan administration's policies, I left the Service.

Though Cuba has played a major role in my life, I came to it quite unintentionally. The decision to join the Foreign Service was deliberate enough; on a bitterly cold night in Korea, suddenly overwhelmed by the absurdity of war, I decided to become a diplomat. Surely it made more sense to spend one's life trying to bring some order and rationality to relations among nations—more sense, that is, than lobbing shells at one another. The decision was made on the basis of a flickering insight and without much knowledge of what diplomats actually do, but from that moment forward I never wavered: I wanted to be a Foreign Service officer. To prepare myself, after the Marine Corps hitch ended, I decided to complete college in Mexico City. I spent three wonderful years there, learning Spanish and studying international relations.

Fidel Castro attacked the Moncada barracks in Santiago de Cuba in July 1953, two months before I arrived in Mexico. Amnestied in 1955, he and his followers also headed for Mexico, and prepared to launch a guerrilla war against Fulgencio Batista. Articles about the Fidelistas appeared from time to time in the Mexican press. I read these with little interest; Cuba occupied my thoughts almost not at all. Fate, however, was even then nudging me toward Havana. My professor, Dr. Francisco Cuevas Cancino, a brilliant Mexican diplomat, suggested that for my master's thesis I compare the Monroe Doctrine and the Iron Curtain.* It turned out to be this thesis more than anything else that led me to Cuba, for when I arrived in Washington in early 1957 looking for a job, the Department of State's Bureau of Intelligence and Research needed a junior analyst who knew something about Communist doctrine and movements in Latin America. In fact, I knew very little, but I applied for the job anyway, hoping that my thesis title would suggest (at least to those who didn't bother to read the thesis) that the author knew something about Communism as it related to Latin America and U.S. interests there. I got the job (and began a frantic reading program on Communist movements in Latin America). Given the moment, it was almost inevitable that one of my first assignments was to assist the analyst who handled Cuba, where the revolution against Batista was gathering steam.

Fidel Castro had by then returned to Cuba aboard the yacht *Granma,* landing in December 1956. Once in the Sierra Maestra, he caught the attention of the world. Certain of his lieutenants also caught the attention of American officials. Ernesto "Che" Guevara and Fidel's brother Raúl were said to be Communists. Some said that Castro himself, if not a Marxist-Leninist, was a Soviet sympathizer. In view of such allegations, a number of us were asked to help out the analyst assessing Castro's political persuasions. We were urged to leave no stone unturned in the effort to ascertain Castro's Marxist-Leninist proclivities—or lack of them. We were to analyze every intelligence report we had on Castro, study his statements, and pore over his background. We had little solid information, but after an exhaustive effort in which I had an exceedingly small part, the intelligence community produced a final report that has stood the test of time. We found no credible evidence to indicate Castro had links to the Communist party or even had much sympathy for it. Even so, he gave cause for concern, for he seemed to have gargantuan ambitions, authoritarian tendencies, and not much in the way of an ideology of his own. He was also fiercely nationalistic. Given the history

*The comparison was not so strained as it may sound. I acknowledged that the two instruments were as different as the two body politics which brought them forth, but based the comparison on the fact that the purpose of both the Doctrine and the Curtain had been to shield new and insecure political systems from an outside world intent on influencing them.

of U.S. military occupations, the Platt amendment,* and the outsized U.S. economic presence in Cuba, he did not hold the U.S. in high regard. One could imagine him turning to the Communists. All depended on what he thought would best advance his interests—and Cuba's, as he interpreted them.

Growing Opposition to Batista

As we proceeded with our analysis of Castro, opposition to Batista within Cuba was mounting. His regime was not being overwhelmed militarily; on the contrary, Batista always controlled tremendously superior forces. The problem was within the corrupt and incompetent regime itself. Batista's police overreacted to insurgent pressure by torturing and killing hundreds, innocent and guilty alike. Bodies were left hanging from trees and alongside roadways. Such tactics inexorably swung public opinion away from Batista, and toward the opposition.

Batista's overreactions also endangered his support from the U.S. In September 1957, part of the garrison at the Cienfuegos naval base, joined by civilian elements in the town, rose in arms against the regime. It was a gallant but quixotic gesture. They were soon surrounded and placed in a hopeless situation. In the ensuing counter-attack against the city, which resulted in considerable loss of civilian life, Batista used tanks, armored cars, and B-26 bombers acquired from the United States. He thereby violated the hemispheric defense agreement under which the U.S., in providing such weapons to Cuba, specifically prohibited their use to maintain internal order. When this violation was pointed out, the Cuban government responded that it had been defending itself against Communism, and this view was supported by the ambassador, Earl E. T. Smith. The Department of State asked for evidence that the rebellion was indeed directed by external forces and was Communist in its orientation. No such evidence was presented, either by Smith or by the Cuban government.

The U.S. Arms Embargo

Eventually, Secretary of State John Foster Dulles himself decided that some sanction had to be imposed against the Batista regime, and

---

*This amendment attached to the Cuban constitution of 1902 asserted the right of the U.S. to oversee Cuba's foreign relations and to intervene in its internal affairs "to maintain order."

on March 14, 1958, an arms embargo was announced. Imposed only days after Batista had again suspended constitutional guarantees, the embargo was widely perceived as a response to that latter step. This was not the case, but as the U.S. was unhappy over the suspension of guarantees also, the misperception at least served a useful purpose.

The embargo's impact was more psychological than substantive, a mild slap on the wrist rather than a serious penalty. It irritated Batista and may have helped further erode his support among the Cuban people, but given the corruption and growing brutality of his regime, that support was already falling away and would have dissipated with or without the embargo. Further, Batista's forces dramatically outnumbered Castro's, were much better armed, and could purchase equipment and ammunition from suppliers other than the U.S. In short, had they been well led and had they used their weapons effectively, they could have defeated Castro at any time. But like the rest of the Batista regime, the army was rotten from within. Its senior officers were venal and woefully inept—just how inept was demonstrated in December 1958 when they sent an armored train against the rebels in Las Villas province. One does not kill many guerrillas from a train fixed solidly to its tracks! Increasingly, too, it was obvious to the common soldier that he was not defending a popular cause. Morale suffered.

While the embargo angered Batista, it convinced neither the Cuban people nor the rebels that the U.S. was really distancing itself from the dictator; rather, the embargo was the result of a typical bureaucratic decision, one which, in trying to straddle all sides of an issue, accomplishes nothing. We suspended arms shipments to Batista, yes, but we left our military mission in Havana to train his troops. Hence, as the latest group of army conscripts finished training in May 1958 and went through graduation exercises just prior to marching off to Oriente province to begin an all-out offensive against Castro, our army attaché and members of the U.S. military mission were prominent on the reviewing stand. The Cuban public could only conclude that the American officers were there to train Batista's troops to fight the rebels. That hardly looked neutral, yet we were supposed to occupy a position of strict neutrality. Nor had it gone unnoticed that Cuban air force chief Col. Carlos Tabernilla, the man who had ordered the bombing of Cienfuegos by B-26s, was given the Legion of Merit by a visiting U.S. military delegation. The Cuban public assumed that Tabernilla was rewarded because he had ordered the bombing.

Finally, how could the U.S. appear neutral when the American ambassador in Havana was so warmly and publicly sympathetic to Batista? In fact, we had two such ambassadors back to back in Havana, both appointed by Eisenhower and both wealthy Republican businessmen with absolutely no previous diplomatic experience. Perhaps they would have done no harm had Cuba been quiet and their role ceremonial. As it was, they were entirely out of their depth and must be held partly responsible for the failure of American policy during that period.

Why the United States persists in sending such amateurs to conduct its relations abroad is difficult to understand. One argument made in favor of political appointees is that the president often needs someone in whom he has personal confidence. Perhaps so, but such a representative needs other qualifications as well—experience in government, and at least some knowledge of the area in which he or she is to serve. The question is not whether ambassadors should be career diplomats or political appointees; rather, it is whether they are to be chosen because of some special competence, or simply because they have contributed greatly to someone's campaign and know the right people. Ambassadors Arthur Gardner (in Havana from 1954 to 1957) and Earl E. T. Smith (who replaced him) were political contributors.

If the imposition of the U.S. embargo in March was a setback for Batista, Castro too had suffered a brief reversal. On April 9 he called for a nationwide general strike to demonstrate the strength of his popular support. The strike fizzled. Santiago de Cuba was pretty well closed down, but few workers in other parts of the country heeded the strike call. In Havana, sporadic acts of violence were easily contained by Batista's police.

The Failure of Batista's Summer Offensive

The strike's failure was interpreted by many, Batista among them, as meaning that Castro's strength had reached its high-water mark. Now seemed the time to deal him a knockout blow. This conclusion was a fatal mistake. Whatever the strike's failure may have said about Castro's lack of wide popular support and about the unwillingness of other groups to cooperate with him, the fact remained that Castro's guerrillas fought well while Batista's army did not. Batista's complacency was not to be penetrated, however. In May, with flags waving, he launched what was intended to be the final offensive against Castro's stronghold in the Sierra Maestra. In terms of logistical and numerical superiority, the offensive should have succeeded. But once again, the troops were poorly led and lacked the will to fight. By August, Batista's forces were in full retreat. And with the collapse of Batista's offensive, Castro himself went over to the attack. Batista's eventual defeat became a certainty.

The failure of the summer offensive altered the situation also with respect to Castro's preeminence. Until that point, he had been the leader of one of the several groups opposed to Batista. His group was called the 26th of July, to commemorate the attack on the Moncada barracks back in 1953. There was also the Directorio Revolucionario (Revolutionary Directorate), composed mostly of students. It had been responsible for the March 13, 1957, attack on the presidential palace in Havana, during which its leader, the very able Antonio Echevarría, had been killed. In 1958, the Directorio was led by Fauré Chaumón and maintained a guerrilla force in the Escambray Mountains in central Cuba.

Also maintaining a guerrilla force in the Escambray was a group known as the Second Front—Escambray. Led by Eloy Gutierrez Menoyo, who had the reputation of being something of a brigand, and an American adventurer, William Morgan, the Second Front had almost no popular base outside the mountains. It did, however, give a good account of itself in fighting.

Then there was the Civic Resistance Movement, led by José Miró Cardona, a former president of the Havana Bar Association. An underground group composed largely of professionals, it tended to be sympathetic to Castro in its views but was not organizationally part of the 26th of July.

And then there was the political opposition—those who wanted to oust Batista and refused to participate in elections as long as he was president, but had not taken up arms against him. This included most of the Ortodoxo party, except for an electionist faction led by Márquez Sterling; a break-away faction of the old Auténtico party, which looked mostly to Tony Varona for leadership and to ex-President Carlos Prío Socarrás for financing; a trade union group led by Angel Cofiño; and several smaller organizations.

Perhaps the most serious challenge to Castro's primacy came from Col. Ramón Barquín and his group of army officers hostile to Batista.

Barquín himself was out of action, having been imprisoned on the Isle of Pines. But Castro's fear had been that other army officers might overthrow Batista and install a junta led by Barquín.

Castro's Emergence as Principal Rebel Leader

Castro's supremacy, then, had not been clear, and had been further called into question by the failure of the general strike. Until the summer of 1958, it had seemed entirely possible that Batista at some point might be replaced by a coalition government comprising all the opposition groups, or by a junta headed by Barquín. But Castro was the one who had turned back Batista's offensive, and Castro was preparing the final push against the dictator. The others now had little choice but to follow his lead. From August 1958 on, Castro did not even have to worry about Colonel Barquín. The army was so demoralized that it would not have fought to install him or anyone else. Castro thus became principal opposition leader. This new status was foreshadowed, perhaps unintentionally, in the fact that when all the opposition groups finally got together and signed a unity pact, in Caracas, on July 20, 1958, Castro was named commander-in-chief. It became increasingly clear that following Batista's ouster, he would dominate the political landscape.

The Ineffectiveness of U.S. Policy

Back in March and April 1958, with Batista's end obviously only a matter of time, it had still appeared that the developing vacuum might be filled by moderate forces. There was a good deal of talk in Department of State staff meetings about such a solution. Indeed, William Wieland, the director of Caribbean and Mexican affairs, had prepared a policy-recommendation paper in which he strongly urged just such an approach—i.e., of encouraging Batista to leave and responsible moderates to step in before it was too late. Even a young and totally inexperienced officer such as I was in 1958 could see that Wieland was right. Clearly, we should have sought a middle way, and even in retrospect, it is difficult to understand why we did not. Several opportunities presented themselves. The United States passed up each one. In part, it seemed to me at the time, this occurred because continuing disagreements between Ambassador Smith and the Department of State hamstrung the decision-making process until it was too late. To be sure, both seemed to agree that the best option for the U.S. was to have Batista relinquish power to "responsible" elements who would close the door to Castro, or at least reduce his role in any future transitional government. But there the agreement ended. Smith regarded these elements as including people linked to Batista. His idea seemed to be that Batista should appoint someone, whom the U.S. would then support even if he were a Batista stooge and whether or not Batista left the country. Smith failed to understand that no new government in any way identified with Batista could win acceptance in Cuba, except among the pro-Batista crowd with whom he socialized. The Department of State, on the other hand, was convinced that Batista's departure was key. State was also skeptical that anyone identified with Batista could win popular support, even with Batista out of the way. Ambassador Smith and the Department of State thus proceeded from different assumptions and worked toward different goals.[1] They continued to do so, thwarting one another's efforts, until it was too late to do anything but watch Castro march into Havana. Nor did anyone more senior—such as Secretary of State Dulles—ever step in to set a clear course and put an end to the bickering. American policy in 1958, then, was simply sterile. We talked a bit about what we ought to do, but in fact we did nothing.

An example of opportunities missed can be seen in the U.S. reaction to the efforts of the Cuban bishops in February 1958 to bring an end to the fighting. In a statement issued on the twenty-eighth, the bishops lamented Cuba's chaotic state and called for an end to violence. To Batista's irritation, the statement went further and proposed the formation of a provisional government. "We do not doubt," the statement read, "that those who truly love Cuba will know how to accredit themselves before God and before history, not refusing any sacrifice in order to achieve a government of national unity which might prepare the return of our Fatherland to a peaceful and normal political life."[2]

The key to the statement centered around the meaning of "a government of national unity." Batista assumed the clergy meant for him to resign, and he immediately countered by reasserting his intention to hold "free and open" elections in June (later postponed until November) but to remain in office until his term expired in February 1959.

For his part, Castro responded by asking the bishops to specify the nature of their suggested national-unity government, and by stating flatly that any government presided over by Batista would be unacceptable to the 26th of July.[3] Another armed opposition group, the

Directorio Revolucionario, hailed the Church's call for peace, but added that "there can only be peace if Batista resigns immediately and a provisional government of national unity is formed to return liberty and democracy to the people."[4]

The bishops followed up by organizing a "Harmony Committee" to try mediation. But with Batista refusing to resign and the opposition refusing to consider any solution short of his immediate resignation, there was no middle ground from which to begin negotiations. The committee gave up and disbanded within five days of its organization.

The U.S. had no hand in the bishops' statement. Previous to its issuance, however, Ambassador Smith had been approached by the papal nuncio, Monsignor Luis Centóz, who discussed with him at some length an earlier version of the statement. According to the nuncio's explanation, the national-unity government would include representatives from all segments—the political opposition, the rebels, and the Batista government. But it was to be presided over by Batista. As a matter of fact, the nuncio even spoke of creating a bridge between Castro and Batista—a wildly implausible idea at that stage in the game. According to Ambassador Smith's account of the interview:

When the Papal Nuncio asked if the United States Government would lend its support to the Church's plans, I regretted to say that I was unable to get any commitment from the State Department. The State Department would not permit me to give any indication of support to the Roman Catholic Church. The position of the State Department was that only if the efforts of the Church were proven successful would the U.S. issue any public statement of endorsement. To do otherwise would be considered intervention.[5]

The Department of State may have been rightly skeptical of the bishops' plan. Unless accompanied by Batista's resignation, it could not have worked. Yet, the department probably surmised, it could not count on its ambassador discreetly to insinuate that precondition. Hence, it did nothing and the moment passed. Had State been more energetic in pursuing its goal, one can imagine a different outcome. Neither Castro nor the other opposition groups rejected the bishops' plea; they only rejected Batista as part of a national-unity government. Had the U.S. at that moment chosen to work quietly but energetically behind the scenes, there was at least a chance the bishops might have been persuaded to urge Batista's resignation, and even a chance that Batista, knowing the U.S. as well as the Church stood behind the demand, would have complied. It was at least worth a try.

But immobilized by policy disputes, the U.S. let the opportunity pass.

Another Missed Chance

An even more promising opportunity emerged on March 18, 1958, when the highly prestigious Joint Committee of Civic Institutions, composed of forty-two religious, professional, and fraternal organizations, issued a lengthy statement demanding that Batista resign immediately and relinquish power to a completely neutral provisional government "comprising *citizens of outstanding prestige.*"[6] To many observers this proposal offered a possible way out. The Joint Committee itself was widely respected. Being outspokenly anti-Batista, it could count on popular support, yet its leaders were men of stature and moderation who would also have the support of the business elements, most of the other anti-Batista groups to the right of center, and even wide segments of the armed forces. Too, Batista had been forced to suspend constitutional guarantees, and on March 14 (as previously noted) the United States had imposed an embargo on the shipment of arms to his government. He was thus in a much weaker position than two weeks previously, when the Church had issued its unsuccessful call for peace; it seemed reasonable to believe he might listen to the Joint Committee's demands, particularly if the weight of the United States government was thrown behind them, albeit discreetly. Castro, on the other hand, was still relatively weak (as evidenced by the failure of his general strike only three weeks later), and might at that point have been compelled to accept the provisional government once Batista resigned and left the country.

One would have expected a U.S. leap to the support of the Joint Committee's statement, but there was none. Ambassador Smith's position on this was not only ambiguous, it surpassed understanding. He did seem to recognize the critical need for a transitional government. In his own words:

It was becoming more and more clear that the only way to salvage the situation was eventually to have Batista relinquish the presidency *and concurrently appoint** a broadly based national unity government without Castro and without representatives of the terrorists, but including representatives of the better elements of the opposition.[7]

---

*Emphasis mine. Smith never understood that no government appointed by *Batista* would have been acceptable to the opposition.

In his book, Smith maintains that he had an exchange of views concerning a possible national-unity government with Cuban civic leaders, including Dr. Guillermo Belt, a former Cuban ambassador to the United States. Smith does not mention the date of that meeting, but from the chronology of events it would appear to have taken place either in late 1957 or very early 1958—at any rate, well before the Joint Committee's March 18 statement. "The cooperation of none of these individuals," Smith wrote later of his meeting with Dr. Belt and his associates, "could be obtained without the support of the United States. . . . None of them would dare risk incurring the wrath of both the Batista government and Fidel Castro unless a peace plan had a chance of success. They knew they could not succeed without the support of the United States."[8]

Having led up to that conclusion, Smith sidesteps all responsibility by declaring that "on the grounds of non-intervention, the State Department never seriously explored any suggested plan for a peaceful solution that would exclude Castro."[9] In other words, his hands (he claims) were tied by the Department of State. His argument that the civic leaders were not willing to act without the prior assurance of American support is demolished, however, by the fact that they *did* act, not only without U.S. support, but actually in the face of Smith's opposition. Smith himself seems to see no inconsistency here and describes the incident in his book. On March 14, he writes, he was informed that the Joint Committee of Civic Institutions intended to issue a public statement. Not wanting the committee to impair its future usefulness as a mediative body (a strange conclusion indeed!), he tells us, he felt that "the committee should know, before making a public statement, that Batista was prepared to create a favorable atmosphere in which to hold general elections and to engender a feeling of confidence in the people of Cuba that the elections would be honest."[10]

Smith therefore asked Raúl de Velasco, the chairman of the Joint Committee, to call on him at his residence. According to Smith's account of the meeting, he informed de Velasco that "there might be a chance for success if it was their desire to approach Batista."[11] Smith, in other words, clearly envisaged a solution that in one way or another included Batista or at least enjoyed his blessing.

Smith says nothing else of the meeting, but de Velasco has related his own recollections of it. "I told Ambassador Smith," he says, "that I thought he was wrong and asked him if he did not realize that

so in December. But by December it was too late to do any good.

The fear of appearing to intervene, so often cited by senior officials at the time, was more than anything else a rationale for doing nothing. For example, Dulles had had no qualms at all about intervening in Guatemala, but years later, when it was suggested that we ought to embrace democratic leaders in the hemisphere, Dulles's response was that to so adjust our relations would open us to charges of intervention.[15] In other words, if it suited us to intervene, we did so without hesitation. If on the other hand we wished to support the status quo, then we justified inaction on the grounds of not wishing to intervene. Our nonintervention policy was a sham, and a transparent one at that.

Some might argue that the Joint Committee's proposal had no chance, that Castro would never have accepted the transitional government it called for and the civil war would have gone on even if the U.S. had put its weight behind the peace effort. But was that really true? In March 1958 it might not have been. The Cuban people wanted Batista out; they did not necessarily want Castro in. Not at that point. Had Batista left the country and been replaced by a respected transitional government, public opinion would almost certainly have rallied behind that new government, leaving Castro sitting in the mountains with a handful of followers.

True, Castro's charisma and political adroitness would in time almost certainly have made him a major figure on the Cuban political stage—but in a very different context. A moderate transitional government taking power in March or April 1958 doubtless would have returned to the Constitution of 1940 and held elections. Sooner or later, Castro probably would have decided to come down out of the mountains and participate in the new political process. He would have made his mark, but within the restraints of a constitutional system. That would have been a very different thing.

We cannot know what might have been. Possibly even with U.S. encouragement, efforts to get Batista out and a moderate group in would have failed. Clearly, however, the opportunity was there and was worth our best shot. We made no effort at all.

Our Arrival in Havana

As Batista's all-out summer offensive ground to an ignominious halt, I was packing my bags to head for Havana. During the year I had served in the Department of State, I had taken and passed both the written and oral examinations for the Foreign Service. In May 1958, I was sworn in as a Foreign Service officer. Because of my work on Cuba, when I had finished the short orientation course for new officers, I was transferred immediately to Havana.

I did not go alone. For several months I had been courting Roxanna Phillips, a beautiful and charming young lady who also worked in the Department of State. In late July, we headed south as newlyweds. The slow trip by car from Washington to Key West, where we took the ferry to Havana, was our honeymoon, as were in a sense our early months in Havana. Despite the turmoil around us, it was a time of great happiness—one reason, surely, that Cuba will always be our special place.

There was much more to it than that, however. From the moment we sailed into Havana harbor, I felt a strong attraction to the place. In part, it had to do with the beauty of the island, with the softness of its landscape, and the warm amiability of its people—under any ruler, among the wittiest, most fun-loving, enterprising, and humane in the world. They seemed to dislike no one.

There was some racial discrimination before the Revolution, but the sort of intense bigotry found in the United States was simply unknown. Blacks, whites, indeed all races and nationalities, lived together in harmony. And while Cuban nationalists strongly resented past U.S. intervention in their country's affairs, they did not evince a personal antipathy toward Americans. Quite the contrary, we got on well together.

Certainly we had shared a lot of history, something else I found fascinating about Cuba. As we sailed down the harbor, we passed the spot where the battleship *Maine* had exploded; passed the plaza where a Kentuckian, Col. William Crittenden, and his men had been executed in 1851 after an unsuccessful filibustering expedition; passed the old Spanish Palace of the Captains General, which had been used as American military headquarters during the occupations. One could almost see Gen. Leonard Wood striding out into the plaza to review the troops. We could see also in the distance the district of Lawton, named after Gen. Henry W. Lawton—as had been Lawton, Oklahoma, where I lived as a boy when my father was an artillery officer at Fort Sill.

I seemed that first evening to be entering a city which through some subconscious process was already familiar to me. Years before, when I was a homesick cadet at Gulf Coast Military Academy in

Gulfport, Mississippi, many of my classmates were Cubans. As they gathered during the evenings to talk with deep longing of their homes, I formed mental images of Havana, Trinidad, Santiago de Cuba, and other parts of the island, absorbing also some of their nostalgia for these places. Thus, years later, though seeing Havana for the first time, I had the sense of "coming home."

No slot was open in the embassy political section, so I spent my first year in Havana as a visa officer. I found the work frustrating, but not without advantages. It was, for one thing, strictly a nine-to-five job, so I had plenty of time to do background reading, and to develop a feel for the situation.

One fact was clear: popular rejection of Batista was so strong that one could feel it in the air. Repudiated by his own people and with his army refusing to fight for him, Batista was in an entirely untenable position. The idea advanced recently by some in the Reagan administration that the U.S. should have kept Batista in power is absurd. Short of another military occupation, there was no way the U.S. could have maintained him in the presidency.

During my second month at the embassy, I and other newly arrived officers received a briefing on the political situation from Daniel Braddock, the deputy chief of mission. Our hope, Braddock said, was that the national elections, now scheduled for November 1958, would open the way for some solution. The rebels would not treat with the Batista regime, but they might with a new government. If so, an end to the civil war could perhaps be worked out and an effort at national reconciliation begun.

I remember my incredulity, which I could not resist expressing. I asked Braddock if we should not have tried months before to convince Batista to give up power? But as we had not, was it not too late for the kind of electoral solution Braddock had just described? Clearly, the recent failure of Batista's summer offensive presaged the end of his regime. Castro had the initiative. Were his forces not likely soon to begin advancing up the island? And had Castro not already rejected the elections as a farce? Hence, could even honest elections and an opposition victory—both unlikely—end the civil war? Elections would solve nothing, I noted, if Castro's forces were on the outskirts of Havana by election day.

Braddock insisted that our policy had been and still was the best available course. We could not have tried to convince Batista to leave, he said; that would have constituted intervention in Cuba's internal

29

affairs. The elections now offered the best chance of bringing about positive change.

Following the briefing, however, Braddock called me aside. Speaking personally, he acknowledged that my reservations were not without foundation. Nonetheless, he emphasized, Ambassador Earl E. T. Smith was convinced Batista would live up to his promise that the elections would be clean and impartial. The rest of us in the embassy had to show a unified front in supporting that hope. Braddock concluded that the best outcome we could hope for was that Márquez Sterling, perhaps the most respected candidate in the race—or, more accurately, the least discredited—would win. Although Castro said he would not negotiate with the winner, he might change his mind if Márquez Sterling turned out to be the new president.

I wondered to myself why Castro would negotiate with Sterling or anyone else when he so clearly held the military advantage. I had already played the brash young man to the hilt, however, so I did not argue the matter further with Braddock. In any event, I sensed that Braddock agreed with me in greater measure than his loyalty to the ambassador permitted him to acknowledge.

Shortly thereafter I learned that my intuition about Braddock had been correct. William G. Bowdler, the second officer in the embassy political section (and later assistant secretary of state for American republics affairs) told me at lunch that he had written a long policy-recommendation message following the defeat of Batista's summer offensive. In it, he had pointed out that the defeat clearly presaged the end of the regime. We were now faced with a last chance. If we could get Batista out and a moderate transitional government in before Castro's counteroffensive gathered steam, there was still a slim chance that such a solution would hold. If we waited, our last opportunity would be lost.

Bowdler said Braddock had enthusiastically approved the message, indicating his full agreement with its analysis of the situation. Ambassador Smith, however, had refused to send it. We were not going to pressure Batista to leave, he had said; rather, we were going to support his elections, which he, Smith, was sure would be honest.

Ambassador Smith's confidence in Batista was misplaced. The November elections were marred by obvious fraud. Batista's candidate, Andrés Rivero Agüero, was elected to the presidency on the strength of stuffed ballot boxes and tombstone votes. Even Ambassador Smith seems to have understood the implications—at least in retrospect. Writing a few years later, he said: "Batista's failure to live up to his solemn promise to me that he would hold full and open elections was his last big mistake. . . . As a result of the elections, he lost whatever followers he had left."[16]

A Trip into the War Zone

Election day, November 3, found me in Preston, a United Fruit plantation town on the north coast of Oriente province. Another consular officer and I had been sent there to bury the American victims and bring out the sole American survivor of a plane crash. The plane, a Cubana airlines Viscount bound from Miami to Varadero, had been hijacked in midair by men who claimed to be members of Castro's 26th of July movement. They had forced the pilot to fly to Oriente province, apparently intending to land at a rebel-held airfield in the mountains. The rebels, however, had refused to light the field even though the plane buzzed it several times. Survivors could only surmise that the hijackers had been acting on their own and were not expected by the rebels on the ground. Whatever the case, they flew on to nearby Preston and after circling for some time tried to land the plane on the small airstrip there. It undershot the runway and crashed into Nipe Bay. All of the plane's crew and most of the passengers had died. According to the few survivors, two of the hijackers had managed to get out and swim to shore. The bodies of three other hijackers, however, were recovered from the submerged wreckage. By the time we reached Preston the next day, the local police sergeant had them on exhibit in a railway boxcar across the road from the small jail. But it wasn't his idea, he insisted. The police commander in Antilla, across the bay, had ordered him to display the hijackers' bodies until he could take accurate pictures of them—with a flash camera, the commander had specified. "But where am I going to get a flash camera?" the sergeant asked.

By next evening, someone in the community had provided one—doubtless to get rid of the grisly sights and smells from the boxcar.

The American survivor was only slightly injured, but was in the hospital with a bad case of shock. He had lost his wife and three children in the crash. Born in Cuba, he had gone to school in the United States, become a naturalized American citizen, and married a girl from Memphis. They had lived happily in the U.S., he said, but the thought gnawed at him that his family should see the island of his birth. He had been bringing them to Cuba when the plane was hijacked.

We buried them at dusk—the wife and three children. None had been outside the U.S. before. They had not lived to see Cuba—except perhaps as a dark mass hurtling up to meet them during those last terrifying seconds. Ironically, and tragically, though they had not known Cuba in life, they would rest there forever, far from anyone who knew or loved them.

Only the town doctor, the priest, and I followed the hearse to the small cemetery near the palm-fringed bay where they had died. As we laid them to rest and walked back to the village in the gathering darkness, the civil war and the sweep of political forces in conflict seemed unimportant. What mattered were the human lives involved, and here were four innocent ones, snuffed out needlessly and most brutally. The melancholy of the moment was almost overwhelming —and not just to me. The doctor, obviously wondering where his own road might end, kept muttering to himself, "Not among strangers; let it not be like this, among strangers."

Like much of Oriente province, the area around Preston was not held by the army after dark. At nightfall, the small garrison barricaded itself in the barracks, leaving the rebels to roam as they pleased until sunrise. Even during the day, the rebels could move through the area almost at will, for the army's principal objective seemed to be to avoid contact; the soldiers retreated at the first sound of gunfire. Shortly after we arrived in Preston, fighting had taken place near the airstrip, almost a mile outside the town. One soldier had been killed and one wounded. The airport for a short time ceased operations. By the evening after we buried the American family, however, it was open again, and Cubana decided to risk sending in a DC-3 to pick up the bodies of the crew members, and any survivors in condition to fly out. Our American citizen was pronounced fit to travel. His wounds were mostly emotional; the farther he got from the scene of his personal tragedy, the better the chance that they might heal, or at least form a protective crust. I accompanied him back to Havana, and what a flight it turned out to be. The pilot, anxious to take off before we attracted rebel fire, was revving his motors even before the passengers—both alive and deceased—were aboard. Some seventy-two hours had passed since the crash. None of the bodies had been embalmed, and several had been in the water thirty-six hours or more. Carpenters had done what they could to make the wooden coffins airtight, but to little avail. Within minutes after take-off, a ghastly smell filled the entire plane. The hostess at first moved up and down the aisle with an aerosol can of Pine Scent, but that only made the smell worse. Before the plane had been in the air twenty minutes, we were all pressed wretchedly against the windows, handkerchiefs clutched over our mouths and noses. To make matters worse, we could not fly directly to Havana; we had to refuel in Camagüey, about a third of the way up the island. We arrived there only to find that a military aircraft, badly shot up by rebel fire as it flew out of Oriente province, had crashed on the runway. We circled the airfield for what seemed like hours, waiting for the debris to be cleared away. Then it was down for half an hour's respite before the last leg to Havana, another hour of sheer misery. By the time we arrived in the capital, our senses were so numb that most of us stepped off in something of a trance.

A Meeting with Ambassador Smith

The next morning, I repeated to Ambassador Smith the account of the hijacking we had heard from the survivors. Tall and always immaculately dressed, Smith looked like what he was, a successful financier. This was my first talk of any length with him. That Smith did not speak Spanish was well known, but I was nonetheless surprised to discover that he could not pronounce the simplest Spanish name. How could he possibly gain any feel for Cuban reality if he had to work entirely through interpreters?

On this occasion, Smith was interested only in determining that the hijackers had indeed put on 26th of July armbands after taking over the plane. Having satisfied himself on that point, he lost interest in my report. I informed him of the Cuban army's defeatist tactics in the Preston area and ventured the opinion that if these was representative of the way the army was fighting, the rebels would soon win by default.

Smith shrugged his shoulders and said there were still ways of keeping Castro out of power. I was then dismissed.

Smith was not highly regarded by the majority of staff; rather, they considered him a dilettante. He, in turn, was not only rude to the staff but obviously distrusted them. He would barely speak to John Topping, the embassy's chief political officer. Topping, a cool professional with years of experience in Latin America, knew what was happening in Cuba. However, he was not permitted to send a word to Washington that Smith had not first seen and approved—and Smith approved very little. In the consequent bickering between them, Topping—the subordinate—was always the loser. Bill Bowdler, Topping's assistant, often tried to play peacemaker, but usually succeeded only in diverting the ambassador's wrath his way.

The atmosphere in the embassy, in short, was poisonous. It got worse as the Batista regime neared its end and the certainty grew that divergent assessments and predictions would soon be tested by history.

Last-Minute Efforts to Persuade Batista to Leave

In mid-December, Batista sent his children's passports to the embassy for U.S. visas. Under normal circumstances that would have caused no antennae to quiver. Most upper-class Cubans kept their U.S. visas up-to-date; a request for visa revalidation did not necessarily mean imminent travel. Under the conditions in December 1958, however, the request was taken as sign that Batista was poised to flee the country.

What we in the embassy did not know—except for the CIA station chief, Jim Noel—was that on the night of December 9, William Pawley, a Republican businessman long connected with Cuba (he had founded Cubana de Aviacion), had seen Batista and urged him to leave the country. Not even Ambassador Smith had been informed of Pawley's top-secret mission by the U.S. government. He was aware of it, however, having been told by a Cuban citizen in November that such an emissary was to be sent.[17] So much for the mission's confidentiality!

Pawley had been sent by the Eisenhower administration, but was not authorized to identify himself as an official emissary; rather, he had been told to say that he came as a concerned private citizen representing a group of influential friends in the U.S. Realizing that such credentials would carry no weight with Batista, Pawley fudged, hinting but not stating explicitly that he came on behalf of President Eisenhower. His proposal was simple: Batista himself should turn power over to a caretaker junta and leave the country. If he did so, he would be allowed to take up residence in his Daytona Beach mansion.[18]

Batista immediately detected the ambiguous, semiofficial nature of Pawley's mission and flatly rejected the proposal. He must nonetheless have understood its significance: it signaled the end of American support. If he still had any doubts, they were dispelled the next day.

Actually, sending a message through a private emissary like Pawley would have been unnecessary if Ambassador Smith had carried out instructions he had received in November. In Dispatch 292 of that month, he was told to inform the Cuban government that U.S. support for the regime of President-elect Rivero Agüero would depend upon a number of things, the most important being the regime's ability to win the acceptance of broad segments of the Cuban people, including the nonviolent opposition. He was also to have expressed U.S. doubts that any internal solution could be worked out as long as Batista was in the country. And, finally, Smith had been instructed to tell the Cubans that the U.S. would provide no more arms.

Although urged by John Topping to carry out these instructions, Smith, incredibly, sat on them. He expressed the view that to transmit the contents of the dispatch might simply open the way to chaos. He intended first to get a clarification from the White House itself. Meanwhile, Dispatch 292 remained in his hold box.[19] At the same time, despite his acknowledged perception that the questionable nature of the November elections had lost Batista any support he might have enjoyed, and despite the reservations he knew his own government to have about supporting the fraudulently elected Rivero Agüero, Smith inexplicably sent telegrams to both Batista and Rivero Agüero congratulating them on the outcome of the elections! How could they avoid concluding that this signaled continued U.S. support despite the fraudulent elections and Batista's expressed intention to remain in Cuba? In other words, Smith directly violated the instructions in Dispatch 292.

On the evening of December 10, Smith was in Washington on consultations—in fact seeking the clarification of Dispatch 292. Acting in Smith's place, Braddock called on Cuban prime minister Gonzalo Guell and saw an opportunity to get across the gist of 292 without usurping the ambassador's privilege. Braddock simply noted to Guell his personal belief that Rivero Agüero would have to win the support of the Cuban people as a whole before the U.S. government would provide any backing. To do that, it seemed clear, he would have to negotiate with the nonviolent opposition, including the pro-Castro civic organizations. He also believed, Braddock said, that Batista would have to leave the country before the U.S. would endorse the Rivero Agüero government. Otherwise, the American public might conclude that the U.S. was simply backing a continuation of the Batista regime in a new guise.[20]

Guell doubtless reported the conversation immediately to Batista, who would have had little choice but to interpret it as another gun in a building U.S. campaign to get him to leave the country.

The next gun was sounded on December 17. In Washington, Smith had argued vehemently in favor of resuming arms shipments to Cuba and throwing U.S. support firmly behind a national-unity government appointed by Rivero Agüero, even if Batista did not leave the country. The choice, Smith had argued, was simply between Batista and Castro. But the Department of State remained adamantly opposed, convinced that no national-unity government identified with Batista had any chance of success. In its view, the only way to keep Castro out of power was for Batista to turn power over to a respected coalition government, in no way identified with him, and then to leave the country. Smith was therefore sent back to Havana with orders, in effect, to carry out the instructions he had been given in Dispatch 292. On December 17, Smith reluctantly delivered the messages in question to Batista.[21] The latter did not indicate agreement. He did not say he would leave. One can imagine, however, that mentally he began to pack his bags.

Nothing in the military situation could have encouraged Batista. The rebels had cut the island in two and were attacking in Las Villas province. Batista's own army was nearing disintegration. Castro's final triumph was clearly only weeks, even days, away. Was it realistic, then, to expect Pawley's mission, or Smith's request to Batista to leave, to accomplish anything more than advance the inevitable by a few days? Obviously not. Momentum had passed to Castro with the failure of Bastista's summer offensive. By December, there was no longer any chance for a moderate government, one falling between what many regarded as the two extremes, Castro and Batista. The U.S. had lost its opportunities. As 1958 came to a close, thoughtful observers could only look back in pain, as on a bridge player who had held his aces too long, until they were all trumped.

Ambassador Smith subsequently charged that Department of State officers such as William Wieland, the director of Caribbean and Mexican affairs, had really been Castro sympathizers and deliberately sidetracked all efforts to keep him out of power. This was not true. I attended a meeting in 1958 at which Wieland stated categorically that while Batista was "bad medicine for everyone, Castro would be worse." Wieland, moreover, had urged that the U.S. encourage Batista to leave and responsible moderates to take over, precisely so as to deny power to Castro. If anyone had failed to work for such a policy, it was Smith, not Wieland.

It was also clear that Smith, not Wieland, had sabotaged our neutrality policy. Smith had been unmistakably and publicly sympathetic to Batista, as had his predecessor, Arthur Gardner.

Who had appointed these two amateurs? And who had permitted Smith to ignore or violate his instructions? The answer is unavoidable: President Eisenhower and Secretary of State Dulles. Responsibility ran all the way to the top. Indeed, senior levels of U.S. government had given little attention to Cuba, or to the rest of Latin America. If Secretary Dulles thought about them at all, it seemed to be simply to assure himself that their governments were anti-Communist, no matter what else they might be. Thus, in the name of democracy and liberty, we had warmly supported brutal dictatorships. Few outside the United States could understand how the two things squared. How could one further democracy by backing repressive regimes that created the conditions for revolution and the rise of dictatorships of the left? Any but the most superficial analysis suggested that one could not, but superficial analysis was about all the U.S. could spare for the Third World. The failure of U.S. policy in Cuba prior to 1959 was a reflection of much wider deficiencies in U.S. decision making, as will be seen in the next chapter.

Life in Havana during the War's Last Days

If tensions were high in Havana those last weeks of the civil war, life went on much as before. The night clubs and casinos prospered. Restaurants were crowded and streets throbbed with the unique and compelling music of Cuba. Not to be outdone by the Cubans, Roxanna and I spent many of those last evenings out on the town. One of our favorite spots was the Bodeguita del Medio, a small bohemian bar-restaurant around the corner from Cathedral Square. The Bodeguita had for years been one of Ernest Hemingway's hangouts. His picture hung on every wall. Errol Flynn was in Havana in December and at a corner table at the Bodeguita most evenings. Flynn later claimed—though not very insistently—that he had been in the mountains during the fighting. If so, his was a fast trip up and back, for the corner table was rarely unoccupied.

The owner and employees of the Bodeguita did little to hide their sympathies for Castro and his bearded guerrillas. One could often hear music there associated with the rebel cause—such as *Cama de piedra* ("Bed of Stone"), an old Mexican revolutionary song, and *Mamá, son de la loma* ("Mama, they're from the hill"), which was so closely identified with the 26th of July that its clandestine radio station, Radio Rebelede ("Rebel Radio"), had adopted it as something of a theme song. The government had banned the song from commercial radio channels. Even at the Bodeguita, the musicians played it only at the request of foreigners, and only after looking around nervously.

Another of our favorite hangouts was El Colmão, a Spanish nightclub featuring flamenco music and wine drunk from a goatskin. As at the Bodeguita, the crowd at El Colmão was decidedly pro-rebel. Instead of playing *Mamá, son de la loma,* however, the musicians there played civil-war songs of the Spanish Republic—the lost cause. The audience would often join in singing these sad but stirring melodies and sometimes made it clear that the lyrics had as much relevance for Cuba as for Spain. One evening a patron became so carried away by the music—and perhaps by the wine—that he leaped to his feet and began shouting, "Abajo el tirano, abajo el dictador!" ("Down with the tyrant, down with the dictator!"). He was quickly silenced and hustled outside. Waiters then went around insisting to the other patrons that "he was referring to Franco, of course."

El Colmão was not closed down in the days that followed, so either spies from Batista's secret police had not been there that evening, or they had believed the waiters' story.

The Flight of Batista

As we enjoyed ourselves at the Bodeguita and El Colmão, the rebels down the island continued to advance. By the end of December, the Batista regime was a walking corpse.[22] Bets were being taken as to when the dictator would flee. In what can only be seen as a last cruel joke on his fellow Cubans, Batista decided to leave secretly on New Year's Eve. The rest of the country woke up the next morning to face not only a hangover but an uncertain future.

Roxanna and I had attended the diplomatic corps' ball that evening. Having had a wonderful time and probably too much champagne, we returned home about 2 A.M., and we had just dropped off to sleep, it seemed, when there came a pounding on the door. Opening it, I faced a groggy embassy officer leaning precariously against the doorframe. The ambassador, he said, wanted all officers to report to the embassy immediately.

With that, he stumbled off down the stairs, the smell of New Year's heavy in his wake. "What is the meeting about?" I shouted down the stairs after him. His only response was an unsteady wave. Suddenly coming wide awake, the obvious hit me: Batista had fled the country! I rushed to the radio. Confirmation spilled out in the form of *Mamá, son de la loma.* That this song was on the radio again meant the rebels had won.

Dressing quickly and heading for the embassy, I got full confirmation on the car radio. Batista had fled just after midnight, leaving the government in the hands of Gen. Eulogio Cantillo. I remember feeling a wave of excitement, and relief—relief because at last the civil war was over and the killing could stop, excitement because to face the unknown is always an intense experience. And at that moment in Cuban history we *were* looking down an unknown road. Batista had been a given quantity, albeit an unacceptable one. About Castro, no one could know for sure. We, and the Cubans, could now only hope for the best.

I wasn't to get home again for three days. During most of that first day and night I was busy making the rounds of the big hotels, reassuring American tourists and suggesting that they stay put until some means was found to get them back to the States. They were in no real danger, and there was no shortage of food or drink.

Meanwhile, the city had exploded with joy. Cars flying the 26th of July flag raced through the streets honking. People milled around, shouting, singing, and hugging each other. There was little fighting. A few Batista supporters who had holed up at various locations around town shot it out with 26th of July militants, but most were subdued within a few hours. My wife was trapped in a neighbor's apartment by one such shoot-out and had to wait until dusk to return home. It was almost funny as she told the story later. The neighbor she was visiting, Mrs. Sonia Mullin, was very pregnant. Mrs. Mullin, Roxanna, and another lady were talking in the living room, which was entirely exposed at the front, the glass doors leading to the balcony having been folded back against the outside wall. As they talked, they heard what they took to be fireworks. It must be the 26th of July celebrating Castro's victory, one commented. The popping noise added a festive note to the conversation until an American military attaché who lived on a floor above shouted down the air shaft, "For God's sake, Mrs. Mullin, get down on the floor; that's gunfire."

The tea-party atmosphere evaporated instantly as the three ladies did a quick crawl toward an interior room. There they felt relatively safe, but as the firing went on, Mrs. Mullin became increasingly agitated. Visions of a premature delivery with herself as the midwife flashed through Roxanna's mind—and probably through that of the other lady as well. The three sat huddled together for several hours, not fearing the guns outside so much as nature's way inside. But all turned out well. The firing stopped by dusk. Mrs. Mullins did not go into labor until two weeks later, when she delivered a lovely baby girl.

Some looting of the homes of Batista supporters occurred before the new authorities put a stop to it. The principal targets of the crowds that first day, however, were the parking meters and the casinos. Every meter was knocked off its metal pole; there hasn't been a parking meter in Havana since. Why? Because they were associated in the public mind with graft. It was well known that a Batista relative had the concession and every centavo from the meters went into his pocket.

The casinos too were associated with corruption. Most were operated by the Mafia. All but one were ransacked that morning. George Raft, who operated the casino at the Capri Hotel, was there as the mob started up the stairs of the hotel's main entrance. According to eyewitnesses, Raft faced the crowd alone and said in his best gangster snarl, "Yer not comin' in my casino."

Apparently having seen enough American gangster movies to fear cement shoes if they ignored him, the crowd turned around and moved off toward the casino at the Hotel Nacional, a block away.

Efforts to Evacuate Americans

Cantillo resigned almost immediately, and Castro was still in Oriente province, so liaison with the new authorities—or even finding out who they were—was exceedingly difficult. By the second day, nonetheless, John Topping and Bill Bowdler had managed to reach the 26th of July organization in Havana and get authorization to evacuate American citizens by charter flights. Those who wished to leave were told to gather at the Hotel Nacional. Convoys were to pull in every hour or so to take them to the airport. Along with Ernie Duff, another young vice-consul, I was sent over to the Nacional to keep order as the Americans waited to board the convoys. Simple enough. The problem was that after the first convoy pulled out about 10 A.M., we didn't see another until nightfall. Meanwhile, the line got longer and the sun hotter. Obviously we couldn't keep everyone standing there, as we had been instructed, so we started going down the line taking names and urging those listed to remain in the vicinity, so that when a convoy came they could board in their original order.

When a page was filled with names, I would mark it with a symbol —a lightning flash, a star, a square—before going on to the next. Why I did not simply number the pages I don't know; using symbols instead was a spur-of-the-moment whim. As the day wore on and tempers frayed, however, the symbols came in handy. In midafternoon a prosperous-looking man of about fifty began to complain that the wait was intolerable. He had important business in New York the next day, he said. Why couldn't we get him out to the airport and onto a goddamned plane? He clinched his argument by saying he paid more in taxes in a year than I earned, and didn't feel he was getting his money's worth.

"But, sir," I answered, "we all know you're important; that's why you're on the star list."

He glared at me a moment, but when I kept a straight face, he mumbled, "I'd better be," and left.

After that, I dealt with all complaints—which I couldn't have done anything about anyway—by referring to the symbols as if they solved everything. "Don't worry, lady," I'd say; "you're on the lightning-flash list." Or, "Not long now, sir; you're on the triangle list." It didn't mean anything, but seemed to make them feel better. I hope that some of my charges, looking back, remember with smiles having been on the zigzag list.

The next morning the planes did begin to land regularly. Duff and I worked most of the day loading the convoys, and then went off to escort some five hundred people to the Key West ferry, which had docked in the late afternoon. By January 4, most Americans who wanted to leave were gone. I went home and slept around the clock.

2

Early Days
1959–1961

Thus began two fascinating, painful years. Castro was soon in Havana. Ambassador Earl E. T. Smith was just as soon out, resigning before the new government could declare him persona non grata. In February, an experienced professional diplomat, Philip W. Bonsal, arrived to take over as ambassador. Wonder of wonders! An ambassador who could speak Spanish and had some idea of how to run an embassy and conduct relations with another government. Picked because as ambassador to Bolivia he had got on well with the government of the National Revolutionary Movement, Bonsal had credentials that might enable him to establish rapport with the new Cuban government.

During the summer of 1959, I finally left visas behind and moved up to the political section, where I worked directly under John Topping and Bill Bowdler. As junior man in the section, I also served as the equivalent of ambassador's aide-de-camp. I accompanied Bonsal on calls, took notes, and handled a variety of protocolary chores. Bonsal was an astute diplomat, a man of moderate instincts, and a gentleman in every sense of the word. Working for him was a distinct pleasure. Certainly he did what he could to develop a cordial relationship with the new government. He was patient and forebearing. Right up until he was finally withdrawn from Cuba in 1960, he urged that the U.S. keep the door open to some future accommodation and that it not try to handle the problem with force. Good advice. Unfortunately, few possessed Bonsal's patience.

Early Relations

It is often forgotten that relations between the United States and Cuba were rather good during the first half of 1959. The first revolutionary government was moderate, headed by Manuel Urrutia as president, and including such respected figures as Roberto Agramonte of the Ortodoxo party as foreign minister, Regino Bottí as minister of economy, and Rufo Lopez Fresquét as minister of the treasury. Nor were its programs radical. The tax reform put through in the spring of 1959 was sensible, as was the first draft of the agrarian reform, though the U.S. was concerned over the matter of compensation to American citizens who lost property under its provisions. Representatives of U.S. companies in Cuba even expressed satisfaction with the tax reform. An American butane-gas distributor put it to me over lunch in June 1959: "With this government, we at least know where we stand. Under Batista, we sometimes paid no tax at all, but we were constantly being hit up for bribes. I'm sure we paid far more under the table than we'll now pay over it. And we will now know precisely how much we'll have to pay and what the ground rules are. Under the Batista crowd, we couldn't be sure from one day to the next."

The press was free during those first months under Castro, and there were no significant restrictions on freedom of expression. Nor did the new government make any overtures to the Soviet Union. On the contrary, though the latter extended recognition to the Castro government in January 1959, the Cubans did not bother to reciprocate, or even to reply. Further, while the Communist party, called the Partido Socialista Populár (Popular Socialist Party), or PSP, was legalized and allowed to publish its newspaper, *Hoy,* there was no mistaking the contempt with which most 26th of July members viewed the Communists, who had done almost nothing to aid the struggle against Batista. The comment often heard among Castro followers was that "we fought the revolution while the Communists hid safely under their beds."

Castro's Shift to the Left

A few of our Cuban friends expressed concern during those first months over Castro's failure to hold elections and over the circuslike atmosphere of some of the trials of Batista followers. Most, however, were euphoric and willing to place all their trust in this bearded young man with the mesmeric voice, the savior who would at long last bring democracy, honest government, and social justice. The dream was short-lived. By the fall of 1959, Castro was shifting toward a more radical course, and toward an association with the Soviet Union.

Of course, there were those who said there really had been no shift. Ambassadors Smith and Gardner, and ultraconservative figures such as Sen. James Eastland of Mississippi, had all along labeled Castro a Communist. They saw his shift in the fall of 1959 as proof that they had been right.

But had they? Our assessment back in 1957 had turned up nothing to link Castro to the Communist party or to Moscow. Nor was any evidence to that effect developed subsequently, as CIA Deputy Director C. P. Cabell confirmed during testimony before a Senate subcommittee in November 1959. "Castro," he said, "is not a Communist . . . the Cuban Communists do not consider him a Communist party member or even a pro-Communist. . . ."[1]

Much has been made of Castro's leftist associates as evidence of his own position, but this argument is hardly persuasive. Castro's brother Raúl had indeed traveled behind the iron curtain to a youth meeting and seems at one point to have been a member of the Communist youth organization in Cuba. Ernesto "Che" Guevara was a convinced Marxist, but he was just as clearly not under party discipline. Far from being Moscow's man in the Castro camp, Guevara was never trusted by Moscow and came to be regarded as something of a bête noire, or, even worse, a Trotskyite.[2] In any event, the fact that Castro had several radical figures in his camp was hardly evidence of Marxist-Leninist affiliations on his own part. Few are the youthful leaders in Latin America who do not spout leftist slogans and have such friends in their entourage. Castro was no exception.

As he came to power, Castro himself consistently denied any Communist links, any Communist sympathy, or any intention of adopting a Soviet model for Cuba.[3] During his April 1959 trip to the United States, for example, he stated categorically that he was not a Communist, and did not agree with the Communist system.[4] Democracy was his goal, he said, but a democracy that provided both bread and freedom.[5]

In denying that he was a Marxist-Leninist, Castro could of course have been dissembling. Indeed, that is what he claimed in a televised speech on December 2, 1961. He had, he said, been a Marxist while in the Sierra Maestra and had already been planning to implement a Marxist program; he had not informed the Cuban people of these plans at the time because they were not ready to evaluate them properly.

But would a dissembler have described the Soviet Union as a class dictatorship, and then gone on to say, "We are against all kinds of dictatorships, whether of a man, of a country, or a class, or an oligarchy, or of the military. That is why we're against Communism"?[6]

Would he have emphasized over and over again that Communism withholds liberty while capitalism withholds bread?[7] And would he have suggested, as he did in his February 4, 1958, interview with newsman Andrew St. George, that the Communists had some sympathy for Batista? "Cuban Communists have never opposed Batista, for whom they seem to feel a close kinship," he had commented.

No, the assertion that he was dissembling is too self-serving and too much an after-the-fact argument to be accepted at face value. Clearly, once Castro decided to line up with Moscow and convert Cuba into a Marxist-Leninist state, he had to suggest that this had all along been his intention, to insinuate a consistency of purpose where in fact there had been a sharp change.

To have said that much, however, is simply to be left with a more complicated question: If Castro was not a Communist when he came to power, why did he subsequently become one?

The Role of the U.S. in Castro's Shift

The reason most often put forward for Castro's metamorphosis by both Americans and Cubans is that U.S. refusal to accept his economic and social reforms forced him to turn to Moscow. In this regard, much is made of a diplomatic note of June 1959 in which the U.S. raised questions about the compensation feature of the new agrarian-reform law. Such U.S. reactions, it is said, demonstrated that Washington would not tolerate reforms in Cuba leading to the expropriation of American properties and possibly endangering other U.S. economic interests.[8] Castro quickly perceived this, so the argument runs, and concluded that if he was to carry out his revolutionary program, he would have to break with the U.S. and turn elsewhere for protection and economic assistance.

There may be some truth to this thesis, but it is, in my judgment, an insufficient explanation. It leaves aside the question of Castro's foreign policy, which is crucial to an understanding of his motives and of the U.S. reaction to them. Further, in ways I shall indicate, it does not correspond to the sort of mind-set I observed and the policy options under consideration during the first year of our dealings with Castro.

One can readily understand, nonetheless, why many intelligent analysts might assume that the U.S. rejected Cuba's internal reforms, and might then find in this rejection the source of Castro's alienation. Intense antagonism toward reformist regimes had indeed been a salient characteristic of U.S. policy in Latin America during most of the 1950s. Seized by a cold-war mentality which hatched McCarthyism at home, the U.S. opposed change almost everywhere lest it lead to revolutionary situations which might be exploited by a supposed international Communist conspiracy.

Thus, the Department of State, under Dulles, had been highly suspicious even of a democratic reformer such as José "Pepe" Figueres in Costa Rica. In 1954, the U.S. engineered the ouster of Jacobo Arbenz in Guatemala on grounds that his regime was Communist-dominated. Dulles could present no real evidence of Communist domination. He needed none. Given the mind-set in the United States, it was enough that Arbenz had begun agrarian reform, legalized the Communist party, and included a few leftists in his government. Many observers thought it likely that Dulles recommended intervention not because of any real Communist threat but because the United Fruit Company seemed on the verge of losing its holdings in Guatemala. Dulles's law firm had represented United Fruit. His brother Allen, who directed the intervention, had been on its board.

This was a period when the U.S. gave full support to dictatorships on grounds that they were a necessary bulwark against Communism. Marcos Pérez Jiménez in Venezuela, Gustavo Rojas Pinilla in Colombia, Anastasio Somoza in Nicaragua, Rafael Trujillo in the Dominican Republic, Fulgencio Batista in Cuba, and various others, were all our good friends.

Even so, initially the U.S. displayed more openness to change in Cuba than one would have expected. That this was so doubtless had to do with a slight shift in official U.S. perceptions beginning in 1958.

Washington had been shocked by the widespread anti-Americanism encountered by Vice-President Richard Nixon during his eight-nation goodwill tour in mid-1958. Deeply offended by U.S. support for oppressive dictators, Latin Americans took out their resentment on Nixon. The vice-president received a warm welcome only in Somoza's Nicaragua. In Venezuela, where the Pérez Jiménez dictatorship had just been toppled, the Nixon motorcade was stoned and spat upon.

A shaken Nixon returned to the U.S. to recommend a new approach based on greater economic assistance and support for democratic leadership. This was seconded by the president's brother, Dr. Milton Eisenhower, and by a number of Latin American specialists in the Department of State. John Foster Dulles was opposed, but by the time Castro came to power in 1959, Dulles's illness was forcing him to turn over the reins increasingly to Christian Herter, and later in the year he gave them to him altogether. Herter favored a flexible approach in Latin America. So did Roy Rubottom, the assistant secretary of state for American republics affairs.

Thus, while official Washington had been suspicious of Castro from the outset, an inchoate shift in our hemispheric approach just as he came to power opened the way to a policy which gave him the benefit of the doubt and promised U.S. acceptance of the socioeconomic reforms he was promising to institute.

It was precisely to implement such a policy that Philip Bonsal had been sent down as ambassador. Bonsal made a sincere effort to establish rapport with Cuba's new leaders and to indicate to them that we were receptive to their reforms. During Castro's visit to the U.S. in April 1959, Rubottom took the initiative in holding out to Castro's advisers the possibility of economic assistance. The U.S., he stated, supported the principle of reform. There might be areas, he added, in which we could be helpful in getting the Cuban economy off to a good start.[9]

This exploratory offer could have led to some concrete agreement if the Cubans had followed up on it. They could not do so, however, for Castro had already ruled out U.S. economic assistance. It had no place in his plans for Cuba's future, he told members of his entourage before emplaning for the U.S. If American officials mentioned the possibility, Cuban representatives were simply to listen and not respond.[10]

If examined objectively, moreover, the famous U.S. note on agrarian reform could hardly be construed as a rejection; rather, it emphasized U.S. acceptance of Cuba's right to impose such reform. This emphasis was not just a rhetorical ploy. From discussions in the embassy at that time, it was clear to me that Ambassador Bonsal, Daniel Braddock, John Topping, and others on the staff accepted the need for agrarian reform and many other changes in Cuba. Their reservations had to do with some of the new reform law's provisions, not with its existence.

The note did question the adequacy of the compensation being provided for the land Cuba was taking. It could hardly have done less. The U.S. government has obligations to its citizens, and at the very least had to ask the Cuban government for fair compensation. There was no sentiment in the embassy—and so far as I could detect, none in the Department of State—for rejecting the agrarian-reform law and taking some punitive action against Cuba even should the Cuban government stick with its original compensation provision—twenty-year bonds at 4 percent. Rather, all other factors being equal, we would have continued to negotiate.

My guess is that in time we would have offered loans so that Cuba could have adequately compensated our citizens. Indeed, the note suggested continued discussions of the matter. In his initial response, moreover, Castro accepted the need for a dialogue and even described the U.S. approach as "respectful."[11] This was hardly, then, the turning point it was later labeled.

What I can say, in short, is that nothing I saw in the cable traffic between the embassy and the Department of State at that time, and nothing in the embassy's own internal discussions and memoranda, led me to believe that the U.S. intended to reject Castro's internal reforms in the same way it had rejected those of Arbenz. On the contrary, I would say that at least within the embassy and in the Bureau of American Republics Affairs back in State, everyone wished not to repeat the mistakes of Guatemala.

The crux of the matter, then, was really not some Pavlovian U.S. response to Castro's social and economic reforms. One might argue nonetheless that no matter what the U.S. intentions, Castro's *perception* was that the U.S. would not accept his reforms and that he reacted on the basis of that perception, which was strengthened by the U.S. note of June 1959. This may be closer to the truth. Castro was, after all, a product of history and of his environment. He believed that in defying Yankee imperialism he was following the teachings of the revered José Martí. The U.S. had rarely favored liberal reforms in Cuba or anywhere else in Latin America. Castro may have been convinced it would be as intolerant of his social revolution as it had been of others. One can only note, however, that if this *was* Castro's preconceived conviction, it was one he held against considerable evidence to the contrary. There were overtures from the U.S. that Castro did not choose to explore. Rubottom offered to discuss economic assistance. Castro ignored him. Bonsal emphasized our acceptance of agrarian reform. Castro subsequently behaved as though we had rejected it.

Why did Castro rebuff or ignore such overtures? One reason perhaps was that to galvanize the Cuban people behind the task of national reformation, it was convenient to have an external threat against which to rally them. The U.S. was certainly the most credible threat around, and the one most likely to draw an emotional response from the Cuban people. More, as national reformation by definition included a drastic reduction of American influence in Cuba, Castro's instincts would have been to confront the U.S., not to make a deal, even if the U.S. *was* prepared to live with his internal programs.

The Real Reason for Castro's Shift

Such calculations doubtless played a role in Castro's decisions regarding U.S.-Cuban relations. In my judgment, however, they were not at the epicenter of the problem; rather, Castro's turn away from us and toward the Soviet Union was essentially a function of his foreign-policy objectives, not of his domestic programs.[12] I believe that Castro's objectives were all along international in scope. He had not fought his revolution just to implement agrarian reform in Cuba. Indeed, given his ambition and ego, it is difficult to imagine Castro content on the small stage that was Cuba. One of Castro's most sympathetic chroniclers has noted: "There is also a Messiah complex. Fidel has all along felt himself to be a crusader, if not a saviour. He is out to achieve a second liberation of Latin America."[13]

This messianic vision is crucial to understanding Castro's actions in those early days. It was this vision that drove him. Foreign-policy objectives outweighed all domestic goals and considerations, and the centerpiece of his foreign ambitions was the "liberation" of Latin America, a goal encapsulated in the slogan "The Andes will become the Sierra Maestra of South America."

Castro seems to have understood clearly, moreover, that the Third World was a proper arena for his charismatic style. In the Third World, after all, a leader's political style and talents counted more than steel mills or the number of armored divisions. Ghana might be a small country, but Nkrumah had played center stage. Egypt was not powerful economically or militarily, yet Nasser bestrode the Middle East. Ideas, charisma, force of will, were what mattered. That suited Castro ideally.

At the same time, simple logic suggested to Castro that his role would be greater as leader of a Latin American revolutionary bloc than as leader of a small Caribbean island. The "liberation" of Latin America was not only an objective but also a means to an end. Its accomplishment would enable Castro to enjoy the same prestige as Nehru, Nasser, Tito, and Sukarno—perhaps even to surpass them.

Castro saw clearly that the pursuit of his objectives in Latin America was likely to carry him, in time, into a confrontation with U.S. power. He hoped to do no less than impose sharp limitations on U.S. economic interests and to challenge U.S. political leadership in the area. The U.S., he surmised, would not look on passively. It might tolerate his domestic programs; his foreign policy was something else again. Unless other restraining factors came into play, sooner or later it would move against him.

Initially, Castro counted on a show of Latin American unity to provide such a restraining factor. Cuba standing alone against the Colossus of the North was one thing. Cuba as the leader of an alliance of revolutionary states would be another. Cuban survival, then, was seen to depend on the triumph of other Latin American revolutionary movements in the near future.

Time was of the essence. New revolutionary regimes had to emerge quickly, before the U.S. had time to react. In the euphoria of his victory, Castro seems to have expected other revolutions to flower overnight. He was also convinced that the same guerrilla tactics that had won for him would succeed throughout Latin America. Guerrilla fronts would spring up spontaneously. In a few neighboring countries—Panama, the Dominican Republic, and Haiti— Castro tried to accelerate the process by sending armed expeditions.

Castro was wrong. Other revolutions did not occur. Where he tried to help them along, his efforts failed miserably. By the latter half of 1959, Castro was forced to reassess the situation. The Cuban Revolution might not be spark enough. Nor, apparently, could one always produce an instant guerrilla front simply by landing a few Cubans. Native cadres would have to be trained, armed, and funded. The process would take longer than anticipated, and would require more effort and resources.

Meanwhile, the other Latin American governments and the U.S. had grown wary. The Fifth Meeting of Foreign Ministers of the OAS (Organization of American States), held in Santiago in August 1959, took up, *inter alia*, the cause of tensions in the Caribbean. It did not mention Cuba, but did strongly uphold the principle of nonintervention, and directed the Inter-American Peace Committee of the OAS to take steps to prevent one state from attempting to overthrow the government of another.

Castro could draw his own conclusions. With the OAS preparing to meet his challenge, and the Inter-American Peace Committee alert to future incursions, he faced a daunting situation. New Cuban efforts such as those against Panama and the Dominican Republic would almost certainly be met with force. Even clandestine support to insurgents might be exposed. In time the U.S., working through the OAS, would surely build up a formidable case against Cuban intervention. It would then have a free hand to confront the Castro regime, and as it would be acting in the name of the OAS, its actions would be cloaked with a convincing mantle of legality. Castro's prospects must have appeared to him bleak indeed. If he continued to pursue his objectives in Latin America, he would find himself all alone face to face with the most powerful nation in the world. His alternatives were to give up his foreign-policy objectives, or to seek a shield against U.S. power. A credible shield required a powerful ally. To which of the world's powers could Castro turn with any hope that his request would be honored? Obviously, only the Soviet Union had the power and the will to undercut U.S. influence in the area.

Wily political fox that he was, Castro must have had the Soviet Union in mind all along—in case the other revolutions didn't occur. This did not mean that he intended to become a Marxist-Leninist. Other Third World leaders had turned to the Soviets for help without converting to Moscow's faith. Nasser had done it. So had Sukarno. Castro thought that if need be, he could follow their example. With such a scenario in mind, he had in early 1959 suggested to various members of the PSP, and to some of the more pronounced leftists in his own group, that when the time came, he would welcome a coalition with the Communists and the friendship of the Soviet Union. Simultaneously, he assured moderates that he would do no such thing. These conflicting signals simply meant that Castro was keeping paths open in both directions, with his choice to be

51

determined by the prospects for other revolutions. When he realized that their short-term prospects were near zero, Castro's choice became obvious, and he made it.

Whatever the precise moment of Castro's decision, by October 1959 most of us in Havana recognized that he had made it. In that month, Huber Matos, a respected revolutionary and the military commander of Camagüey province, denounced Communist infiltration of the Revolution. He was immediately arrested, subjected to a scathing tongue-lashing by Fidel, and sentenced to imprisonment for twenty years. In November, *Revolución*, the organ of the 26th of July movement, moved from restrained hostility toward the Cuban Communists to cautious approval. By the end of the year, all of Cuba's moderate cabinet ministers were gone. Manuel Urrutia had been forced out in July and replaced by Osvaldo Dorticós, known to be more amenable to a relationship with the Communists, if not a Communist himself. Che Guevara replaced Felipe Pazos as president of the National Bank. Manuel Ray, the minister of public works, was replaced by Osmani Cienfuegos (Camilo's brother), who was generally regarded as sympathetic to the Communists. Roberto Agramonte was replaced as foreign minister by the more radical Raúl Roa.

Significantly, a Soviet trade union delegation arrived in Havana in November and was given red-carpet treatment. At the Labor Union Congress, which the Soviet delegation had been invited to observe, Fidel Castro personally intervened to impose upon the Cuban Confederation of Labor a slate that included the Communists.

Also in November, *Revolución*, often Castro's personal mouthpiece, pointed out that Soviet Deputy Premier Anastas Mikoyan was to open a Soviet trade exhibit in Mexico just after the turn of the year. It suggested that advantage should be taken of his presence in a neighboring country to invite him to Cuba. This was done, and Mikoyan's visit to Havana in February 1960 marked the first official public contact between the two governments.[14]

On May 7, 1960, Cuba and the USSR established diplomatic relations. By the summer of 1960, the Soviet Union was beginning to supply most of Cuba's petroleum needs. By the time the U.S. terminated Cuba's sugar quota in July 1960, Cuba was already receiving large quantities of weapons from Eastern Europe—principally from Czechoslovakia. The Soviet bloc became Cuba's principal backer and ally against a common foe, the United States.

It should be noted, however, that during the period from the fall of 1959 until April 1961, Castro saw the Soviets as allies but not as ideological soulmates. The Cuban Revolution was becoming more radical, yes, but as Guevara himself suggested at the time, it remained essentially left-wing nationalist in orientation.[15] Anti-American Castro was, in spades, but that had not carried him to an acceptance of the socialist model—at least not yet.

On April 16, 1961, however, Castro suddenly shifted leftward again, declaring that the Cuban Revolution indeed *was* socialist.[16] Having maintained a non-Communist position even while grasping for a Soviet shield, why did he now declare his movement to be socialist —and subsequently go on to describe himself as a convinced Marxist-Leninist?[17]

In my judgment, he did so because no Soviet shield had materialized. True, in July 1960, Nikita Khrushchev had suggested that Soviet rockets might be used in Cuba's defense, but he had quickly noted that he was only "speaking figuratively."[18] Moreover, when Raúl Castro was dispatched to Moscow to explore the possibility of a bilateral military agreement, and Soviet defense guarantees, the Soviets would have none of it. They emphasized that they could undertake such obligations only with socialist states.[19]

As Castro reviewed the Soviet response, he must have realized that at work here was the key tenet of Marxism-Leninism: the irreversibility of the historical process. In a sense, the validity of the whole doctrine of Marxism-Leninism rested on this irreversibility, for it was virtually the only empirical evidence the ideologues could point to as "proof" of the doctrine's correctness. Once having attained power, no ruling Communist party (with the dubious exception in 1919 of Béla Kun's regime in Hungary) had lost it. This fact seemed to bear out the doctrine. The collapse or overthrow of a Marxist-Leninist state would have dealt a severe blow to that keystone. Castro must therefore have perceived that in a doctrinal sense, the survival of Marxist-Leninist states transcended even their emergence—though, to be sure, the one did not become an issue without the other. Hence, by proclaiming himself a Marxist-Leninist, Castro might force the Soviets to come to his defense.[20]

It was not by accident that Castro declared for socialism on the very eve of the Bay of Pigs invasion. He knew that an invasion was on the way, and doubtless expected to face the full impact of U.S. power—with marine divisions as well as Cuban exiles landing on his beaches. The motive behind his identification with socialism, then, was transparent. He was in effect saying to the Soviets: "I am a good Marxist-Leninist just like you; if the Americans attack me, you must come to my defense."[21]

That step having been taken, all else flowed from it. Over the years, Castro did indeed transform Cuba into a full-fledged Marxist-Leninist state.

Not that the Soviets went along with him—at least not at first. Castro's assertion of socialism went unacknowledged by a Soviet government most reluctant to accept increased obligations. The Soviets continued for some time to refer to Cuba simply as a "progressive" country rather than as a socialist state. Only in May 1962, when on the verge of positioning missiles in Cuba, did they accept Cuba's socialist credentials. Cuba that year was listed among the socialist countries in the May Day slogans.[22] Nevertheless, not much changed. The Soviets continued to avoid making a military alliance or providing an express guarantee to defend the island. Even when Moscow placed missiles on Cuban soil, it did so for Soviet purposes, not for Cuba's defense (Khrushchev's argument to that effect notwithstanding).

Might a more cordial relationship between Cuba and the U.S. have been possible if not for Castro's geopolitical objectives? Could the two countries have coexisted peacefully if he had left his neighbors alone? Perhaps. Certainly it was his foreign-policy goals that were of most acute concern to the U.S. government; by contrast, as has been indicated, a strong group within official circles sympathized with the need for reform in Cuba. Others, however, would have wished to confront Castro even if he had stuck to internal reforms. In time, these zealots might have gained the upper hand against the Bonsals and the Rubottoms in the Department of State. Richard Nixon's aversion to Fidel Castro is well documented. Relations might have deteriorated, then, even if Castro had met the U.S. halfway. But he did not. As Castro's verbal vitriol rose and his ties to Moscow strengthened, the Eisenhower administration, concluding that it simply could not deal with him, wrote him off.

The Last Chance for a U.S.-Cuban Understanding

Unfortunately, the only modestly promising opportunity for accommodation came too late, after the U.S. had already decided to launch a clandestine military operation to remove Castro from power. On January 11, 1960, Ambassador Bonsal handed the Cuban government a note which complained that implementation of the agrarian-reform law was unfairly harming the interests of U.S. citizens. Nothing in the note could have been unexpected to the Cubans and yet their response was so intemperate, so loaded with invective, that the Department of State called Ambassador Bonsal home for extended consultations. A total rupture in relations seemed imminent. While in Washington, however, Bonsal recommended to Secretary of State Christian Herter and President Eisenhower that the latter issue a statement emphasizing U.S. adherence to the principle of nonintervention in its dealings with Cuba. Eisenhower agreed, and a conciliatory statement was issued on January 26. At that point, Eisenhower could truthfully say that the U.S. was not planning to intervene; he had not yet approved the formation of an exile invasion force. Importantly, Eisenhower concluded the statement by suggesting that disagreements between the two countries should be solved through negotiations.

Back in Havana, our chargé d'affaires, Daniel Braddock, quietly suggested to the Argentine ambassador, Julio Amoedo, who had an excellent personal relationship with Castro, that he urge the latter to open his mind to a negotiated *modus vivendi* with the U.S. Castro seemed to react favorably. In any event, he lowered his voice for several weeks, and the Cuban response to the Eisenhower statement, articulated by President Osvaldo Dorticós, was measured but positive. Differences should indeed be worked out through diplomatic means, Dorticós said, and went on to stress Cuba's desire to improve relations with the U.S.

But then the Russians entered the picture. Soviet Deputy Prime Minister Anastas Mikoyan arrived in Cuba on February 4 to an effusive reception by the Cuban government. The attention shown to Mikoyan, the warmth of the speeches, and the bilateral economic agreement signed before he left, all seemed to indicate a *fait accompli:* Cuba had already cast its lot with Moscow. In retrospect, this view was probably an overreaction, of which I was as guilty as anyone. Because of it, we concluded that the rather conciliatory Cuban response to Eisenhower's statement had been insincere, a mere play for time.

Hence, the U.S. government was in a foul and suspicious mood when on February 29 the Cubans handed us a note expressing complete willingness to negotiate all issues in disagreement. The Cuban negotiating team had been named and was ready to travel. Talks could begin immediately, the note said. The single condition was that during the course of the negotiations, the U.S. take no unilateral action to damage Cuba or its economy.

The U.S. was not in a frame of mind to listen. Convinced that this too was simply a Cuban delaying tactic and that there was no longer any chance of coming to terms with Castro, the U.S. immediately rejected the Cuban proposal, noting that its single condition was unacceptable. The Cubans responded hotly, pointing to our turn-down as proof of U.S. plans to commit economic aggression against Cuba. In the midst of this highly charged atmosphere, on March 4, the French munitions ship *La Coubre* exploded while unloading at the Havana docks, causing heavy loss of life. It seems likely that the explosion was the result of carelessness. Castro, however, immediately labeled it sabotage and accused the U.S. government. All chance of rapprochement evaporated in the bitter invective that followed. On March 17, Eisenhower formally (but secretly, of course) approved a program of covert activities aimed at toppling Castro. Eventually, this led to the Bay of Pigs.

Was the U.S. right to turn down the Cuban offer of February 29? Or did it miss an opportunity? Was Castro sincere, or just stalling for time?

Patient though he was, Ambassador Bonsal felt that the Cuban proposal was "advanced for propaganda purposes," and should have been rejected.[23] Most of us in the embassy agreed. Looking back, I wonder if we were not too hasty. Had we not already written Castro off, and had we examined the Soviet-Cuban economic agreement more dispassionately, we might have concluded that Castro had reason to be disappointed, no matter what his public mien. The Soviets had not been generous. They had agreed to buy just under five million tons of sugar from Cuba over a five-year period, but at a price *below that of the world market.* While Cuba would have a $100 million credit, this could be used only to purchase Soviet goods. The agreement was useful, but hardly impressive in magnitude or pricing arrangements.

It is also possible—even probable—that Soviet-Cuban disagreements over revolutionary tactics had emerged even in that first meeting. If so, Mikoyan's visit, while on the surface reflecting a warming of Soviet-Cuban relations, may in fact have caused Castro to wonder whether turning to the Soviets was a good idea after all. He may have

been in a mood to deal with the U.S. And neither party had much
to lose by trying.

Deteriorating Relations

After the breach, both sides lost a lot. Blow followed blow. On June
7, 1960, Esso, Texaco, and the British oil company Shell, refused to
refine Soviet crude oil imported by the Cuban government. Cuba
responded on June 28 by nationalizing all three foreign refineries.
The U.S. Congress, in turn, on July 3 authorized the termination of
Cuba's sugar quota, and on July 6 President Eisenhower, acting on
that authorization, announced that the U.S. would not buy the 700,-
000 tons of Cuban sugar remaining in the 1960 quota. Cuba retaliated
by nationalizing all U.S.-owned industrial and agrarian enterprises
on August 6 and all U.S.-owned banks on September 17. Then on
September 26, Castro made a speech before the U.N. General Assembly that was bitterly critical of the U.S. and was enthusiastically
applauded by Nikita Khrushchev.

On September 30, the U.S. government advised American citizens
not to travel to Cuba and urged those living in Cuba to send their
wives and dependents home. Finally, on October 19, the U.S. imposed a partial embargo on trade with Cuba, prohibiting all exports
except foods and medicines.

All this was accompanied by the shrillest kind of invective on both
sides. Various U.S. newspapers and members of Congress blasted
Castro as a "Communist madman." The Cuban press, in turn, portrayed Eisenhower as a senile old man who had to have a nurse wipe
his chin before cabinet meetings.

The atmosphere could hardly have been more poisonous. Members of the embassy staff were frequently asked to sleep in the building, to be on hand in case of flash demonstrations or other mishaps.
These all-night vigils sometimes had their lighter moments. I remember one long weekend when an extra-strength crew stayed in the
building, halfway expecting a mob to attack. The trigger for Cuban
ire on this occasion was that a missile fired from Cape Canaveral and
destroyed shortly after launch had crashed in Oriente province, causing some property damage and supposedly killing a number of cows
belonging to the National Institute of Agrarian Reform (INRA).
Castro had called for a protest demonstration at the embassy. We
expected the worst. Barricaded inside, our marines poised to launch

tear gas at an instant's notice, we all felt a little foolish when the demonstration turned out to be a hundred or so INRA employees leading a few dozen INRA cows around and around the building, each cow with a placard protesting the incident in rather imaginative terms. "Yankees, you killed our sisters," said one; "We demand compensation," read the next; "INRA cows also fight to the death," announced a third. After parading around the building for an hour or so, the bovine procession moved off toward the *Maine* monument. Laughing with relief, we wondered if they were going to march around that too. But no, we were told later, they had moved on to the lawn of the Hotel Nacional, where the cows were left to graze.

Not all demonstrations were so jocular. One in particular—on July 26, 1960—was decidedly unpleasant. Glowering militia marched around the embassy chanting anti-American slogans. A nasty crowd on the other side of the street looked as if they would like nothing better than to take us apart. No one laughed that day.

And what of the Cuban people? How had they reacted to Castro's Moscow move? As one might expect, they were sharply divided. Some were, in spirit at least, with that hostile crowd across the street from the embassy. Others were very much opposed to the new Marxist-Leninist tenor of their revolution. When Castro marched into Havana in January 1959, he had had the overwhelming support of the Cuban people. As the months had gone by, however, and he reneged on promises to restore the Constitution of 1940, to hold fair and honest elections and guarantee freedom of expression, doubts arose. After Castro played his Soviet card, these doubts hardened into outright opposition. Castro doubtless still enjoyed majority support —and enjoys it today—but the the minority that came to oppose him in 1960 was large and its dissent was profound.

Many Cubans were convinced that the U.S. would intervene as Castro moved further toward the Communists. Marines would land, as they had landed in 1909 and 1916. Why not in 1960? What had the Platt amendment been about if not that? Hence, the best thing to do, many reasoned, was to sit things out in Miami until the U.S. got rid of Castro.

This line of thought resulted in a rush for visas, which simply overwhelmed our visa section. By mid-1960, over a hundred thousand Cubans waited on a list merely to apply. Hundreds more lined up at the door to the consular section each morning to add their names to the list. Others jammed the embassy's main entrance, sent by friends of friends to see officers working in other sections of the embassy in hopes of getting an early turn to apply for visas.

In a typical case, I would be called by the receptionist and told that, say, José González, supposedly a friend of someone I knew, was at the door. He had to see me about an urgent matter. Inevitably, the urgent and confidential matter turned out to concern getting a visa. José González would explain that he couldn't wait his turn; he had to leave the country immediately because he was anti-Communist. Frequently it would surface that my supplicant knew no one of my acquaintance; rather, perhaps a cousin of a friend of his knew someone I knew.

I would respond that the great majority of those waiting in line at the other entrance were also anti-Communist. It certainly wouldn't be fair to them to move Mr. González to the head of the list simply because he knew a friend of a friend, or, indeed, even if he himself were my best friend. Personal relationships had nothing to do with the matter. Mr. González should, I would conclude, join the line.

Some, we did help. There were the ill in need of medical attention in the U.S. Others had actually taken a public stand against the trend toward Communism and were in trouble with the regime. Prison might have cut short their wait in line had we not expedited their visas.

Not all who opposed Castro simply left. A few stayed to express their dissent more directly. By mid-1960, a very active anti-Castro underground had sprung up throughout the country. Rarely did a night go by in Havana that we did not hear bombs, and occasionally we even heard gunfire. Going to the movies—or any other public place—became something of an adventure. Roxanna and I were in a movie theater one evening when suddenly, a few rows in front of us, there was a loud pop and hissing flare. Thinking this was the fuse of a bomb that might explode at any second, we dashed out into the lobby in world-record time. My recollection is that I lagged behind to shield Roxanna from the blast. Hers is that I beat her up the aisle by a full second. In any event, the "bomb" turned out to be nothing more than a small phosphorous flare—intended to do just what it had done, clear the theater.

During another evening at the movies, Secretary of State Herter and President Eisenhower appeared in a newsreel. Although the Cuban narrator condemned the two as imperialist enemies of mankind, the great majority of the audience broke into loud applause. A lady in the rear tried to silence them by shouting "Traitors!" and "Viva, Fidel!" at the top of her voice. She was met by hisses and jeers. She had the last word, however. Within minutes, the lights went on and police cleared the theater. Several people were arrested and the theater shut down for a week.

I hasten to add that the reaction of this audience was not typical. The theater was in a well-to-do residential area. Had it been in a working-class district, the audience would probably have hissed Herter and Eisenhower, not the lady in the rear.

We could virtually follow the course of the Cuban Revolution on the faces of our friends. All had favored the Revolution. Some had had reservations about Castro himself, but had crossed their fingers and worked for his cause. Several had held positions in the revolutionary government during 1959. By the end of that year, however, many had either resigned or were thinking of doing so. "We had such high hopes," one commented to me over dinner one evening. "We thought that at last Cuba might have its first really honest and democratic government, and one, moreover, which put the welfare of the people first. Now we see it is not to be. We have traded one dictatorship for another."

This same friend sent his family to the U.S. and stayed on to join the anti-Castro underground. He was imprisoned during the Bay of Pigs. Released several years later, he eventually joined his family in the U.S. His story thus had a happy ending. Few such stories did.

Another good friend was Father Francisco Guzmán, a huge Jesuit priest who had been in the mountains with Fidel and was a staunch advocate of social and economic reform. He had expected Castro to implement reforms within a democratic framework. When Castro did not, and moved toward Marxism-Leninism instead, Father Guzmán joined the underground. He was careful not to compromise my diplomatic status by telling me this directly, but it was obvious from his words and actions. A man without much concept of time, Guzmán was in the habit of dropping by our house at all hours for a drink and a chat. As 1960 wore on, his visits came more and more often in the middle of the night. There would be a tapping on our bedroom window. Outside loomed a huge figure in a white cassock. I would get up and let him in. We'd have a brandy and he would give me a mimeographed leaflet protesting some new government action. As his hands were covered with ink, there was no doubt as to who had been running the mimeograph machine, but he never said so.

One evening, he mentioned to me just as he was leaving that he had heard through the grapevine that the underground might try to knock out the Havana power station the next afternoon. "You just might want to make sure the emergency generator at the embassy works," he winked.

The attempt on the power station was indeed made, but power was only very briefly interrupted. I heard later that Guzmán had driven the getaway truck. I didn't doubt it for a moment. Not long after that, Guzmán left Cuba for good and I lost track of him.

A few of our friends remained staunchly loyal to Fidel, not because they were Communist sympathizers but because they believed in him and because they so desperately wanted the Revolution, writ large, to succeed. "Yes," one of them argued with me at lunch in late 1960, "I am a democrat and I had hoped Fidel would hold elections. He could have won by a landslide had he done so. As Fidel has now explained to us, however, even if he and other revolutionary leaders had been elected and reelected, without some change in the system and in the mentality of the people, sooner or later the old political hacks would have managed to get back in and corrupt everything again. The only way to make the necessary changes in our society is to have the Revolution in power over a long period of time. Elections therefore are a luxury for the future. I am not a Communist; on the contrary, I disagree with their philosophy and style of politics. Still, if Fidel says the Revolution needs their cooperation, I am willing to work with them. Fidel is our last hope. I'll stay with him no matter what," he concluded.

This was a very accurate statement of the views held by many former democrats who remained loyal to Fidel. The friend who made it continued to serve in the Cuban government until the early 1970s, when he died, still loyal to Fidel Castro.

Such sharp differences of opinion were bound to produce personal conflicts throughout the society. Families were divided, classmates fought on school grounds. Frequent fights, sometimes near riots, erupted in bars and other public places.

Our Cuban employees at the embassy were also divided. The majority were appalled by the prospect of a Marxist-Leninist Cuba, and also felt a certain loyalty to us. A significant minority, on the other hand, put all their trust in Castro and called those who did not traitors.

One afternoon I found two of the typists in the visa section crying.

They had been inseparable friends, but one now opposed Castro, the other was fanatically loyal. They had just quarreled bitterly and vowed never to speak to one another again. The separation obviously pained both, and I tried to persuade them to make peace. They would have none of it. The parting was final; so far as I know, they never exchanged another word.

A few employees quit, saying that under the circumstances they could no longer work for us. One of them, a chauffeur with whom I had been close, came by my office to say good-bye. With tears in his eyes, he said he hoped I understood that there was nothing personal in his decision. He liked me and a number of the other Americans, but our government was now the imperialist enemy. He could no longer take its "tainted money."

I did not argue. Obviously I could not change his mind. I embraced him, said I regretted the circumstances and hoped we did not meet some day over the point of a bayonet. Wishing one another *buena suerte,* we parted. The scene summoned memories of a cold night in Korea and a young man pondering human absurdity.

Initial Plans for the Bay of Pigs

Having concluded that we could not coexist with Castro, the Department of State in mid-1960 began reviewing other policy options—options that had been aired in contingency papers as early as 1959. If we could not deal with him, how could we get rid of him?

In the course of the review process, the embassy was asked for its recommendations. Daniel Braddock, Harvey Wellman (who by then had replaced Topping as chief political officer), Bill Bowdler, and I discussed the matter at some length, and were in basic agreement. Essentially, our recommendation in late 1960 was as follows: It was of key importance that any solution come from within Cuba. The perception among the minority of Cuban people who tended to be anti-Castro was that the internal opposition to Castro was progressive and democratic, while the opposition in exile was made up in large part of former Batista supporters and was controlled by the CIA. Hence, while the introduction of a force from the outside had worked in Guatemala, it would almost certainly backfire in Cuba.

Our best hope was to ride with the forces for change released by Castro himself, but to channel them in a direction less ideological and less antagonistic to enlightened U.S. interests. That meant that in the limited ways open to us, we ought to encourage the internal opposition, which wanted reforms within a democratic system and without any ties to the Soviet Union. Meanwhile, as we encouraged these nationalist forces inside Cuba, we ought also to work with the OAS to throw a *cordon sanitaire* around Cuba. As long as we could prevent Castro from exporting revolution to his neighbors, he would pose no serious threat. We would have time for the opposition inside Cuba to grow and eventually to solve the problem itself. In no event should we be perceived as intervening with force to turn back the clock and undo the popular reforms Castro had instituted.

We could not know, of course, that wheels rolling toward the Bay of Pigs were already in motion. As far as I was able to determine in later years, the embassy's recommendations slowed those wheels not a whit. Perhaps it was already too late, but why then was the embassy's opinion even asked?

That some kind of paramilitary operation lay ahead was obvious just from the street talk in Miami. During the late summer of 1960, Roxanna and I spent several days in Miami and heard plenty of such talk. The CIA had recruited men for a special operation. Every Cuban in Miami seemed to have found out about it within a few hours.

While in Miami, we went to a party given by an American businessman we had known in Havana. Whether actually CIA, we weren't sure, but clearly he had had a special relationship with the CIA in Havana. It soon became apparent that the relationship continued, for many of the people at the party were obviously CIA operatives. Once I was introduced as part of the embassy political section, they spoke almost as freely as if I had been one of them. A phrase I heard over and over again that evening was "Operation Guatemala."

"We're going to take care of Castro," one of them told me, "just like we took care of Arbenz. It was easy then and it'll be easy now. The only difference is that this time our boys will have to come in by sea rather than walking across the border."

I commented vaguely that it might not be so easy. I then asked point-blank, did the CIA really plan to invade Cuba, or was this just a lot of talk?

No, he answered smugly, it wasn't talk. Operation Guatemala was real and was going to solve all our problems in Cuba.

No one at the party, however, would discuss the operation itself. Possibly they were too junior to have been informed of anything except its over-all outline, and even that they weren't going to impart to me.

Roxanna and I returned to Havana convinced that the CIA was indeed preparing a paramilitary operation, but we thought it was a contingency plan, to be used only as a last resort. I still had difficulty believing we would actually invade Cuba. One thing was certain: if we did, it would come as no surprise to Castro. If every Cuban in Miami knew about it, so did he.

Last Days in Havana

Growing tension between the U.S. and Cuba culminated in the suspension of diplomatic relations on January 3, 1961, after Castro had demanded in a speech the previous day that the U.S. reduce its embassy staff in Havana. Those last days are vivid to me. Daniel Braddock, Bill Bowdler, a number of other officers, and I had gathered on the top floor of the embassy to watch the speech and report to Washington anything of immediate interest. Bowdler and I, as was our custom, alternated in sending to the Department of State a running account of the speech. The first hour was dull stuff. The crowd in front of Castro grew restless. The watchers at the embassy, equally restless, drifted down to the snack bar, leaving me alone in front of the TV, scribbling my notes. Suddenly, Castro mentioned the U.S. embassy—a "nest of spies," he called it. I am convinced this was an off-the-cuff remark, not a theme he had intended to weave into this speech. But the crowd liked it and began to wake up. They wanted some fireworks. Responding to their mood, Castro himself became more animated. Cuba wasn't going to put up with the nefarious activities of the embassy any longer, he declared. No. Cuba would demand that the embassy staff be reduced to eleven officials, the same number Cuba had in Washington.

With that, I ran to the phone, summoning Braddock and the others back from the snack bar. As soon as I had briefed Braddock on what Castro had said, he called the Foreign Ministry for clarification. How were we to define "officials"? Did that perhaps mean eleven American diplomats, plus clerical support staff?

At the same time, we fired off immediate-action cables to the Department of State, reporting Castro's words and asking for guidance. For its part, the embassy recommended that if the Foreign Ministry allowed us eleven diplomats (those of officer rank carried on the diplomatic list) we ought to remain. The embassy staff had already been reduced. By restricting the visa operation and dispensing with agricultural, commercial, and treasury attachés, among others, we could continue to function as a channel of communication to the Cuban government and as the eyes and ears of the U.S. in Cuba during this time of upheaval and confusion. A listening post was especially important just then. Why give Castro the satisfaction of driving us out with a mere affront? After an all-night exchange of cables, Washington seconded our recommendation, but all for naught. On the following morning, the Foreign Ministry informed us that "officials" included all embassy employees; we would be permitted a staff of eleven, including secretaries, code clerks, guards, and so on. From the tone of the reply, moreover, it was clear that the noose would soon be tightened. Our choice seemed to be between an immediate break and an eventual one. Reluctantly, Braddock, with the concurrence of the entire staff, recommended an immediate break. Washington agreed, and that afternoon we notified the Foreign Ministry that diplomatic relations between our two countries were henceforth suspended. The embassy staff would be withdrawn.

It had been obvious for some time that a break might come. In talking about it among ourselves, we had speculated that the U.S. would ask Great Britain to look after our affairs in Cuba. The British had the only Western embassy large enough to do so comfortably. Our working relationship with them, moreover, was so close that we often read one another's cables. The British embassy staff seemed also to expect, without much enthusiasm, that they would be tapped. It therefore came as a surprise to us and distinct relief to them when we were instructed to turn pending business over to the Swiss. The Swiss! Their embassy in Havana consisted of an ambassador and a first secretary. The latter, Jakob Etter, was a close friend with whom I often went skin diving on weekends. I called immediately to tell him the news. It *was* news. Berne's cable had not yet reached his ambassador. Etter was stunned. I could almost see him blench. I would have blenched too. The American embassy was so big! Was its work load really to fall squarely on Jakob Etter? Fortunately not, as we should have known. The Swiss were very experienced in such matters, and the first cable was soon followed by a second, explaining that Switzerland would send a special team headed by an ambassador to take over U.S. interests. Etter was decidedly relieved.

Departure was simple. Because of the trend in our relations, household effects, cars, and other encumbrances had been returned to the U.S. during the summer of 1960. All personnel had been ordered to reduce their belongings to what could be carried in two suitcases. Families had been evacuated in July 1960. One of those evacuated was Kathleen Turner, star of *Jewel of the Nile* and *Prizzi's Honor*, whose father, Dick Turner, was the chief of our visa section. Little did we know that among us in the person of that scrawny four- or five-year-old, we had a future Hollywood star and Academy Award nominee.

After July, Roxanna was the only dependent left, and she remained only because she worked in the embassy and was considered an employee rather than a dependent.

Thus, when the break came, we merely packed our bags, turned out the lights, and were ready to go.

We gathered at the embassy on the afternoon of January 4 to be bussed to the dock, where the *City of Havana*, an old railway-car ferry chartered the previous day by the Department of State, was waiting to evacuate us. As the final indignity (though one which more amused than angered), the Cuban authorities had sent a company of woman militia "to protect the Yankees from the enraged crowd." But the only crowd around the embassy that day consisted of desperate visa seekers imploring us to stamp their passports before we closed down.

As we boarded the bus, an American newsman snapped a photo of my wife exchanging looks with one of the militiawomen. The picture appeared in various U.S. newspapers the following day over imaginative captions. One, for example, assured its readers that the "cold look" passing between the two women symbolized the break between the two countries. Maybe so, but that was not what had caused Roxanna to do a double take; rather, she had noticed that the militiawoman had a stunning black mustache!

That was the day's only light note. Most of us realized that an era was ending, that any future *modus vivendi* would not close the rift. Relations between us could never be the same.

Dick Valeriani and a sprinkling of other U.S. newsmen were on the dock to see us off. So was Daniel Braddock, who was to remain in Havana a few more days, literally to lock the door and give the key to the Swiss. We sailed just at dusk, and as we passed Morro Castle, all eyes were on the embassy building, standing on its headland to the west of the harbor entrance. There, as we cleared the channel, the lights on all floors began to blink on and off, on and off, the last farewell from our Cuban employees. As we watched the city that had been our first home drop below the horizon, Roxanna and I had little hope of ever seeing it again.

3

The Years of Divorce
1961–1977

We landed in West Palm Beach the next morning and took an afternoon train for Washington. Not until we were seated in our compartment with cocktails in hand did fatigue overcome me. I had slept only six hours since the morning of January 2. As the tension drained away, I collapsed. Even after sleeping around the clock, I was still groggy when we pulled into Washington's Union Station the next morning. We arrived, however, in the midst of a driving snowstorm, and as I was still attired in tropical wash-and-wears, the cold had me painfully awake before we reached the Department of State.

Personnel returning from Havana had expected to be immediately reassigned to other posts. Most were, but a few of us were held in Washington on temporary assignment. I was put to work writing a daily Cuban-situation report, simply a compilation of press clippings and open-cable traffic that as far as I could see, served no useful purpose and wasn't read by anyone. After a week or so, I asked for leave; it was denied. "Sorry," I was told, "you're needed here." I couldn't see that I was needed at all, but one does not argue such matters. I returned to my daily report.

Others of the Havana contingent churned out management studies and economic reports—anything to keep us busy. An office for the embassy Havana paymaster materialized on the first floor, and for a time we drew our paychecks as though still assigned to Havana.

The Bay of Pigs

As January passed and February turned to March, we of course began to wonder what was going on. Why were we being held in Washington? In late March, I found the answer. Cuban friends called from Miami to tell me of mounting rumors that an invasion was imminent. There had been press reports of a secret base in Guatemala where Cuban exiles were said to be training for an attack on their homeland. Most of us in the Department of State knew no more than the average American. Invasion rumors buzzed about the corridors, but few of us had any solid information.

A few days after the call from Miami, I and several others were summoned by Assistant Secretary of State for American Republics Affairs Thomas C. Mann to discuss the draft of a white paper on Cuba. After the session and out of earshot of the others, I played the brash young man again. Were the invasion rumors true? I asked Mann.

Mann, a hard-eyed Texas conservative, became even stonier-faced than usual. Such matters, he responded, were not to be discussed.

"Okay," I said to myself, "if Mann won't deny the rumors even in private, they're probably true, and *that's* why we are being held here. We are to be the nucleus of a new embassy in the wake of the invasion."

I felt a rising sense of apprehension—not at the prospect of returning to Cuba, but at the idea of an invasion. I was still convinced that the embassy recommendation in late 1960 had been correct: any solution had to come from within; it could not be introduced from the outside, and certainly could not be masterminded by the U.S. That kind of "solution" would never be accepted by the Cuban people, whose nationalist batteries had been charged to the full by Fidel Castro. An internal solution would be longer in developing and might take directions not altogether satisfactory to the U.S., but in my view it was our only sensible alternative.

I tried to reassure myself that even if an invasion was planned, there had to be wrinkles to it I couldn't imagine. Surely the secretary of state and the joint chiefs of staff would have seen the pitfalls. Who was I to doubt their good sense and competence?

On April 7, Tad Szulc's now famous article in the *New York Times* reported that a CIA-organized invasion was indeed near at hand. By then, I had become almost relaxed about the whole thing. "Have confidence in your superiors," I kept telling myself.

Even with all the forewarning, I was shaken by the actual invasion. As planes supposedly piloted by defecting Cuban air force officers bombed Cuban airfields, Roxanna and I were in New Haven, Connecticut, visiting friends we had met the year before in Cuba. The next day, mutual acquaintances called from Miami to say that the word in the streets was that the invasion force would land within hours. (Some well-kept secret!)

"It looks like this is really it," said our host, as he hung up.

We were silent for a few moments; then as if to some unspoken signal, we simultaneously raised our wine glasses. "Let's hope to God they know what they are doing," I said.

"Amen," our friends murmured.

The Bay of Pigs invasion was described at the time as that rarest of all things—a perfect failure. I was depressed for weeks afterward, the more so as the details surfaced. It was difficult to believe that intelligent people had concocted such a scheme. I admired the bravery of the men in Brigade 2506 who had gone ashore. (Indeed, as far as I was concerned, the only bright spot was that most of them survived and were subsequently returned to the U.S. in exchange for farm machinery desperately needed by Castro.) But my respect faltered for the senior American officials—those who had actually approved the operation. It was the first profound disillusionment I suffered in the Foreign Service. I had willed myself to believe that those in the senior levels of government knew what they were doing. At the Bay of Pigs, they demonstrated quite conclusively that they had not.[1]

President Kennedy accepted the responsibility, as he should have, but the blame lay elsewhere. He inherited the operation and had been in office only three months when it was launched. He had to rely on his military and foreign-policy advisers—those in the CIA. All failed him miserably. Of those at the meeting which gave final approval, only Sen. William Fulbright expressed reservations. CIA Director Allen Dulles, Gen. Lyman Lemnitzer, chairman of the joint chiefs of staff, Secretary of State Dean Rusk, Assistant Secretary of State Thomas C. Mann, and A. A. Berle, chairman of the President's Latin

American Task Force, were all present. All said "go." All were dead wrong and ought to have known it.

Nor was the failure of the operation due to President Kennedy's decision that American forces could not provide air cover or become directly involved in any other way. If this restriction cast doubt on the operation's success, the CIA and joint chiefs of staff ought to have urged the president to cancel the whole thing, for he had made it clear all along that he would not approve the use of American forces. Nevertheless, Allen Dulles had predicted victory and urged the president forward.

Even if air cover had been provided and ensured a tiny bridgehead —which is problematical—the operation would have failed. The Brigade itself could not have held out against Castro's immensely superior forces, which now included Soviet tanks and artillery. The planners assumed that the invasion would spark a popular uprising against Castro. The Brigade would gain a foothold. The Cuban Revolutionary Council led by José Miró Cardona would then be flown in from Miami to establish itself as the revolutionary government and rally the Cuban people to its banners. Hope of the victory hung on the response of the Cuban people. It was a wildly implausible hope. No objective official who knew the situation inside Cuba could have harbored any such illusion. But none of the men sitting around the table had firsthand knowledge of Cuba, and they failed to consult with those who did. I was too junior to be involved, but Ambassador Bonsal and Dan Braddock were not—nor were John Topping and Bill Bowdler. Consulting them might have made a difference, for they would have killed the notion that a popular uprising would occur. Most Cubans continued to support Castro. A sizable minority did not, but except for the very few active in the underground, the members of this minority were unarmed and unorganized. How and with what were they supposed to rise up? In time, had disgruntlement increased and had the underground itself grown in strength and capability, it might have become a potent force for an internal solution. That possibility died at the Bay of Pigs.

With so much riding on reaction within the island, one would have expected the CIA to coordinate with the Cuban underground. The CIA, however, tended to distrust the underground, first because it was well penetrated by Castro's counterintelligence forces, but also because many of its members were too liberal for the CIA's taste. I recall an argument with one of the CIA men in Havana before we broke relations. If the CIA helped anyone, I ventured, it ought to be Manuel Ray, Castro's former minister of public works, who in 1960 had turned against Castro and organized a small but effective underground force.

"Absolutely not," the CIA man answered. "Ray is anti-Castro, but he's something of a socialist himself. Why, he says he'd do away with the inheritance of wealth!"

So there was little communication with such forces. Many underground members were totally unaware the invasion was being launched. The first they heard of it was when they were arrested. Tens of thousands were picked up. Some were released after they had been investigated, but many others remained in prison for years, and some died there. If the Bay of Pigs fiasco had any lasting result, it was the destruction of the anti-Castro underground, which never recovered from the blows it received in April 1961.

With the failure of the invasion, those of us in the "shadow" embassy were dispersed. In May, I was sent upstairs to be A. A. Berle's staff aide. The grand old man of Roosevelt's good-neighbor policy in Latin America, Berle had been dealing with Cuba's political problems when I was still literally wet behind the ears. Liberal by inclination and background, Berle was close to a coterie of progressive Latin American leaders—Rómulo Betancourt of Venezuela, Luis Muñoz Marín of Puerto Rico, and José "Pepe" Figueres of Costa Rica. The cold-war mentality of the 1950s, however, had left its mark on Berle. Some said he was now more anti-Communist than pro-democrat. I never found him to be so. He had supported the Bay of Pigs, yes, and in its wake he advocated a tough line toward Castro. But Berle's aversion to Castro arose from his abhorrence of all forms of dictatorial rule. He acknowledged that there might be a positive side to the Cuban Revolution, but felt it was far outweighed by the destruction of political freedoms in Cuba. Too, Berle was a moving force behind the Alliance for Progress. "How can we expect these societies not to turn to radical solutions if opportunities are not created within their present systems?" he often asked.

Berle was, in sum, a man of strong conviction not easy to categorize. Although we differed on many things, especially on the Bay of Pigs, I came to have great respect for his sincerity and devotion to principle, and great affection for him as a human being.

I worked for Berle only about three months. The interlude was most enjoyable, and I learned much from this man who had devoted so many years to public service. My satisfaction with the job was marred only by a certain feeling of discomfort over the circumstances related to my transfer to his office. Friends in the front office of the Bureau of American Republics Affairs (ARA) confided that I had been assigned to Berle as a signal to him. I was, in effect, being used as a pawn, and a most insignificant one at that, in an intradepartmental struggle. During those first months of Kennedy's presidency, the lines of command for Latin American affairs were tangled. As far as Berle was concerned, as chairman of the Latin American Task Force, he answered directly to the president, from whom he felt he had a mandate to direct U.S. relations with Latin America. In Berle's view, everyone else involved in Latin American affairs was subordinate to him. That was never clear, however, to the Department of State's ARA, which resented Berle and circumvented him at every opportunity. In truth, it was not difficult to do so, for Berle never really took charge. For one who had been so astute a strategist in earlier times, he seemed curiously unable to move effectively within the bureaucracy. As the months passed, Berle's influence eroded, and with our failure at the Bay of Pigs, corridor gossip had it that his days in office were numbered.

For the first five months of Berle's chairmanship, Bob Sayre, a senior Foreign Service officer, had been his staff aide. (Sayre was soon to become deputy assistant secretary of state for Latin America and subsequently to serve as ambassador in Uruguay, Panama, and Brazil.) By May, Sayre (for obvious reasons) wished to move on to another job. In assigning me, a junior officer, to replace him, ARA apparently hoped to suggest to Berle that his influence was slipping. It didn't work. If Berle ever took my assignment to him as a putdown, he certainly never let on. Quite the contrary, he seemed delighted that I was there and always treated me with kindness and consideration. He seemed above such petty infighting—which eased my mind considerably. If it was of no concern to him, there was less reason for me to worry about it.

Another compensation was that along with the job came the grandiloquent title Executive Secretary of the President's Latin American Task Force, an office with a sofa, and a secretary to bring my morning coffee. All the symbols of success in the bureaucracy. These perks, unfortunately, were taken away all too quickly. At the beginning of my fourth week in Berle's office, someone must have checked my rank rather than my title. I came back from lunch to find my secretary gone, my name removed from the door, and someone else sitting at my desk.

"Your stuff is in that box," said the new occupant. "We packed you up to save time; you're sitting across the hall now."

I went across to Berle's suite of offices to find I was now to be ensconced in a tiny cubbyhole off the reception area. "Back to the real world," I mumbled to myself, glad at least that I had invited all my junior-officer friends to come up and see my grand digs while I still had them.

By July, Berle was preparing to return to private life and I was released for onward assignment. The Brazilian Northeast was much in the news those days as the most likely "new Cuba." A sprawling, backward area characterized by incredible poverty and social injustice, the Northeast was indeed ripe for revolution. Lowell C. Kilday and I both indicated an interest in serving there. We had served together in Havana, and since we had witnessed the development of revolution in Cuba, the department thought it made sense to assign us to the American consulate general in Recife, the principal city in the Brazilian Northeast. Thus began a frustrating two-year assignment. There was no revolution. Few on the left really seemed to want one; rather, they wanted desperately to bring about change within the existing system. The Brazilian military, however, seized power before either revolution or evolutionary change could take place. Certainly, during our two years in Recife, no change occurred in the grueling life of the masses. The Alliance for Progress was supposed to help, but in fact accomplished almost nothing.

Despite the assignment to Recife of more than a hundred officers of the U.S. Agency for International Development, and the lavish outlay of dollars, at the end of two years the Alliance for Progress office in Recife could not point to a single project even begun. In part, this had to do with politics. Our Alliance for Progress people did not wish to cooperate with the Brazilian agency, the Superintendency for the Development of the Northeast (SUDENE), which was considered too leftist. Yet, without such cooperation, the Alliance could not possibly work. In part, too, our style worked against us; we sometimes behave only slightly less arrogantly than the Russians. Most of the Americans, it seemed to me, spent more energy on the importation of luxury cars and food for themselves than on the development of the Northeast.[2]

Sergei Kudryatsev (center), the first Soviet ambassador to Cuba, leaves the American embassy in Havana after calling on Ambassador Philip Bonsal, in September 1960. He is escorted by Wayne Smith, third secretary of the American embassy (right), and Gennady Sazhenev, third secretary of the Soviet embassy. Years later, Sazhenev was Soviet ambassador in Grenada when U.S. forces invaded the island.

A church in the old colonial city of Trinidad, at the foot of the Escambray Mountains.

Looking east from San Juan Hill, Santiago de Cuba, with the Sierra Maestra in the background.

Roxanna Smith at the foot of the memorial to the American soldier, San Juan Hill.

Wayne Smith amidst the cannons at the peak of San Juan Hill.

Morro Castle, Havana.

A typical Cuban sunset, seen from Morro Castle, Santiago de Cuba.

Cathedral Square, Havana.

Plaza de Armas, Havana. The old Palace of the Captains General, used as military headquarters by the U.S. during its occupation of Cuba.

Meanwhile, several horizons away, the U.S. and Cuba were again at sword's point. Following the Bay of Pigs, the U.S. had adopted a twofold policy: to isolate and contain Castro, and to improve economic and social conditions in the hemisphere so as to deny him targets of opportunity. The concept was sound enough. Although the Alliance for Progress failed to achieve most of its development goals, it did—by signaling our acceptance, even encouragement, of change—have an important symbolic and psychological value. The humanitarian instincts behind it were right, even if the effort itself achieved little.

Some of the extreme measures we tried to take against Castro—such as efforts to assassinate him, or at least make him ill by putting itching powder in his shoes—were of course absurd and reprehensible. And in helping other countries to defend themselves against Castro's expected guerrilla onslaught, we tended to go overboard in strengthening the hand of the military—a mistake that came back to haunt us as civilian government after civilian government was overthrown by the generals during the 1960s.

Still, the basic idea behind the policy of containment and isolation was sound. So long as Castro was vowing to overthrow other governments and to turn the Andes into the Sierra Maestra of South America, it behooved his neighbors to say, "Then you will not be treated as a member in good standing of this community of nations." At the meeting of OAS foreign ministers held in Punta del Este, Uruguay, in January 1962, they did just that. Cuban membership in the organization was suspended. Castro's vitriolic response simply further alienated the other Latin American governments of the hemisphere, which he said had sold out to U.S. imperialism.

Nikita Khrushchev meanwhile had mistaken U.S. prudence at the Bay of Pigs (i.e., Kennedy's refusal to use U.S. forces) for weakness. He had also misjudged President Kennedy at their meeting in Vienna. Thinking that U.S. resolve was faltering and that this was a weak-willed young president who could be pushed around, Khrushchev tried to do that by placing missiles on Cuban soil.

The 1962 Missile Crisis

I saw the missile crisis from afar, from Recife. Only later did I have the chance to read through all the documents and analyze Kennedy's handling of the crisis. The more I read, the greater my respect for him. With the world poised on the brink of war, and with no assurance at all that the Soviets would not push the button rather than back down, Kennedy maneuvered with cool calculation, never taking his eye off the principal objective: the removal of Soviet offensive-weapons systems that might threaten the United States. Detractors on the right have subsequently criticized him for not trying to force a total Soviet withdrawal from Cuba. To my mind, such talk is foolish. The key to Kennedy's success lay precisely in leaving the Soviets a way out that avoided complete humiliation. It is easy to say now that he should have pushed them to the wall, but the fact is that had he done so, the outcome might have been very different. Left no choices other than abject capitulation or pushing the button, they might have opted for the second. While a few may pointlessly cavil, most of mankind remains grateful to Kennedy for the responsibility and good sense he showed in guiding us through that tensest of moments. The principal U.S. objectives were achieved, and war was avoided.[3]

Though the deal cut by Kennedy and Khrushchev was simple and direct, subsequent discussion of it has made its provisions sound like unfathomable enigmas. People who should know better have alleged that the Cubans and Soviets therein committed themselves to halting all "export of revolution," that they promised to withdraw Soviet ground forces from Cuba, and that the removal of U.S. missiles from Turkey was an integral part of the deal. None of this is true.

Why there should be such confusion is difficult to understand, since the crucial documents were declassified years ago under the Freedom of Information Act and are available to anyone who cares to examine them. Indeed, the most important documents were published in Robert Kennedy's book *Thirteen Days* back in 1969. The agreement was outlined in a message sent by Khrushchev on October 26, 1962, and in Kennedy's response of October 27. Its essential parts were that if the Soviets would withdraw their offensive weapons from Cuba under UN supervision, the U.S. would lift its naval blockade of the island and pledge not to invade it.[4]

That was the sum of it. There was no prohibition on the stationing of conventional forces in Cuba. Nor was there any stipulation that Cuba refrain from encouraging revolution elsewhere in the hemisphere. President Kennedy certainly understood that we would have to contend with Cuba's efforts to foment revolution, and the problem weighed heavily on his mind. But he also understood that it was a problem to be dealt with at a level below nuclear confrontation. Soviet missiles in Cuba represented such a clear challenge that it had to be taken up even at risk of a nuclear exchange. Just as clearly, it would have been irrational to risk such an exchange over every Cuban shipment of rifles to guerrillas in a neighboring country. To warn the Soviets and the Cubans that we nonetheless intended to challenge such activities, albeit through conventional means, Kennedy stated in a news conference on November 20 that there "could be peace in the Caribbean so long as the offending Soviet weapons were withdrawn and not returned, *and so long as Cuba was not used for the export of aggressive Communist purposes*." (Emphasis mine.)

As for the U.S. missiles in Turkey, it is easy to understand why Khrushchev subsequently chose to interpret their removal as part of the understanding. In fact, however, as he knew, it was a separate issue. Kennedy had decided the year before to remove our missiles from Turkey because they were outmoded and vulnerable. Discussions with the Turks regarding their removal had begun in the spring of 1961. In October 1962, however, the missiles were still in Turkey. Khrushchev asked that they be removed as part of the settlement. Kennedy did not believe it appropriate to include this matter in the agreement, though he was going to take them out anyway. He therefore deliberately excluded them from the points of the understanding outlined in his message of October 27 to Khrushchev, but that evening had his brother Robert inform Ambassador Anatoly Dobrynin of our intention to go ahead with our previous decision to remove the missiles, once the present crisis had been resolved.[5]

The Reagan administration has tried to suggest that the 1962 understanding is no longer valid, or perhaps never was. In a speech, on September 14, 1983, for example, President Reagan stated categorically that the understanding had been "abrogated." He did not explain what he meant, but the word "abrogated" was left on the record.

Shortly after the president's statement, his friend ex-Governor William P. Clements of Texas, a member of the Kissinger commission on Central America, added a personal footnote to the commission's report in which he stated his conviction that "there was no understanding or agreement." Elaborating on the theme at a February 1984 luncheon in Dallas (which I happened to attend), Clements suggested that Kennedy and Khrushchev had not even referred to one another's messages; hence, how could there have been an understanding? Their messages had simply passed one another like ships in the night, unaware of one another's positions. He then promptly contradicted himself by going on to say that "the understanding" had not become operative because UN inspection of the missile withdrawal in Cuba was not permitted.[6]

Then, at the Republican National Convention in Dallas later that year, Jeane Kirkpatrick reiterated earlier charges that Soviet submarines were operating from Cuban bases, thus giving the impression that the understanding had been violated.

These declarations, had anyone taken them seriously, would have cast considerable doubt on the continued validity of the 1962 understanding. One can only assume that they were intended to do so. Whatever their purpose, the fact is that there is not a true statement in the lot. As we have seen, there most certainly *was*, and still is, an understanding. It has not been abrogated or violated. In 1970, the Soviets tested its limits by setting up facilities in Cienfuegos, Cuba, from which they could operate nuclear submarines. The Nixon administration reacted strongly, insisting this operation would constitute a violation of the 1962 understanding and demanding that the facilities be dismantled. They were.

In talks between Washington and Moscow at the time of the 1970 mini-crisis, it was agreed that isolated port calls by Soviet submarines would not be considered violations, but that their servicing in or operation from Cuban ports would be. Apparently to assert their right to do so, the Soviets sent a submarine into a Cuban port in 1972, and another in 1974. The U.S. was aware of those calls and did not consider them violations of the agreement. Since 1974, no Soviet nuclear or missile submarines have called at Cuban ports except for one towed in briefly in distress. Clearly, then, Kirkpatrick was in error. Soviet submarines are *not* operating from Cuban ports.

As we shall see, the Carter administration also honored the accord. In 1978, it questioned whether the addition of MIG-23s to the Cuban air force was an infringement, but eventually concluded that no violation was involved, since the planes were not capable of carrying nuclear weapons.[7]

True, because of Castro's refusal to cooperate in 1962, the provision for UN verification was not fulfilled. To give us the next best thing, the Soviets removed the missiles—and later the IL-28 bombers which they had just provided to the Cubans—as uncovered deck cargo, so that we could count them as they came out. One might argue that our *nolo contendere* acceptance of that substitution, and our subsequent insistence on U-2 overflights in lieu of on-site verification, amounted to implicit acceptance of the validity of the understanding, as amended.

Leaving that argument aside, however, the unassailable fact is that U.S. administrations have for at least fifteen years taken the position that the understanding is binding. We can hardly turn back the clock and say now that we never regarded it as valid because the verification provisions were not fulfilled.

Whatever motivates the Reagan administration to cast doubt on the 1962 understanding, it would be better advised to mark that understanding as one which has well served U.S. interests and ought to be sustained, not debased. As long as it is upheld, no significant threat to U.S. security can emanate from Cuba.

Castro's Offer of the Olive Branch

A few months after the missile crisis, my two years in Recife ended. In the summer of 1963, Roxanna, our new baby daughter, and I returned to the U.S. I was again to be assigned to the Department of State, but first I spent a year in Latin American studies at Columbia University. It was a good year, but by August 1964 I was anxious to get back to work.

My new assignment turned out to be not new at all. Bill Bowdler, my Havana office mate, was serving as deputy director of the Office of Cuban Affairs. He wanted me to join the office as political officer, and I jumped at the chance to get back to things Cuban.

I came back just in time for the tail end of a U.S. turndown of a Castro overture. That Castro had made such an overture might in itself have appeared strange. One would have expected increased hostility in the wake of the missile crisis. From Castro's vantage point, however, his olive branch to the United States made sense, for Soviet behavior during the missile crisis must simply have confirmed to Castro what he had already come to suspect at the time of the Bay of Pigs: in a crunch, the Soviets would *not* come to his defense.

Further, Castro was now finding that his association with Moscow impeded rather than furthered his objectives in the hemisphere. He had wanted a Soviet defense umbrella behind which he could promote his own brand of revolution in the rest of the hemisphere. He had assumed the Soviets would give him a free hand. To his consternation, he found that they had their own objectives, tactics, and allies. They were supremely suspicious of his insistence on armed struggle, preferring the slower but safer popular-front tactics. They also disliked the undisciplined revolutionary groups he wished to support, insisting instead that he work through orthodox Communist parties, which Castro considered mere suit-and-tie cadres more intent on collecting party dues than on leading a revolution. Almost from the beginning, then, there was friction between Moscow and its headstrong new friend, with Moscow trying to rein him in and Castro shaking the traces in fury.

Castro was also experiencing economic trouble. The U.S. economic embargo hurt. Almost all machinery in Cuba was still American-made—elevators, cars, generators, industrial plants, sugar-grinding machinery, everything. Where would spare parts come from? How was the whole apparatus to be kept running? Phasing over to Soviet equipment, a colossal undertaking, would greatly disrupt the Cuban economy.

For all these reasons, Castro may well have reconsidered his burned bridges to the U.S. In any case, in 1963 and 1964, he reached out for an accommodation.

The campaign began in the fall of 1963, when Cubans in the UN let the Americans know through third parties that they were interested in discussions leading to an accommodation. One of our UN delegation's special advisers, Bill Attwood, acting on instructions, then held a series of conversations with the Cubans with a view to setting up a meeting between himself or some other U.S. official and Castro or one of his representatives. There seemed to be a good deal of enthusiasm on the Cuban side. After some discussion back and forth over the site, the U.S. side was ready to agree to a secret meeting in Cuba, provided Castro would first have his ambassador to the UN propose and discuss an agenda with Attwood. Attwood was waiting for the ambassador to get in touch with him when President Kennedy was assassinated.[8]

The Attwood channel, it turned out, had not been the only one used. Intrigued by the Cuban signals and perhaps becoming impatient with the delays in setting up a meeting, President Kennedy had sent an emissary of his own to Castro. In late October, at the suggestion of Attwood and Ben Bradlee of the *Washington Post,* he saw Jean Daniel, a French newsman who was soon to visit Havana, and asked him to give Castro a message, the gist of it being that Kennedy was prepared to explore the possibilities of an accommodation between the two countries.

According to Maurice Halperin's account of the Daniel mission:

Castro's reaction to Daniel's report on his conversation with Kennedy was euphoric. In his reply to Kennedy via Daniel, he expressed enthusiasm over the prospect of an accommodation for which he was prepared to make important concessions. President Kennedy was assassinated on November 22, 1963, on the very eve of Daniel's departure from Havana. With Kennedy's death, the new administration broke off communications with Castro on both the diplomatic and White House levels.[9]

Had John Kennedy lived, he might over time have reached a *modus vivendi* with the Cubans. At the very least, he would have explored the possibilities. Lyndon Johnson, however, was not inclined even to probe, and was encouraged in his negativism by his assistant secretary of state for American republics affairs, Thomas C. Mann, the same rock-ribbed Texan who had said yes to the Bay of Pigs. Even so, Castro did not give up. During the winter and spring of 1964, he dropped several hints that he was still open to a deal with the U.S.[10] Receiving no reply from Washington, Castro in July made a new offer, which in retrospect appears astounding in its scope and relative explicitness. The first part of the offer came in a marathon series of interviews with *New York Times* reporter Dick Eder. To Eder's surprise, Castro said that bad relations between the U.S. and Cuba were the fault of both sides. The time had come to seek a more normal relationship. He would be willing to discontinue any material aid to Latin American revolutionaries if the U.S. and its allies would halt their own support of efforts to bring down the Cuban government. Castro also informed Eder that to lessen tensions around the U.S. naval base at Guantánamo, he would pull Cuban troops back several hundred yards from the base perimeter and position them in secure bunkers.

Cuban threats to shoot down one of the U-2 overflights that regularly penetrated Cuban airspace were another cause of intense concern in Washington. Here too, Castro was conciliatory. Rather than repeating threats to shoot down a U-2, he told Eder that Cuba would take its case to the UN General Assembly in the fall. Diplomatic means ought to be pursued first, he said; only if they were exhausted would Cuba consider military options.

Castro did not condition these concessions on an immediate end to the U.S. embargo. He did, however, make it clear that lifting of the embargo should flow from the normalization process and that it would be welcomed by Cuba. He spoke in optimistic terms of future trade between the U.S. and Cuba, and, addressing another key U.S. concern, said that once such trade had begun, Cuba would be willing to negotiate the compensation of U.S. owners for goods and properties nationalized by the Cuban government in 1959 and 1960.

Finally, Castro told Eder that an easing of tensions with the U.S. would enable him to release most of the political prisoners then held in Cuban jails. Some of the Cuban Revolution's harsher methods, Castro suggested, had been linked to Cuba's life-and-death struggle with the U.S. If Cuba no longer had to fear the U.S., he implied, internal discipline could be relaxed.[11]

This was a major policy shift on Castro's part. One would have expected the U.S. government to weigh it carefully and to ask for clarifications before responding. Nothing of the sort happened. The day after the Eder report appeared in the *New York Times,* without taking time to digest or ponder the Castro initiative, let alone discuss it with Congress or our allies, the Department of State issued a sharp rejection of the Castro overture. The department simply reiterated its standing position: if Castro wanted to improve relations with the U.S., he must *first* end his dependency on the Soviet Union and his support for revolutionary groups in Latin America. Only *after* such steps would the U.S. talk.

Castro did not give up. He had the gist of the Eder interviews reproduced in *Revolución,* the official organ of the 26th of July, an almost unprecedented step, and in his annual commemorative speech on July 26, he again took up the matter of détente with the U.S., which he told the Cuban people could be based on mutual nonintervention and adherence to the norms of international conduct. "Our position," he said, "is that we are disposed to live in peace with all countries . . . of this continent. We are disposed to live under a system of international norms to be complied with on an equal basis by all countries."

Castro acknowledged that under these "international norms" Cuba would have to refrain from giving material aid to revolutionary groups in other countries, but that would be a trade-off. Cuba would respect the sovereignty of countries which respected Cuba's, but would consider that it had every right to aid revolutionaries operating against governments which intervened in Cuba's international affairs. Tit for tat, in other words.[12]

Castro's July 26 message, while phrased less moderately than his talk with Eder, still left the door open to an accommodation. It received the same response, however, as had the interviews.

By the time I joined the Office of Cuban Affairs, Castro's overture was a dead issue. I was bothered by the hardness of our demands. How could Castro break ties with the Soviet Union *before* reaching an accommodation with us? How could he renounce Soviet military assistance when he still faced a hostile United States? How could he renounce Moscow's economic aid without being certain of finding another benefactor? Obviously, he couldn't. Clearly, we did not wish to talk to Castro. Our hard reply was simply a way of saying no without appearing to do so.

On the other hand, Castro had sent no more than a verbal signal. He was continuing actively to foment revolution in Venezuela and several other countries. And he had been caught at it. In December 1962, Venezuelan authorities had uncovered a cache of arms on their coast—arms subsequently traced to Cuba. The OAS was in the midst of examining evidence and considering sanctions against Cuba. It was only to be expected that Castro would seek to head off joint action against him by adopting a more conciliatory posture.

If this was a factor in Castro's peace offensive, it didn't work. On July 26, as Castro made his conciliatory speech in Santiago de Cuba, the OAS was voting in Washington 15 to 4 (with Bolivia, Chile, Mexico, and Uruguay opposed) for mandatory termination of diplomatic and trade relations with Cuba. The U.S. had worked hard to get that vote. It did not believe for a moment that Castro's olive branch just before the meeting was coincidental. As one of my co-workers put it: "Imagine the confusion and the loss of momentum had we responded positively to Castro! We would never have gotten the Latin Americans back together again in a united front against Castro. Our containment policy would have suffered irreparable damage."

One cannot dismiss the logic of this argument. It was especially persuasive if one was already convinced that Castro really had no intention of restraining himself in Latin America—at least for more than a tactical moment. And all of us in the Office of Cuban Affairs at that time, myself included, were so convinced. Even if we had not been, those at the senior levels of government, where the decision to reject Castro's proposal was made, were in no mood to discuss anything with him. They were still intent on bringing about his downfall and believed that it might be within grasp. Asked on February 25 why the U.S. traded with the Soviet Union but not with Cuba, Secretary of State Dean Rusk replied that the Soviet government was a permanent fixture; the Castro government, on the other hand, was regarded by the U.S. as strictly temporary. To people with that kind of mind-set, Castro's peace feelers appeared to be a sign of weakness and encouraged the hope that with the application of a little more pressure, he might topple. This, then, was not the time for easing tensions. Quite the contrary. The obvious thing to do was to throw Castro's olive branch back in his face.

I did not disagree with this rationale at the time, and I suppose I argued the case for rejecting Castro's overture as energetically as anyone else. I remember having lunch with Dick Eder several times during that period and on each occasion insisting to him (almost condescendingly, I'm afraid) that Castro had simply been using him.

Eder felt otherwise, of course. He would patiently point out that he was not inexperienced and that we ought to give him some credit for being able to tell when he was being had and when he wasn't. In his long talks with Castro, he said, he had sensed a certain sincerity and urgency in Castro's wish for better relations with the U.S. He was only a reporter, he would conclude, and would not presume to tell us our business. He could only say that if he were in the Department of State, he would find some way at least to explore the matter thoroughly.

Another who advocated cautious exploration was Adrian Basora, a young analyst in the Bureau of Intelligence and Research. "Castro *may* indeed be dissembling," he would say, "but what if he isn't? Aren't we then passing up an opportunity that may not come again for a long time?"

I would of course insist that there wasn't a chance Castro was serious about giving up the export of revolution, so there was nothing to explore.

Who can say who was right? The Castro overtures of 1964 may have been only a ploy. Perhaps we ought indeed to have rejected them. In retrospect, however, I am not so sure. Over the years, I have read over the Eder interviews and Castro's July 26 speech many times, and I have often looked back on those discussions with Eder and Basora with the painful suspicion that they were right and I was wrong. I console myself with the realization that what I thought mattered not a whit. The decision had already been made, and nothing I could have done would have changed it. Still, I wonder why we did not at least send a secret emissary to sound Castro out. We could have done so without delaying the vote in the OAS. Then, had our soundings been encouraging and Castro still interested *after* the July 26 action in the OAS, we could have followed up with acknowledged but still confidential conversations. With the benefit of hindsight, then, I now think we should at least have looked at the proposal more seriously. I think we at the working level would have been more inclined to do so if we had known about the Kennedy-Castro communications and been aware of the seriousness with which Kennedy treated the matter. We were not aware. Only years later did I find out about Jean Daniel's mission and about Bill Attwood's conversations in New York. When I learned of them, my immediate reaction was to wish we had weighed Castro's overtures of 1964 as carefully as Kennedy had obviously weighed those of 1963.

1964–1973

With the rebuff of his 1964 overtures, Castro turned back to the export of revolution as a policy and to armed struggle as a tactic. At least in a symbolic sense, this aggressiveness reached a peak with the Tri-Continent Congress in January 1966, at which Castro in effect called for world revolution and even maneuvered the ever-cautious Soviets into a verbal endorsement of his tactics—however quickly (much to Castro's disgust) they disavowed them in practice.[13]

There was one other significant development during my two years in the Office of Cuban Affairs. This was the Camarioca sealift, practically a dress rehearsal for the Mariel exodus of 1980. With the termination of air service between the two countries after the 1962 missile crisis, the number of Cubans fleeing to the United States by small boat increased dramatically, a fact played up by the Voice of America as confirmation that Castro's Cuba was an island prison from which most of its people wished to escape. This irritated Castro greatly. On September 28, 1965, he tried to turn the tables by announcing that participation in the Cuban Revolution was strictly voluntary. Anyone who wished to leave could simply go to the port of Camarioca, a small inlet west of the major beach resort at Varadero. Friends or family members from the U.S. could pick them up there in small boats.

Within a few days, thousands of people were gathering at Camarioca and hundreds of boats converged from the north to pick them up. Camarioca remained open for only a month. During that time, however, some five thousand Cubans left for the U.S. The Coast Guard did all it could to keep the constant flow of boats under surveillance and to provide for their safety, but it was a losing battle. Too many people totally inexperienced in handling boats were putting to sea in small and unseaworthy craft. At least a dozen boats went down, and by late October, exhausted Coast Guardsmen were predicting a major maritime tragedy unless the operation was halted.

We assumed that Castro wanted us—indeed, was trying to force us—to close off the sealift and to announce that we would accept no more refugees. The onus would then have been squarely on us, and from that point forward Castro could have crowed that not he but the U.S. refused to permit emigration.

We did not want to play into Castro's hands, and for humanitarian reasons too we wanted to keep the doors open to Cuban refugees. But the dangerous and chaotic sealift could not go on. John Hugh Crimmins, the director of Cuban affairs and one of the brightest officers ever to serve in ARA, came up with the idea of a refugee airlift— several flights a day to bring out Cubans who had applied to their own government to leave and had also been documented by the Swiss embassy in Havana. The idea was quickly proposed to Castro, through the Swiss. Some in the department were certain he would reject it. Instead, he immediately accepted and pressed for discussion of the mechanics.

Two weeks earlier he might not have jumped at the airlift, but by late October the Camarioca sealift had proved more disruptive than Castro had expected. Too many Cubans were taking him at his word by simply walking off their jobs and heading for Camarioca, without any notification to the Cuban government. Castro needed a way of controlling the flow as much as we did. The airlift gave him one. It also gave him an emigration safety valve as effectively as did the sealift, and it was likely to function for a longer period of time.

In the summer of 1966 I left the Office of Cuban Affairs and began a six-year stint in the Soviet section, including two years in Moscow. I did not lose sight of Cuba, however. Analyzing and reporting developments in Soviet-Cuban relations was always one of my responsibilities, whether at the embassy in Moscow or back on the Soviet Desk in Washington. The principal reason for giving me Soviet experience, moreover, was so that I would be better prepared to return to Havana someday. But it seemed that "someday" might never come, for Castro continued to press ahead with his aggressive policies and tactics in this hemisphere. Relations between Washington and Havana remained tense.

Nothing much was working for Castro. Guerrilla movements failed in country after country. Che Guevara was defeated and killed in Bolivia in 1967. Nowhere in Latin America did armed struggle replicate the Cuban model. Soviet tactics, by contrast, were bearing fruit by the late 1960s. In 1968, a progressive military government took power in Peru. It initiated land reform, nationalized foreign petroleum holdings, and took other measures that even Castro had to acknowledge were revolutionary in nature. The Soviets moved quickly to offer assistance to the new Peruvian government, which responded by establishing diplomatic relations with Moscow. Castro had always contended that the forces of progress could come to power in Latin America only through a rifle barrel. He now had to admit that there might be other ways.[14] The Peruvian experience, moreover, was soon followed by the victory of Salvador Allende's popular front in Chile. It came to power through elections, not through armed struggle.

As the Soviets pressed Castro to swing in behind their lead, tensions grew in Soviet-Cuban relations. In his speech of July 26, 1966, Castro scathingly denounced the Latin American Communist parties as pseudo-revolutionary and strongly hinted that the Soviets were no better. In reaction, the Soviets tightened the screw further. By late 1967, they began to hold back desperately needed petroleum shipments to Cuba.

With his own tactics a failure, with other methods apparently succeeding, and under heavy pressure from the Soviets, Castro bowed to the inevitable as the decade drew to a close. He had made his first obeisance to Moscow in 1968 by endorsing (however convolutedly) the Soviet invasion of Czechoslovakia. In the months that followed, he de-emphasized export of revolution and armed struggle, moving instead to break out of his hemispheric isolation through diplomatic and trade relations with "progressive" governments. By 1970, Cuban assistance to guerrilla groups in the hemisphere had been drastically reduced.[15]

Against this background, other Latin American governments began to resume diplomatic relations with Havana and to insist that the OAS multilateral sanctions be lifted. Cuba's policies had changed, they argued; the response of other nations should be adjusted accordingly.

Beginning of a U.S.-Cuban Thaw

Even the U.S. attitude toward Cuba—until then characterized by intense hostility—began to soften. In 1973 the two sides signed an anti-hijacking agreement. Each agreed to prosecute hijackers or return them to the other country for prosecution. Over the years, hijacking had become a serious headache for both sides. Many hijackers failed to adjust to Cuba's more regimented society and ended up in trouble with the authorities. Hijackings, moreover, were increasingly equated with terrorism, and Cuba no longer wished (if it ever had) to be identified with such acts. And of course the U.S. also desired a halt to these dangerous acts of air piracy.

It is now public knowledge that the hijacking negotiations were followed in late 1974 by an overture from Henry Kissinger to Fidel Castro suggesting that secret talks be held to explore the possibilities of improving relations on a broader spectrum. Castro responded positively, and several rounds of talks were held, sometimes in rather bizarre circumstances. One session, for example, was held in the coffee shop at La Guardia airport.

There were other, more visible signs of a thaw. On January 9, 1975, commenting on what seemed to be growing interest in the U.S. in contacts with Cuba, Castro remarked that he viewed this with pleasure.[16] Kissinger was even more forthcoming. Two months later, during a major policy speech in Houston, he said that the U.S. was willing to move in a new direction if Cuba would meet us halfway. He added that we saw no virtue in "perpetual antagonism between Cuba and the U.S."[17]

On July 29, 1975, the United States voted with the majority in the OAS to end the multilateral diplomatic and economic sanctions that had been in place against Cuba for eleven years. Member governments were now free to maintain diplomatic and trade relations with Cuba if they wished. The U.S. itself did not establish such relations. In keeping with the spirit of the OAS vote, however, it did lift a number of third-country sanctions. Henceforth, foreign subsidiaries of U.S. companies would be permitted to trade with Cuba under certain conditions. Various bans against providing economic aid to countries that traded with Cuba were also lifted.

As late as September 1975, Assistant Secretary of State William D. Rogers reaffirmed U.S. willingness to improve relations with Cuba.

Resolution of the various areas in disagreement would not be easy, he said, but the U.S. was prepared to try.[18]

Angola

This promising movement toward more normal U.S.-Cuban relations was cut short by Cuba's intervention in the Angolan civil war in 1975. The Ford administration portrayed this as an unprovoked and criminal act of aggression.[19] The secret talks were halted, and Castro was told we would resume them only if he removed his troops from Africa. Subsequently, American administrations were to point to the Angolan case as evidence that talking to the Cubans is of little avail. We tried to reason with them, the argument runs; they responded by going into Angola.

But is this view accurate? Was the Cuban intervention unprovoked, and did the Ford administration really play a peace-keeping role, as it claimed? Unfortunately, the answer is no. From the eyewitness account of John Stockwell, then chief of the CIA's Angola Task Force, and from various other sources, we now know that the U.S., far from seeking peaceful solutions, had been instrumental in starting the final round of fighting.[20]

As of January 1975, all interested outside powers were backing one or more of the three national-liberation groups in Angola: (1) Holden Roberto's National Front for the Liberation of Angola (FNLA) was backed strongly by Peking, Zaire, and the U.S. (Roberto had been on the CIA's payroll since at least 1962); most of his military forces were camped out in Zaire. (2) Agostinho Neto's Popular Movement for the Liberation of Angola (MPLA) was backed principally by Cuba and the Soviet Union, though Soviet support had been sporadic and in January 1975 was in suspension; it was only resumed in March 1975 in response to U.S. and Chinese aid to Roberto. (3) Jonas Savimbi's National Union for the Total Independence of Angola (UNITA) was supported by South Africa and Peking; U.S. support began only in 1975.

As it became increasingly clear that Angolan independence was near at hand, these groups were in competition—often armed competition—for control of the first government of the new state. The Portuguese, with problems of their own back home, simply wished to wash their hands of the mess in Angola, and had announced in late 1974 that Angola would shortly become independent. In an effort to prevent chaos, they did at least encourage the contending liberation groups to settle their differences peacefully. In January 1975, the three groups met in Alvor, Portugal, and to everyone's surprise, reached an agreement to negotiate jointly with the Portuguese the terms of independence, and to share power in a tripartite transitional government until elections could be held immediately after independence day, now set for November 11, 1975. Announced on January 15, this came to be called the Alvor agreement.

The Alvor agreement offered the best hope that Angola's transition from colony to nation might be accomplished without a civil war and without major outside intervention. One would have expected the U.S. to back it to the full and to urge other interested parties—such as Moscow, Havana, and Pretoria—to respect it also and keep hands off. Instead, incredibly, the Ford administration moved to do the exact opposite, to shred the Alvor agreement. It did not even wait a decent interval to see if the agreement might work; only days after the Alvor agreement had been signed, the National Security Council's 40 Committee (which oversees clandestine CIA operations) authorized some $300,000 in covert aid to Holden Roberto. (The CIA had earlier supported Roberto without the committee's authorization.) Kissinger later insisted that the money was given for political purposes only,[21] but such an assertion is hardly credible. Certainly Holden Roberto did not use it for political purposes. According to John Stockwell, then head of the CIA's Angola Task Force: "In February 1975, encouraged by Mobutu and the United States, Roberto moved his well-armed forces into Angola and began attacking the MPLA in Luanda and northern Angola. In one instance in early March they gunned down fifty unarmed MPLA activists. The fate of Angola was then sealed in blood."[22]

Nor had the U.S. encouraged Roberto to act because of some aggressive move by the MPLA. Quite the contrary: according to John Stockwell, both the MPLA and the UNITA had given evidence of intending to honor the Alvor agreement.[23]

By March, Holden Roberto's forces were driving on Luanda. They were joined by a full battalion of regular troops of the Zairean army, which we had encouraged President Mobutu to provide. Eventually too they were joined by CIA advisers and by European mercenaries paid by the CIA. Outgunned and outnumbered, MPLA forces retreated south. The tripartite transitional government of course collapsed.

The U.S., then, was instrumental in shattering the Alvor agreement and starting the bloody civil war that was to rage in Angola well into 1976. It was an unwise move, which blew up in our faces.

Ford and Kissinger did not inform the American people of what they were doing in Angola, but while the American people did not know, the Cubans and Soviets certainly did. They knew the U.S. and Zaire were supporting Roberto's offensive against the MPLA, and saw no reason to give us a free hand. Hence, in March, the Soviet Union resumed shipments of arms to the MPLA—shipments which had been suspended since 1973.[24] And in June, the Cubans sent some 230 advisers of their own to help the beleaguered MPLA. By July, with Soviet weapons and Cuban advisers, the MPLA had expelled all FNLA and UNITA forces from the vicinity of Luanda and was holding its own on other fronts.

This new situation prompted the 40 Committee, in turn, to authorize larger amounts of covert support (some $30 million in all) to both Holden Roberto and Jonas Savimbi, along with the recruitment of mercenaries and the expanded use of CIA advisers. And on August 9, South African forces intervened for the first time, crossing into Angola and occupying the Cunene hydroelectric project.

In the wake of this South African incursion, the MPLA asked Cuba for increased assistance, and in late August and September, more Cuban military personnel arrived. Whether they were regular troops or simply advisers is still hotly debated. In any event, their number was small, and their arrival was a response to the earlier commitment of regular South African forces.

Up to that point, the involvement of outside forces remained limited. No hard choices had been forced on anyone. The problem was that if matters continued unchanged, independence day would find the MPLA still in control of the capital, a situation that neither the U.S., the South Africans, nor the FNLA and UNITA were willing to accept. Hence, on October 23, the South Africans crossed the border in force and launched an all-out drive on Luanda, and the whole complexion of the struggle changed. South African armed helicopters and armored units swept the demoralized MPLA before them. The road to the capital seemed to be open.

The U.S. was fully aware of this invasion. Indeed, according to ex-CIA officer John Stockwell, there was close liaison between the U.S. and South Africa.[25] The Ford administration voiced not a word of protest as the South Africans poured across the border.

Some two weeks later, however, came a less palatable form of intervention. In response to desperate appeals from the MPLA, Havana began airlifting troops to Angola. In November, these recently arrived forces were instrumental in turning back Holden Roberto and his foreign allies at Quifangondo. They succeeded also in slowing the South African advance and eventually turning the tide in favor of the MPLA.

Inevitably, the CIA wanted to respond to Cuba's intervention by increasing American assistance to the FNLA and UNITA. There was even some talk in Washington, though never very serious, of sending in U.S. troops. Fortunately, some members of the U.S. Senate had had enough. Aghast at the clandestine operation, once they found out about it, and convinced that it would lead to disaster, they had now had their worst fears confirmed. It was obviously another of those slippery slopes one ought avoid. Kissinger and the CIA had already taken us down it part way, but we could still cut our losses and turn back. On December 19, 1975, the Senate acted to do just that, passing the Clark amendment, which forbade further U.S. assistance to the FNLA and UNITA and ruled out the use of U.S. forces. With that, the South Africans began to pull out of Angola, charging the U.S. with defaulting on a promise to give them all necessary support in their campaign to defeat the MPLA.[26] (The American people, of course, had never been told about that promise!) As the South Africans withdrew, FNLA and UNITA resistance crumbled. By March 1976, the war was over for all practical purposes and the MPLA was left in sole possession of power. U.S. bungling had produced exactly what we had wished to avoid.[27]

Rather than proving that dialogue and efforts at pragmatic problem solving with the Cubans availed us nothing, the Angola case demonstrated the exact opposite: we almost certainly would have been better off if we had backed the Alvor agreement and discussed the situation frankly with the Cubans and the Soviets, advising them that we intended to keep hands off and warning that they should do the same. *That* might have worked. The Soviets were pursuing a policy of détente with us, to which they obviously attached considerable importance. Angola, on the other hand, was a low-priority area for them. Cuba too was interested in improving relations with us— though certainly not at any price. Both might have kept hands off *had we also shown restraint.* But we did not—far from it. What was needed was sound diplomacy, but what we got instead from our government was an irresponsible military operation that backfired badly. Apparently we had learned nothing at the Bay of Pigs.

One further comment on U.S. actions in Angola. I suppose it is obvious that I have strong feelings on the matter. Some may therefore ask, "Why didn't you express your reservations at the time, small fish though you were?"

The answer is quite simple. I did not know what we were up to in Angola. Indeed, I would wager that only a handful of people in the Department of State—aside from Kissinger's entourage—were aware of our involvement there. At that point I was serving as political officer of the American embassy in Buenos Aires, and I well remember the series of cables in late 1975 and the first part of 1976 instructing our diplomatic posts around the world to ask the host governments for their support in condemning this "unprovoked Cuban aggression." As I suppose did political officers at a hundred other embassies, I dutifully trotted over to the Foreign Ministry and carried out my instructions with conviction. I *believed* the department's assertions that the U.S. had tried to preserve the peace, while Cuba had committed a flagrant act of aggression. Not until almost two years later, back in Washington, did I began to come across the true story. The more I learned of what we had really done, the greater my sense of outrage. I did not mind so much having been put in the position of misrepresenting the facts to the officer who had received me in the Argentine Foreign Ministry. *That* I had done on instructions and I am sure my Argentine interlocutor would not have thought me a dishonorable man even if he had known (as perhaps in fact he did know) that what I was telling him was the sheerest hogwash. No, what bothered me deeply was the obvious willingness of senior levels of the U.S. government to lie to the American people. And this soon after Watergate, when one would have thought that public officials would be most reluctant to lie.

Other Problems

Angola was not the only new obstacle in U.S.-Cuban relations. In April 1976, extremist Cuban exiles attacked two Cuban fishing boats in international waters. Havana immediately protested, claiming that the terrorists had been encouraged by the hostile rhetoric of senior U.S. officials. On October 6, a Cubana airliner was destroyed in mid-air by a terrorist bomb, the plane plunging into the sea off Barbados. All seventy-three passengers and crew members were killed. Cuba blamed the CIA, and in an emotional speech on October

15, Castro announced that Cuba would allow the 1973 anti-hijacking agreement to expire. Cuba had upheld its commitments under the agreement, he said. The U.S. had not, as demonstrated by its complicity in the downing of the Cubana plane. Cuba would continue to prosecute hijackers but would no longer be a party to an agreement which, Castro said, the U.S. had dishonored.[28]

The Transition Period, May 1976–January 1977

Meanwhile, the war in Angola was over. The MPLA was now the government of the new country. Savimbi still held a strong but isolated position in the south. Holden Roberto's forces had been driven back into Zaire. The MPLA seemed in a position to take care of itself. Hence, in May 1976, Castro advised Prime Minister Olof Palme of Sweden that Cuban troops were beginning to withdraw from Angola at a systematic weekly rate, which would result in a drastic reduction by the end of the year.[29] These were not mere words. American intelligence confirmed that Cuban troop strength in Angola had indeed been reduced.

This had no effect on the Ford administration, which insisted that all Cuban forces had to be out of Angola before it would resume talks. The Democratic party, however, was more flexible. The Cuban plank in its platform for the fall presidential elections suggested that the U.S. should be willing to move toward better relations "if Cuba ceased its provocative international actions and policies." Relations between the U.S. and Cuba could only be normalized, however, if Cuba refrained from interfering in U.S. internal affairs and released all U.S. political prisoners.

As the U.S. moved toward the 1976 presidential elections, the commission on U.S.–Latin American relations headed by our former ambassador to the OAS, Sol Linowitz, made a series of recommendations for the new administration's Latin American initiatives, one of which was that early in his first term Carter should energetically try to improve relations with Cuba. The effort would be based on reciprocity. If we made a gesture, the Cubans should make one in response. The report suggested that such gestures might include, on our side, prevention of attacks by terrorist exiles and a lifting of the embargo on food and medicines; on the Cuban side, welcome gestures would be the release of U.S. prisoners and the withdrawal of Cuban troops from Africa (something the Cubans seemed in the process of doing anyway).

Not everyone in the Carter camp favored an opening to Cuba, however. As the transition team presented its recommendations, Zbigniew Brzezinski, soon to be Carter's national security adviser, raised strong objections. Nothing was to be gained, he argued. There was no cohesive body of public opinion which favored such a move. In contrast, there was a strong body of opinion against it. Furthermore, he said, the Cubans were simply Soviet puppets. Gestures in Havana's directions might be taken by Moscow as a sign of weakness.

Others on the transition team persuaded Brzezinski to accept a more relaxed position by arguing that our Cuban policy appeared anachronistic to many of our closest allies and had come to be an impediment in our relations with many other countries. Problems with Canada and Argentina over their trade with Cuba were but examples. Brzezinski acquiesced, but it was clear from the beginning that he had strong reservations. These would resurface very quickly and sink the new Cuba policy even before it was well launched.

4

The Carter Opening

1977

E ven before the new administration's inauguration, secretary of state designate Cyrus Vance hinted that efforts to improve relations with Cuba would be one of its first initiatives. At his confirmation hearing before the Foreign Relations Committee on January 10, Vance told the senators it was time to begin removing impediments to a more normal relationship between the two countries.[1] And at a press conference shortly after the inauguration, he emphasized that the withdrawal of Cuban troops from Angola would not be a precondition for talks with the Cubans—as it had been for the Ford administration. It was to be hoped, he said, that the two countries could quickly begin moving toward normalization.[2]

A few days earlier, in a letter dated January 24, thirty members of the House of Representatives had urged Castro to release Huber Matos, a prominent Cuban political prisoner, but had also expressed hopes for a lessening of tensions between the two governments.

During the Carter administration's first weeks, reconnaissance overflights, a U.S. staple since the 1962 missile crisis, were quietly stopped. This gesture to the Cubans was one the U.S. could safely make, for the technology of surveillance had improved considerably since 1962. We could now get most of what we needed from peripheral photography and satellites.

Another gesture came in March, when President Carter did not renew the ban on travel to Cuba by U.S. citizens. Again, this was dictated as much by the realities of the situation as by a wish for rapprochement. The U.S. courts had already made it clear that travel bans per se could not be enforced. The U.S. government might tell a citizen not to travel to Cuba, but if the citizen did so nevertheless, the government could do nothing about it. So why maintain the fiction of a ban, which many Americans felt was inconsistent with our value system anyway?

More important than the lifting of the travel ban was the concomitant cancellation of the ban on expenditures in Cuba. If U.S. citizens were to travel to Cuba, they would have to pay their bills. Now they could. No major impediment to tourism remained. Four years later, however, the Reagan administration would restore the ban on expenditures.

The Cubans noted these overtures. In late January, they sent through the Swiss a confidential proposal for talks on the issues of maritime boundaries and fishing rights. These problems needed immediate attention. The United States had just established a two-hundred-mile fishing administration zone. No other nation could fish within those waters without signing an agreement with us. Cuban vessels, along with those of many other nations, had traditionally fished off the New England coast, and Cubans wished to continue doing so. An agreement therefore had to be negotiated. Further, Cuba had itself established a two-hundred-mile economic zone. As the Straits of Florida are at one point only ninety miles wide, we needed to fix a line between their zone and ours.

The Department of State publicly acknowledged the Cuban proposal on February 4. Acceptance was implicit in a statement made the previous day by Fred Brown, the department's spokesman. "There is," he said, "a whole range of issues we want to discuss with the Cubans."[3]

During those early days of his administration, President Carter consistently emphasized that "the human rights issue is the key element in relations between the U.S. and Cuba."[4] He would bury the hatchet if Castro would but ensure the human rights of the Cuban people. Release of political prisoners was the key U.S. expectation in this area.[5]

President Carter's emphasis on human rights was laudable, and I thought his willingness to open a dialogue with Cuba showed not only sincere humanitarian concern but also a fine political prescience.

Unfortunately, the president also quickly displayed the penchant for contradictory signals and policy incoherence that came to characterize his presidency—and eventually led to its failure.

The first flash of this incoherence, within the Cuban context, had to do with Angola. Secretary of State Vance had in January indicated that the withdrawal of Cuban troops was *not* a precondition for talks. On February 16, however, during a visit to the Department of Agriculture, President Carter seemed to contradict that. "If I can be convinced that Cuba wants to remove their aggravating influence from other countries in this hemisphere, will not participate in violence across the oceans, will recommit the former relationship that existed in Cuba toward human rights [*sic*], then I would be willing to move toward normalizing relations. . . ."[6]

What Carter perhaps meant to say was that troop removal would be a precondition for the normalization of relations. But how was one to know?

It was left to Vance to explain that President Carter had not meant to imply that any preconditions had to be met before talks could begin. On the contrary, Vance declared, the U.S. wished to talk to the Cubans about a wide range of issues.[7]

Meanwhile, Cuban and U.S. officials were already talking. Culver Gleysteen, the department's director of Cuban affairs, met several times during the first few weeks of 1977 with Néstor García, the first secretary of the Cuban mission to the UN, initially to work toward formal negotiations on maritime boundaries and fisheries, then to work out modalities for the meeting which actually took place in New York during March.

These first signs of a thaw found me still in Buenos Aires, finishing my five-year tour as embassy political officer. Having been present at the divorce sixteen years before, I had dreamed ever since of taking part in the reconciliation. I had already made known my desire to be assigned as director of Cuban affairs when transfer time came around in the summer. The momentum toward engagement with Cuba seemed to be building so quickly, however, that I began to wonder if by summer there would be anything left for me to do. It appeared that I might miss the day for which I had been preparing for so many years. I felt immense satisfaction and relief, therefore, when on February 26 I received a cable ordering me to take the next plane back to Washington. I was to help prepare for and participate in the first discussions with the Cubans.

Throwing some clothes into a bag and telling Roxanna and the children I'd see them in a few weeks, I left that same night. Late the next afternoon, I walked into the Office of Cuban Affairs, and I almost literally did not see sunlight again for some two weeks. I was immediately caught up in the process of preparing background and position papers for the coming talks.

Directing the operation was Culver Gleysteen, who had headed the office since 1975. A professional with long years of service in Soviet affairs, Gleysteen had been convinced for some time that U.S. objectives in Cuba could be achieved only through dialogue and engagement. Reading over his recommendations and briefing papers for the year prior to the opening of talks, I formed a deep respect for the determination and courage with which he had pushed for such a policy. Now his efforts were about to pay off. What was envisaged in planning these talks had been anticipated in the Linowitz report —a step-by-step negotiating process, which, over time, might lead to normalization. The negotiations on fisheries and boundaries were seen as merely the opening round.

The whole process would be based on the principle of strict reciprocity. If we took a step or a made a concession, the Cubans would be expected to follow suit. Thus, while Castro had told Congressman Jonathan Bingham during the latter's fact-finding visit to Cuba in February that the U.S. would have to lift the embargo before a full negotiating process could begin, our view in the Department of State was quite different.

As we saw it, the embargo had not, after all, been imposed until all U.S. goods and properties in Cuba had been nationalized without a penny of compensation. It would therefore be illogical to discuss the one but not the other. Reciprocity demanded that before the full embargo could be lifted, there would have to be agreement on compensation. (This was not to say, however, that certain elements of the embargo could not be dealt with separately. Many people felt, for example, that the ban on the sale of medicines ought never to have been instituted and should be rescinded as soon as possible.)

It was agreed that in our opening statement at the March talks, we would propose to the Cubans that both sides begin thinking of future discussions on such issues as compensation, release of American political prisoners, resumption of the anti-hijacking agreement, and withdrawal of Cuban troops from Africa. President Carter, ever intent on articulating the human-rights issue within its widest parameters, insisted that we refer to the release not just of American prisoners but of all political prisoners.

Some in the executive branch, and certainly some in Congress believed we should not begin these talks at all. It was inconsistent, they maintained, to chide the Argentine and Chilean military governments for violations of human rights while at the same time moving to improve relations with another chronic violator, Cuba.

In fact, there was no inconsistency. The objective in both cases was the same, but we began from opposite ends in terms of leverage. With such countries as Argentina and Chile we had well-developed relations. Our tactic with them was to indicate that those relations might be reduced unless they improved their human-rights record. With Cuba, we began from zero; we had no trade, no investments, no commercial air links, not even diplomatic ties—nothing to take away. The tactic had to be the opposite of the one used with Argentina and Chile. If you want to develop a relationship with us, we were in effect saying to the Cubans, you must address the human-rights issue, especially the release of political prisoners.

Such an approach, it seems to me, was most sensible. And it worked. Thousands of political prisoners were released, and many Cuban families reunited after years of separation. Those who saw some contradiction between an opening to Cuba and a concern for human rights should examine the record.

By March 24 we were fully prepared to meet the Cuban delegation. The meeting place was to be the Roosevelt Hotel in New York City. Our party flew up from Washington that morning and lunched at the nearby Oyster Bar in Grand Central Station before the 2 P.M. meeting. Led by Assistant Secretary of State for American Republics Affairs Terrence Todman, the group included Rozanne Ridgway, the department's expert on fisheries; Culver Gleysteen, the director of Cuban affairs; Frank Willis, of the department's legal division; Robert Hodgson, the department's geographer; Stephanie Van Reigersberg, our interpreter; and myself, in the role of Cuba expert. Others, from the Coast Guard and the Department of the Interior, participated in some of the meetings, but this core group participated in all of them, both in New York and later in Havana.

To say we were excited at lunch that day would be an understatement. We felt we were about to begin a process with perhaps sweeping consequences. I suppose the Cuban delegation, lunching that day at their UN mission, felt much the same excitement.

The meeting began rather inauspiciously in a small, unlovely room on the Roosevelt's mezzanine. The Cuban delegation, headed by Vice-Minister of Foreign Relations Pelegrín Torras, arrived on time and was escorted up from the lobby by U.S. security agents. Introductions were made, a bit stiffly, and Todman then launched into his previously approved opening statement.

The Cuban side seemed visibly taken aback by Todman's recital but heard him out politely. When he had finished, Pelegrín Torras stated in reply that the Cuban delegation had come to discuss fishing and maritime boundaries. They did not have instructions on any other subjects and therefore could not reply to Todman's proposal of an expanded agenda. He could say, however, that Cuba certainly recognized the need to solve many of these long-standing disagreements. The U.S. side, Torras concluded, should not interpret his inability to answer as a rebuff. On the contrary, he expected that his government would be interested. He would report Todman's remarks and ask for instructions.

We then broke for coffee, which was cold. The room was so crowded that we had to move about carefully, lest in the act of drawing coffee from the urn, we elbow our neighbors in the ribs or slosh coffee on their shoes. The close quarters did at least make for informality, and as the two delegations began to chat with one another, the ice was broken. Few could have resisted the infectious charm of Olga Miranda, a bouncy woman with an irrepressible sense of humor who was the Cuban side's legal specialist. In fact, I was delighted to see, in all the Cubans around the table, that after sixteen years the special zest and humor that had been the hallmark of the Cuban character were still intact.

During the next four days I heard more about by-catches and fishing windows, about straight base lines and low-water coordinates, than I could absorb. Suffice it to say that the experts on such matters were pleased with our progress.

The press soon discovered our meeting place. In view of the number of extremist Cuban exiles desirous of ending the discussions with a bomb blast, we moved first to the Waldorf-Astoria and then to the Plaza. By the fourth day, we had carried the discussion as far as we could without new instructions. The cartographers, moreover, needed time to feed their coordinates and other data into computers. At the morning session, the two delegations agreed to recess and meet again the following month. After lunch, Pelegrín Torras informed us of his government's invitation to continue the talks in Cuba. We could not accept without consulting Washington, but I think there was no doubt in any of our minds that the invitations would be accepted. We parted with warm handshakes and the anticipation of seeing one another again very shortly, next time in Havana.

We had emphasized at the outset the particular desire of the U.S. to discuss reactivation of the anti-hijacking agreement. Castro had indicated in his speech the previous October that he would not sign another such document until acts of terrorism against Cuba were halted. As the Carter administration was now taking measures to halt these acts, we felt that Castro might be persuaded to reactivate the previous agreement, or negotiate a new one. Our hope had been that as soon as the fishery and boundary issues were out of the way, we could focus on the hijacking question. Those hopes were reduced, however, when in a four-hour meeting with Castro in early April, Senator George McGovern was told flatly that Cuba would not consider signing a new anti-hijacking agreement until the U.S. lifted its economic embargo.[8] Disappointment was tempered by Castro's assurances that Cuba would continue to abide by the agreement even though it was not formally in force, and by hints from Defense Minister Raúl Castro to McGovern and Senator James Abourezk a few days earlier that lifting of the embargo on foods and medicines might be enough to get negotiations started.[9] We had no intention of lifting even that much of the embargo just yet, but Raúl's hint at least suggested that there was some flexibility in the Cuban position.

Raúl Castro also told the senators that he hoped U.S.-Cuban relations were entering a new phase. "The war has ended," he said, "and now we are reconstructing the bridge brick by brick, ninety miles from Key West to Varadero. It takes a long time, but at the end of the bridge, we can shake hands without winners or losers."[10]

A poignant moment came during the visit of the American senators, who had accompanied the South Dakota basketball team, the first American sports group to compete in Cuba since 1960. The teams came onto the court, each carrying its national flag, and the crowd stood respectfully as the Stars and Stripes appeared and the U.S. national anthem was played. A Cuban friend who was there that night told me some years later that he and many others in the crowd had wept unashamedly. "It was such a moving moment," he said. "It was like finding something long lost. We would perhaps continue to have political differences, but at least on the level of personal relationships, we could begin to deal with one another like human beings again."

Upon their return from Cuba, Senators McGovern and Abourezk reported to President Carter. Both strongly recommended ending the embargo on foods and medicines, and President Carter apparently responded favorably, saying he would not oppose efforts in Congress to do so.[11] This would lead to some difficulties in the summer—about which more later.

Meanwhile, President Carter and Secretary of State Vance had approved the Havana talks, now scheduled to begin on April 25. The delegation flew down to Fort Lauderdale on the morning of the twenty-fourth, and after lunch prepared to board the small charter aircraft that was to take us across the straits to Cuba. For security reasons, our travel plans had been held in strictest confidence. Nevertheless, Dick Valeriani of NBC had somehow learned the time and place of our departure. There he was on the other side of the fence, filming the delegation as it boarded the plane and requesting a few words from Todman.

For me, history had come full circle. Valeriani had been on the dock to see us off sixteen years earlier, when the embassy staff had sailed from Havana. I wanted nothing so much as to go over to the fence to tell Valeriani how touched I was to see him there. Todman, however, was furious that data on our flight had leaked—and with good reason. Instead of Dick Valeriani, Cuban terrorist exiles might have been giving us a send-off. Still, with the charter company, the airport crew, and various others knowing our plans, we could hardly have expected the media not get onto them. Since Todman was muttering imprecations against the "irresponsible wretch" who had given us away, and I was going to be working closely with Todman in the months to come, I decided discretion was in order. To rush over to talk to Valeriani might simply have suggested to Todman that I was the "wretch." Feeling craven but wise, I climbed aboard without so much as a wave in the direction of the fence.

The plane was small, and I sat directly behind the pilot, peering over his shoulder to see the Straits of Florida slipping beneath us and, finally, the coast of Cuba edging onto the horizon. I could hear the radio conversations with ground control. First Miami tower dropped away, then Key West, and a few minutes later Havana tower picked us up. I could not have imagined a more exciting way to return after sixteen years—at least, not a way I would have wished to try; parachutes are not to my taste.

We crossed the Cuban coast at Varadero, a beach resort some eighty miles east of Havana, where Roxanna and I had spent many lovely afternoons on the sugar-white sands. We then turned sharply west and flew on to José Martí International Airport. Nostalgia swept over me at sight of Cuba's green rolling hills and tall palms. Morro Castle had not changed since Roxanna and I had sailed under it as newlyweds in 1958—or since we had watched it drop behind us on January 4, 1961.

We were met at the airport by the Swiss ambassador, Etienne Serra, by the omnipresent Néstor García, first secretary of the Cuban UN mission, and by a number of officials from the Foreign Ministry. Swept through the formalities of customs and immigration, we were taken directly to the Riviera Hotel, on Havana's ocean drive not far from the old American embassy. There being nothing scheduled for us that evening, Todman asked me to recommend a place where the delegation could have dinner. Without hesitation I suggested the Bodeguita del Medio, and off we went. The Bodeguita was unchanged. The same owner (now the manager, since the establishment was owned by the state), the same good music and food. Errol Flynn no longer lounged at the corner table, but pictures of him and of a few other Hollywood celebrities of the past still hung on the walls.

Todman congratulated me on my good taste—until the bill came. Generations of government employees can thank me for the decent subsistence allowance now paid to official travelers to Havana. One look at the bill, and Todman declared that the first order of business once we were back in Washington would be to raise allowances for Cuba—still pegged at ten dollars per day, as they had been when we broke relations back in 1961. And next time, he added, he'd pick the restaurant.

The talks started the next morning and went smoothly. We had all our coordinates ready and our position on fishing by-catches well orchestrated. We had come with authorization to sign. After only two full days of discussions, agreement was reached. The next day, April 27, we signed both a fishing agreement and a boundary agreement.

While the rest of the delegation was present at the signing ceremony, I was stuck away in the Swiss embassy with an archaic device called a one-time pad, laboriously encoding a message to Washington reporting a conversation between Todman and Foreign Minister Isidoro Malmierca earlier in the day. Malmierca had asked Todman to call on him principally as a courtesy, I believe; he reiterated Cuba's interest in improving relations, but had nothing really new to say. Todman, however, took advantage of the visit to raise a very specific point of our own. Prior to departure, we had received authorization to raise with the Cubans the possibility of opening interests sections in one another's capitals. Todman now put it to Malmierca.

Why interests sections? Basically, because even though we had ruled out formal diplomatic relations until the fundamental problems between us had been resolved, we needed direct communications if those problems *were* to be worked out. On our side, moreover, we wished again to have firsthand reports of what was going on in Cuba. Also, with travel restrictions now lifted and American citizens again likely to be traveling to Cuba in greater numbers, we wanted a U.S. consular office on the ground to extend protective service to them.

We therefore turned to that ingenious institution called an interests section. I do not know who invented it. If not the French, it was someone with their flair for subtlety. Governments frequently sever diplomatic relations but continue to recognize one another. Each then usually requests a third country to protect its interests in the country from which it is withdrawing its embassy. The U.S. had recognized the Castro government in January 1959, and that recognition had not been withdrawn. As noted, when we broke relations in January 1961, we requested Switzerland to look after our interests in Cuba. For sixteen years, three Swiss diplomats and two secretaries had visited American prisoners, protected any remaining American citizens and property, and issued an occasional diplomatic or UN visa to Cuban officials traveling to New York. Cuba's affairs in Washington during those years were managed by designated officials of the Czech embassy.

Our proposal in April 1977 called for American diplomats to take over the handling of U.S. interests in Cuba, as a section in the Swiss embassy. Cubans would replace Czech diplomats in the management of Cuba's interests in the U.S. This was a means of having diplomatic missions in one another's capitals without benefit of diplomatic relations—a means, in effect, of not having one's cake but being able to eat it anyway.

Malmierca immediately took to the idea. He promised to take it up with President Castro and get back to us shortly—possibly to arrange more detailed discussions of the proposal.

Todman also requested permission to visit the American citizens then being held in Cuban prisons. Several of these, arrested shortly after the rupture in relations, had been in prison ever since. It was important, Todman pointed out, that we be able to take back news of these men and women.

As we were scheduled to fly out the following morning, there might not have been time for the Cubans to reach a decision and make the necessary arrangements. Todman therefore suggested that if necessary, one or two members of our party could remain behind to visit the prisoners.

By that evening, we had our answer. Malmierca sent word that representatives designated by Todman would be permitted to interview a number of prisoners the following afternoon. Frank Willis, our legal adviser, and I were tapped. We were delighted, especially as the Swiss ambassador immediately invited us to stay at his lovely residence.

Having raised with Malmierca the question of opening interests sections in one another's former embassy buildings, Todman thought we should inspect ours. The Swiss ambassador took us over that afternoon, and for me it was like entering a haunted house. As we went from office to office, I could almost hear the voices of those who had worked in them all those years before. Faded group pictures hung on the walls. President Eisenhower's portrait dominated the main entryway.

The most poignant moment came as we entered the building. Lined up to greet us were seven Cuban employees who had once worked for the embassy and had stayed on working for the Swiss all during the sixteen years of our absence. I recognized Gabriel, Ambassador Bonsal's old driver, at the same instant that he recognized me. We embraced and then stood smiling at one another as two people do when they can't find words to bridge the years. Finally I asked him, "Gabriel, were you one of those who blinked the lights that night we left?"

He sighed and without really answering said, "Good, good; you did see it then."

As we walked on through the building, I remembered Gabriel holding the door of the car for Ambassador Bonsal one afternoon in late 1959. Demonstrators were milling about in front of the embassy, and the ambassador had been advised to leave by the rear exit. "I never leave by the back door," he had replied, and ordered his car brought around to wait for him—right in front of the demonstrators.

I had been looking down from a fifth-floor window as Bonsal walked out to the car. There stood Gabriel, stolidly ignoring the taunts and threats of the crowd. Bonsal also ignored them, except to nod cheerfully toward the crowd before gliding into the car. This defiance may appear foolhardy—the crowd could have torn him limb from limb. But Bonsal knew his Cubans. They do respond to demonstrations of courage, especially if carried off with a certain style, and Bonsal walked down those steps with all the dignity and style one could have hoped to see. A few in the crowd continued to shout insults, but a few others actually applauded. No one made a threatening move.

Bonsal's gesture was fine, but it was the image of Gabriel that had stayed with me most vividly over the years. This had been no display of bravado on his part; rather, he had simply been doing, faithfully and well, what he felt his job demanded. Somehow, that was even more moving than Bonsal's obvious courage and dash.

The next morning, Frank and I said good-bye to the rest of the delegation and were then driven out to Combinado del Este prison for the promised interviews. We were disappointed to learn we would see only four of the more than twenty Americans. The Cubans had, however, trotted out a representative group: one political prisoner, two drug smugglers, and one hijacker. We found them to be in good health and spirits, the latter raised by the hope that our visit presaged their early release (as in fact turned out to be the case).

The political prisoner, Carmen Ruiz, had been in the longest of the four. A naturalized American citizen, she had been accused of working for the CIA, had acknowledged her guilt, and had been in prison ever since. During those years, she had married another prisoner. Recently, she told us, she and her husband had been given periodic furloughs from prison. Carmen was nearing the time she might be released. Like the others, she was moved at being visited for the first time by a representative of her own government. Her only request, however, was a novel one. When we got home, she said, she wanted us to raise with the CIA the matter of compensation due her for her years in prison. (Eventually, the CIA did quietly take care of her.)

Returning from Combinado del Este, I called the Foreign Ministry to request interviews with all the other American prisoners. Vice-

Minister Pelegrín Torras informed us the next morning, however, that these would not be possible. We were not consular officers and were in no way accredited to Cuba, he noted. Even our truncated visit had been a special concession. The Cuban government could go no further. Swiss diplomats regularly visited the prisoners, he pointed out; if we wished to check on the welfare of individual prisoners, we should consult the Swiss.

Having no further reason to remain in Havana, Frank and I booked the first flight to Mexico, leaving two days later. Meanwhile, we enjoyed the Swiss ambassador's hospitality and acted like tourists. On Sunday, the ambassador suggested a tour of the former American ambassador's residence. Like the embassy building, the residence was filled with memories. Standing in the small dining room I recalled my last meal there, in December 1960. Daniel Braddock had moved in after Bonsal was called home, and he was throwing a farewell dinner for some Latin American diplomat whose name I have long since forgotten. Most of the guests were Latin American. Raising his glass in a farewell toast to the guest of honor, Braddock had looked around the table and predicted rather sadly, "Probably none of us will be here much longer." How right he had been!

The old house was as stately and beautiful as ever. Certainly it was well graced by its current inhabitants, the three lovely young secretaries assigned to the Swiss embassy. One of them told me over drinks at poolside that afternoon that because of the availability of our residence, Havana had become a popular posting for Swiss foreign-service secretaries. "Who wouldn't want to live in this house?" she asked. I agreed. Since 1958 it had been my distant dream to do just that.

A few days after our return to Washington, the Office of Personnel confirmed what I had already been told informally: I was to replace Culver Gleysteen as director of Cuban affairs when he went on to another assignment in July. Meanwhile, I ought to return to Buenos Aires to pack up and bring my family.

In my absence, U.S. and Cuban delegations met in New York and agreed upon modalities for the establishment of interests sections. The two sections were to be inaugurated simultaneously on September 1. Each would be staffed by up to ten diplomats; each would have direct communication with the host government; the senior officer of each section would be treated as a chief of mission, being invited to all gatherings of the diplomatic corps, for example; each would be located in its country's former embassy building; and each was to enjoy all diplomatic privileges and immunities. Indeed, as one examined the ground rules, it became clear that the interests sections were to operate as embassies in all but name. They were to do everything an embassy would do except fly their own flags and call their chief "ambassador." And for the U.S. chief of section, at least, any pain at not having the title would be eased by an ambassador's salary and life in the former ambassador's residence. Sometimes there may be a lot in a name; in this case, there wasn't much.

During the summer, I returned to Havana as part of a team to iron out the administrative details involved in reopening a post—finding housing for our personnel, putting the old embassy building into full operating condition again, and working out with the Cubans a way to bring in all the needed equipment, household effects, and vehicles.

Otherwise, my role was confined to Washington. I found that certain elements of our own bureaucracy were less cooperative than the Cubans. The Department of the Treasury, for example, at first refused to grant licenses enabling our diplomats to have bank accounts in Cuba to pay their monthly living expenses. I pointed out to the reluctant official that the refusal would create a situation in which we sent diplomats to Havana but then told them that if they paid their bills by check, they would be subject to arrest upon their return to the U.S.

"Maybe so," he replied, "but that's the way I read the regulations." Fortunately, he was overruled by a superior.

There was also the matter of the American deposits. Many American citizens leaving Cuba back in 1960 and 1961 had left their valuables behind, not by choice, but because jewelry, paintings, silver services, coin collections, and the like, were often confiscated at the airport on grounds that they were part of the Cuban national patrimony. Until the break in relations, these American valuables were safeguarded by the embassy staff. After the break, the Swiss accepted valuables for safekeeping. Much of this property was in sealed boxes, so there was no way to determine exactly what it consisted of or how much it was worth. From a number of depositors who had contacted us, however, we knew there were gold coins, silver, crystal, and some very valuable paintings. A conservative estimate placed the value at over a million dollars. During the years of our absence, most of the deposits had been stored in the basement and in other rooms of the embassy building. Now that we were to manage our own interests again, the Swiss, logically enough, wanted us to assume charge of them.

In my view, we had no choice but to do so. The only question was whether we should try to secure Cuban agreement to returning the deposits to their owners in the U.S., or simply leave them where they were.

Culver Gleysteen had informally raised the matter with Néstor García, who had hinted that the Cuban authorities might look the other way as we removed them. But of course we could not proceed on that basis. First of all, García had spoken without instructions. That the Cubans might look the other way was a mere possibility, not a firm commitment. Second, even if García had been authorized to suggest it, we could not have accepted so informal and potentially risky an arrangement. What would have protected us if the Cubans changed their minds in the midst of the removal? One can almost visualize the international wire-service reports:

Only days after reopening a diplomatic mission in Cuba, American diplomats were apprehended red-handed at Havana airport attempting to smuggle out jewelry, silver, and valuable paintings. Americans claim they had been told Cuban authorities would overlook such a smuggling operation. Rest of world laughs.

No. The alternatives were to get Cuban authorization in writing or leave the deposits where they were. Or so it seemed to me. The Bureau of Consular Affairs had a different idea. I had sent a memorandum explaining the matter of the deposits and asking for advice. The reply I got back a few days later was simply astounding. According to the Bureau of Consular Affairs, our regulations did not provide for the acceptance of such property; hence the Swiss had improperly received the deposits and the U.S. would not accept them now. Our interests-section staff could tell the Swiss to take the deposits over to their own building, or they could dump the deposits in the street!

Outraged, I called the bureau to protest. Did they realize that scores of newsmen would be in Havana to cover the opening of the interests section? Did they want the dumping of deposits to be recorded on film? And how could we possibly explain to our own citizens that the Swiss had been better stewards of their property than we were?

Unfazed, the consular officials replied that regulations were regulations. Perhaps, I shot back, but I defied them to show me a regulation that said we had to remove the property of U.S. citizens from a diplomatic mission once that property was on the premises.

They couldn't, but even so, during the next few weeks I spent whole work days arguing the matter. It finally became apparent that the consular officials' greatest fear was that the deposits might be returned to the U.S., for then the bureau would have to accept responsibility for their safekeeping and return to the owners. Sorting it all out was certain to involve litigation: many of the depositors would have lost their receipts, while others would have died, and heirs would squabble over ownership.

I could understand the bureau's apprehension even if I did not agree with it. What baffled me was the fierce opposition even to leaving the valuables in the basement of the embassy. The impasse was finally broken by Phil Habib, the undersecretary for political affairs, who saw the point and in less than two minutes ruled that for the time being the deposits would stay put. And so they have, to this day.

Meanwhile, we were carefully choosing the ten members of the Foreign Service who would form the interests section's first staff. Often, Assistant Secretary Todman did the choosing.

Lyle F. Lane, the deputy chief of mission in Lima, was to head the mission. An experienced diplomat with long service in Latin America, Lane proved an excellent choice. Another was Tom Holladay, to be consular officer. Holladay had worked under Culver Gleysteen in the Department of State and knew consular issues backward and forward—protection and repatriation of American citizens, visits and mail for American prisoners, visas, passports, and dozens of other such matters.

And then there was Barbara Hutchinson, the cultural officer. A crusty and straightforward woman with a number of Latin American posts already under her belt, she was not a favorite of the bureaucrats in the United States Information Agency. Fiercely independent and competent, she did not suffer fools easily. Once in Havana, she did a first-rate job, quickly winning a wide circle of friends in Cuban cultural and intellectual circles. This memorable woman was mourned by those Cuban friends as well as by her American colleagues when she died in January 1984.

Both sections were opened on schedule, with the usual fanfare and champagne. In keeping with the spirit of reciprocity, the two inaugural receptions were held simultaneously, ours in the old embassy building, where Lyle Lane and his crew were now busily setting up shop, the Cuban in the Czech embassy in Washington. At both, the tone was decidedly upbeat. One theme ran through all the toasts—much might continue to divide us, but now we could at least discuss our disagreements face to face.

I do not believe our optimism that day was naive. At the risk of sounding parochial, I can only say that even in retrospect it seems to me that we in the Department of State approached the new relationship with Cuba realistically. Neither Todman nor I expected Castro to stop being Castro or Cuba to stop being a Marxist-Leninist state. Certainly Undersecretary Phil Habib, did not, nor did David A. Newsom, who subsequently replaced Habib. We assumed that Cuba would remain allied with the Soviet Union. That was a given. Cuba might show a greater sensitivity to U.S. security concerns, but we were under no illusions that it would abandon its steadfast foreign-policy objectives. And since Cuba and the U.S. had very different world views, we fully expected that its objectives and ours would often clash.

The premise underlying the new approach was that we were likely to accomplish relatively more by trying to negotiate our disagreements than by pushing them to confrontations, and more by reducing tension than by increasing it. Our hope in the Department of State was that as we reached agreement on various issues and developed somewhat more confidence in one another, the atmosphere between the two countries might gradually change, and eventually hostility and suspicion might give way to a realistic *modus vivendi.*

We were convinced, moreover, that important American interests could be served by improving relations with Cuba—but the process would take time.[12] Only over a period of years could we hope to bring about conditions under which Cuba might begin to show greater independence of the Soviet Union. Certainly it could not do so so long as it needed constant reassurance of Soviet support against the threat of U.S. attack. And only as the two countries worked out an accommodation might we hope to see some real moderation of Cuba's foreign policy.

The opening to Cuba, finally, was part of the Carter administration's broader strategy of establishing a much closer rapport with the Third World. Calling off the cold war with Cuba was intended to signal a more flexible, pragmatic U.S. approach and to make it clear that we no longer intended to respond to all situations in the developing world as though each were a zero-sum game with the Soviets.

As we had moved toward the inauguration of the interests sections, our expectation had been that the next major step would be to negotiate a timetable for lifting the embargo, and for Cuban compensation of American citizens who had lost properties and businesses in Cuba. The Cubans had never denied that they ought to compensate the American claimants. Only the amount was at issue, but on that there was no meeting of the minds. Even to open negotiations, the matter of timing was crucial, for the Cubans, understandably, had said nothing could be negotiated until the embargo was lifted, and we, just as sensibly, had said we couldn't lift the embargo until our citizens were compensated.

After the new chief of the Cuban interests section, Ramón Sánchez-Parodi, arrived in Washington in late August 1977, the two of us discussed the matter over several lunches, looking for a way around the impasse. The scenario we agreed to put forward to our governments was hardly inventive; we intended simply to propose that we negotiate the two issues simultaneously—the embargo at one site, compensation at another. Agreement on the two issues, once reached, would be announced simultaneously.

Within the Department of State, we did not envisage any particular difficulty in dismantling the embargo, whether piece by piece or all at once. Congress had given the president authority to impose it, and conversely, to lift it. Carter was under no obligation to ask for new congressional authority—though of course he would want the support of Congress for such a move. During the summer of 1977, there seemed no doubt that Congress would go along. Indeed, a number of key congressional figures had urged that the embargo on foods and medicines be lifted as a unilateral concession. The Department of State advised the president not to take such a step, which we felt would simply give away needed bargaining chips for the negotiations we expected to begin in early autumn. Accepting that reasoning, the president lobbied successfully in the Senate Foreign Relations Committee to turn back the proposal.

In late September, I discussed the simultaneous-negotiations scenario with Assistant Secretary Todman, who gave it his approval—in principle—pending a go-ahead from the secretary of state and the National Security Council (NSC). I never saw the latter's response, but was told in October that the White House wanted to hold off

Cuban negotiations until the Panama Canal treaties had been ratified by the Senate. The administration needed to concentrate its efforts on getting the treaties through the Senate. To open new talks with the Cubans right in the middle of the ratification fight might have divided those efforts, and might also needlessly have antagonized certain wavering Republican senators whose votes were needed for ratification. So negotiations with Havana were put on a back burner, temporarily, we thought. As it turned out, it was for good, for old problems were resurfacing to roil anew the waters between us.

A minor—but deeply resented—problem had come up in August, just as we were moving toward the inauguration of the interests sections. About that same time every year since 1972, Cuba had urged the UN Committee of 24 (the body that handles questions of decolonization) to take up the status of Puerto Rico. The U.S. always resisted, pointing out that as a self-governing territory, not a colony, Puerto Rico was none of the UN's business.

It was not new, then, for the Cubans to raise the Puerto Rican question, but apparently many in our government had assumed that given the friendlier relations we were then in the process of developing, they would choose not to do so this year.

The Cubans, however, not only raised the Puerto Rican issue but pushed it hard. They presented a resolution calling on the UN to actively pursue self-determination for Puerto Rico, and urged the Committee of 24 to forward it the full General Assembly. The resolution really steamed many Americans, who noted that the Puerto Rican people already had the right of self-determination and could vote, which was more than the Cubans could do.

As it turned out, the Committee of 24 simply voted to postpone consideration of the matter until the following year, so a clash was avoided. Even so, Cuba's insistence on presenting a resolution it knew would offend the United States at the very time we seemed to be making some progress in improving the atmosphere left a sour taste in the mouths of many who favored rapprochement.

I understood why this issue was so deeply felt by the Cubans. José Martí, the revered father of Cuban independence, had championed independence for Puerto Rico as well. With the defeat of Spain in 1898, American forces had occupied both Cuba and Puerto Rico. They had marched out of Cuba in 1902, leaving it an independent republic. Puerto Rico, however, has ever since remained a U.S. territory. The idea that this was unjust, that Puerto Rico ought to be a sister republic, had become an article of faith for Cuban nationalists.

Even though relations between Cuba and the U.S. were now improving, it was not realistic to expect much change in Cuban attitudes with respect to Puerto Rico. Nor, in my view, was that very important. Cubans could *believe* to their hearts' content that Puerto Rico ought to be independent, as long as Cuba did not actively support the tiny Puerto Rican independence movement.

I emphasized this distinction to Sánchez-Parodi when the two of us discussed the issue at length a few days after the inauguration of the interests sections. I pointed out that Cuban meddling in our internal affairs, such as funding the Puerto Rican Independence party, or, even worse, supporting Puerto Rican terrorists, could only have the most unfortunate consequences for our relations.

Sánchez-Parodi replied that Cuba would certainly not meddle in Puerto Rican politics; it would limit itself to expressing its opinion in the UN, which was supposed, after all, to provide a forum for the discussion of conflicting interests and points of view. The U.S. might object to Cuba's point of view, but surely would not deny Cuba's right to express it.

Of course, I countered, but the people of Puerto Rico had expressed their preference in a plebiscite. When had the people of Estonia been able to do that? If Cuba wanted to champion a people's right to self-determination, why not start with Estonia?

Sánchez-Parodi replied that Estonia was not part of Cuba's collective subconscious; Puerto Rico was. Cuba would raise Puerto Rico. If the U.S. wished to raise Estonia, he suggested, it was free to do so.

That was a good idea, I retorted, but if we did, would Cuba vote with us?

"Raise it, and you'll find out," Sánchez-Parodi concluded with a laugh.

The Puerto Rican issue was a minor problem. Greater trouble lay across the sea, in Angola. Events there had been moving in a favorable direction. Castro had begun withdrawing troops in the summer of 1976. The drawdown stalled near the end of the year, but Havana indicated its intention to go ahead with reductions as circumstances permitted. That was Cuban policy until March 1977. Ironically, in the same month that we had our first talks with the Cubans in New York, that policy changed, after Katanganese gendarmes armed and trained in Angola invaded Zaire's Shaba province (formerly Katanga). These gendarmes were the troops, originally organized by European mercenaries and supported by the West, who had fought under Moise Tshombe for an independent Katanga during the Congolese civil war. After that effort failed, they had gone into exile in Angola, and for a time fought for the Portuguese against the various Angolan nationalist forces. During the last stages of the Angolan civil war, however, they had thrown their support to the MPLA, probably because they saw it would be the winning side.

Our information was that while the Angolan government had allowed the incursion into Zaire to take place, it had not inspired or directed it. There was no credible evidence at all of Cuban complicity. To be sure, the Cubans had given the Katanganese some training, but there was nothing to indicate they had encouraged them to cross the border. Certainly the Cubans would have had more to lose than to gain from such a move. Angola's security was Cuba's principal concern in the area, and the Katanganese incursion might well have invited countermoves from Zaire which would have threatened that security.

President Mobutu of Zaire requested assistance in turning back the Katanganese attack, and received it from several countries, including Belgium, France, Egypt, the Sudan, and Morocco. Morocco even provided some 1,500 crack troops. Thus strengthened, Mobutu might have been tempted not simply to drive the intruders out of Zaire, but to pursue them across the border and attack their base camps inside Angola, an action which could have led to clashes with Angola itself. In fact, Mobutu did not do so, but the threat that he might clearly concerned the Angolan president, Agostinho Neto, who requested that no more Cuban troops be withdrawn from Angola. He may also at that point have requested the return of several thousand of those already withdrawn. If not, he certainly made such a request after an abortive coup against him in May carried out by an MPLA faction headed by Nito Alves. The Cubans responded by sending several thousand reinforcements in June and early July.

The U.S. was aware of this action and understood it. No protest was lodged with the Cubans. Our hope was that once the dust had settled from the abortive Nito Alves coup, and once Neto was certain Mobutu did not intend to invade, the drawdown might resume.

Perhaps we should have taken the initiative at that point in suggesting an exchange of views with the Cubans on the Angolan situation, both to clarify their position and to emphasize again the strength of our own feelings on the subject. In retrospect, I have often reproached myself for not sending forward an action memorandum to that effect. At the time, however, there was no sense of urgency, especially since the movement of Cuban troops back to Angola had halted in midsummer. The interests sections were going to open in September; there would be ample opportunity after that, it seemed, to raise the Angolan issue again.

The interests sections *did* open, and in the two months that followed, no significant changes occurred either in the situation in Angola or in Cuban troop levels there. Then, in early November, Ramiro Valdés, a vice-president of the Cuban Council of State (and soon again to be interior minister), announced during a visit to Angola that the number of Cuban technicians in that country would be increased by several thousand during 1978. The U.S. had no particular objection to the presence of Cuban technicians—as long as they were only that. The concern, however, was that they would be followed by new contingents of troops. On November 12, President Carter signaled this concern by reiterating U.S. hopes that Cuba would cut back rather than increase its involvement in Angola. In an off-the-record remark, he acknowledged that the increase seemed to involve no military personnel, only civilians, but observed that, even so, this would make it more difficult for the administration to expand the limited new relationship with Havana.[13]

This was the right thing to say. It was straightforward and in line with our previous position. The Department of State had been consulted beforehand and was in agreement with the president's comment.

I myself thought it would have been better to discuss the matter privately with the Cubans before airing it in a more public way. Still, I understood why the president wished to be frank. And as his statement did not basically alter our earlier positions, I thought there was still time to arrange a full exchange of views with Havana through our interests section. I informed Todman of what I thought we should do and got his go-ahead to begin working on the necessary instructions. Before I was well started, however, Brzezinski, in an unattributed statement on November 16, rendered the whole effort irrelevant.

The president's comment had been one thing; Brzezinski's was something else again. Having breakfast the morning of November 16 with a number of journalists, Brzezinski gave them a background briefing in which he was described as a "high-ranking administration official." A new CIA study, he told them, revealed that there had been a steady military buildup in Angola and Ethiopia during the summer and fall, and that there were now Cuban military personnel in some thirteen African countries.[14] Just since July, he said, some 4,000 to 6,000 Cuban troops had been sent to Angola. Normalization with Cuba was therefore now "impossible."[15]

I had been in Williamsburg, Virginia, the evening of November 16 giving a talk on U.S.-Cuban relations. I heard about the "high-ranking" official's announcement on the car radio driving back to Washington the next morning. I was stunned. What "steady buildup in Angola" was he talking about? And how could such a statement have been made without the knowledge of the Office of Cuban Affairs? I had spoken to the office by phone the afternoon of November 16. At that point, no one had been aware that such a statement was to be issued—that, indeed, it had already been made.

Arriving back at the Department of State and reading Hedrick Smith's article in the *New York Times,* I was more puzzled than ever, for "administration officials" were quoted as saying we had informed the Cuban government through diplomatic channels of our displeasure over the buildup. As far as I knew, we had done no such thing. To be sure, we had consistently made known our concern over the continued presence of Cuban troops in Angola. But we most certainly had not protested any troop buildup since July, for the simple reason that *there had been no buildup.* I called an analyst at the CIA to confirm this. Did we, I asked, have any evidence of the arrival of significant numbers of Cuban troops in Angola since mid-July?

The answer was no. I was told, however, that on the basis of new evidence, the CIA had revised upward its estimate of how many Cuban troops were in Angola. What was involved, in other words, was not a buildup but a revision in our own bookkeeping.

I then called Todman to see if he knew what was behind the White House statement. His secretary told me to come upstairs immediately; Mr. Todman was angry at me. As I walked into his office, he glared and asked, "Did you clear that statement without informing me?"

No, I said emphatically, I did not. No one had consulted me either. What about the secretary of state? I asked. Had he been consulted?

No, Todman replied, he had not. Todman sank back in his chair and shook his head glumly. This was no way to run foreign policy, he muttered. He then instructed me to get from Bob Pastor, the Latin American adviser on the NSC, a read-out on the statement and what was behind it. I did so and found Pastor evasive. Why should there have been any consultations on the November 16 statement? he asked. It really contained nothing new. It simply reemphasized long-standing U.S. concerns over Cuba's military presence in Africa, which seemed to be increasing. The purpose was to warn the Cubans against any further increase.

I protested that this was neither an accurate description of the statement nor a fair prediction of its effect. Saying that normalization was now "impossible" obviously went far beyond what I had understood our position to be. The statement was, moreover, filled with inaccuracies. For example, there had been no "steady buildup in Angola since July." And in view of all this, the statement was more likely to puzzle the Cubans than to warn them.

I concluded by pointing out that no one in the Department of State had even seen the new CIA report to which Brzezinski had referred. Might Pastor at least send me a copy?

Pastor agreed to do so. When it arrived that afternoon, I was appalled. It consisted of two pages, the first a list of countries, with the CIA's estimate of how many Cuban civilian and military personnel were in each, and the second a map showing where the countries were. Some study!

In all fairness, the fault was not the CIA's. Apparently asked by Brzezinski for its latest estimates of Cuban personnel in various African states, that is what the agency gave him. And as already indicated, the CIA had just revised those estimates upward. Some of the figures were dead wrong. There were nothing like 450–600 Cuban military advisers in Mozambique, as the "study" suggested, none in Uganda, and none in the Malagasy Republic. The "high-ranking administration official" had been incorrect in saying that Cubans had recently spread into these countries. In most other cases, the Cubans had been in the listed countries for several years—they had been in Guinea and Congo (Brazzaville) since the mid-1960s. One had to wonder why the Carter administration was making an issue of that presence now.

The only development of any significance reflected in the CIA estimates was the reported presence of 400 Cuban military advisers and 300 medical personnel in Ethiopia. A warning to the Cubans not to intervene in Ethiopia would have made sense. Subsequently, the

NSC claimed it had been issuing just such a warning. If so, it went about it the wrong way. By referring also to twelve other countries and by talking about troop buildups in Angola that were in fact fictitious, Brzezinski simply confused the issue and left the Cubans wondering what we were in fact getting at. And as we shall see, by making his case in public before it had been discussed with the Cubans through diplomatic channels, Brzezinski may, on balance, actually have *increased* the chances of Cuban intervention in Ethiopia.

Shortly after Brzezinski's breakfast briefing, Ramón Sánchez-Parodi asked to see me. He wanted an explanation of the White House statement. "Why did your government say this?" he asked. "You know there has been no increase in our troop strength in Angola since July. And even with those increases in June, we still have far fewer men there now than we did at top strength—about 40 percent fewer. We would like to reduce further, but we cannot until the situation is more stable. We understand that this is a matter of concern to you. We accept that. But if you thought we were building up in Angola, why did you not raise the question with us through the diplomatic channels we now have? You claim you used them, but in fact you did not. Why? We thought it was for situations like this that you wanted to have them."

As the NSC had not, after Brzezinski's November 16 statement, provided us with any rationale or guidelines for handling such questions, I was at a disadvantage. Still, as a good soldier, I had to support the White House position. I therefore answered Sánchez-Parodi by saying that while we might argue over how many troops had been in Angola six months before, the fact was that the number had increased since then. Moreover, I pointed out, these new reports of Cubans arriving in Ethiopia were of great concern to my government.

Sánchez-Parodi noted that I hadn't explained why the U.S. had failed to discuss the problem through private communications.

I admitted that I was uncertain and that I, personally, thought there might have been a tidier way to proceed. Nonetheless, I added, whether made publicly or through diplomatic channels, the warning of the U.S. government was serious and should be so treated.

A few days later, Sánchez-Parodi was received by Undersecretary for Political Affairs Phil Habib to discuss the same issue. Habib gave him essentially the same answers I had—not surprisingly, since the Office of Cuban Affairs had written the briefing paper on which Habib based his response.

But the Cubans did not accept our advice that they take the warning seriously. Rather, as they mulled over the highly public nature of the November 16 statement, they concluded that it must have been made for domestic public consumption. The Carter administration was being attacked by the right wing on the issue of the Panama Canal treaties. Perhaps it was seeking to shore up its right flank by adopting a tough posture toward Cuba.

A number of Cuban diplomats put forward this thesis to me at a dinner party in Washington in early December: "If your government were really as concerned as it says it is over our activities in Africa, it would have discussed them with us privately. Diplomatic channels are for serious business; public statements are for striking postures with some domestic political consideration in mind."

I felt a grudging admiration for the political acumen behind the latter statement, even as I tried to disabuse them of its validity in this case. I made little headway. I am sure they continued to believe for several more weeks that they need not take as seriously as they once had U.S. expressions of concern over their African policies.

I do not mean to suggest that the Cubans subsequently intervened in Ethiopia *because* of Brzezinski's November 16 statement. In the final analysis, the Cubans went in because of circumstances there, and probably would have done so even if the statement had not been made. What I do say, however, is that to the extent that the Brzezinski statement had any effect at all, it reduced rather than increased the degree to which concern over U.S. reaction might have acted as a restraint on Cuban actions. After all, he had said normalization was already impossible. Cuban policy makers would therefore have concluded that in terms of their relations with the U.S., they had nothing to lose by going in. Normalization would be no more "impossible" whether they intervened in Ethiopia or refrained from doing so.

The Brzezinski statement of November 16 had implications for our relations with Angola as well. In effect it meant that the Carter administration would not follow the approach many of us had expected toward Angola. Neto was still energetically seeking to establish a more amicable relationship with the U.S. Gulf Oil, and a number of other U.S. companies, were doing business in Angola. Why not add diplomatic relations to the commercial ties that already existed? Many of us felt that it was time for the U.S. to make its own presence and influence felt in Angola. But this was not to be. Brzezinski pressed instead for a hard line toward Angola and for a policy of trying to drive the Cubans out of Angola. This had not the slightest chance of success and ran counter to everything most of us in the Department of State believed the Carter administration should be doing in the area. As Cyrus Vance was later to put it:

My hope of increasing our leverage in Angola had disappeared with the administration's decision not to recognize the Neto government as long as Cuban forces remained in Angola. Some proponents of this move believed that U.S. support for the UNITA insurgency in the south, led by Jonas Savimbi, would provide a way to drive the Cubans out of Angola. On the contrary, I believed the reason the Angolans kept the Cubans in Angola was because they feared further incursions by South Africa and South African support of UNITA. I felt that the solution lay in removing these Angolan concerns that, in African opinion, legitimized the Soviet and Cuban presence.[16]

In fact, we never got around to giving Savimbi any significant support, but by the end of 1977, Brzezinski had succeeded in so changing the administration's mind-set that the idea of expanding our relationship with Angola could not be resuscitated. Indeed, by then our whole approach in the Third World was shifting back toward the more rigid East-West oriented responses of the past.

Developments in Africa would continue to bedevil U.S.-Cuban relations. That was perhaps inevitable, but I never felt the Carter White House, particularly the NSC, understood the nature of the problem or how best to address it. By failing to provide any progress toward a solution, they became a part of the problem.

5

Cuba, the United States, and Africa

Two principal characteristics seemed to govern the National Security Council's approach to Cuba's presence in Africa. The first was marked indifference to the facts, as demonstrated by Brzezinski's claim of a Cuban buildup in Angola, when in fact none existed, and his suggestion that the Cubans were now moving into countries where in fact they had been operating for years. The NSC seemed to believe that Cuba's interest and involvement in Africa were new—as though taken up just to bedevil the Carter administration. On the contrary. Cuba had played a minor role in the first Algerian-Moroccan war in 1963—on the Algerian side. When Che Guevera left Cuba in 1965, he had gone first to the Congo, to work (unsuccessfully) toward an anti-Western guerrilla force. Only after he failed there did he go on to Bolivia. Cuban troops had been in Congo (Brazzaville) since 1965, and Castro had enjoyed a close relationship with the MPLA in Angola since that time also. Only the magnitude of Cuban involvement changed in 1975. To be sure, it should have concerned us all the same, but if one is to deal with a problem, one ought to understand its nature and genesis. I never was aware of any real effort at the senior levels of the NSC to understand either.

Second, Brzezinski tended to interpret most political and military events in terms of some Soviet blueprint for world conquest. Even local conflicts were seen in an East-West context. Whatever the Soviets or Cubans did, Brzezinski believed that they were "testing" us and unless we responded vigorously, they would think us lacking in will. It seemed never to occur to him that the other side might be reacting to some thoughtless move of our own, convinced that *we* were testing *them*. Ethiopia was a case in point.

The Intervention in Ethiopia

The abrupt change of partners in the Horn of Africa in 1977 is a case study in the cynicism of politics—on both sides. Somalia had long been a close ally of the Soviet Union and Cuba. The Russians held a major naval base at Berbera, on the Gulf of Aden. Ethiopia, on the other hand, had been one of *our* staunchest allies in Africa. Even after the overthrow of Emperor Haile Selassie in 1974 by a military junta —the Dergue—the U.S. was allowed to keep its military facilities, including the large air base at Kagnew. The Dergue put out no feelers to the Soviets or Cubans; rather, the junta wanted continued good relations with the West.

For their part, Moscow and Havana showed little interest in events in Ethiopia—at least, not until February 1977, when Lt. Col. Mengistu Haile Mariam, the leader of the Dergue's radical wing, emerged as the new head of government. Then Castro's antennae suddenly began to quiver. He issued an unusually enthusiastic greeting to Mengistu and indicated a desire to pay him a state visit.

Mengistu was more assertively Marxist than the previous leaders of the Dergue had been. Even so, he did not break with the West; a problem with Eritrea complicated the development of relations with Moscow and Havana. Eritrea, a province of Ethiopia, had long sought to win its independence. The United States and most other Western countries supported the central government in Addis Ababa, emphasized the territorial integrity of Ethiopia, and denied Eritrea's right of secession. Moscow and Havana, on the other hand, pushed self-determination for Eritrea and provided material support to the rebels there.

Hence, as Mengistu came to power and tackled the problem of holding Ethiopia together, he had some reason to be wary of Moscow and Havana, and to look to the U.S. for support. With patient and adroit U.S. management, it is possible that Mengistu would not have become closely associated with the Soviets and Cubans; rather, he might have followed a nonaligned path and kept his doors open to both East and West. Secretary of State Vance saw that possibility and wanted to capitalize on it, noting that "there was some evidence that Mengistu was unhappy with the Soviets and was still willing to maintain contact with us."[1]

Vance says President Carter approved such an approach. If so, we had a strange way of implementing it. On February 24, 1977, only days after Mengistu had assumed power, the U.S. drastically reduced its aid to Ethiopia on grounds that Ethiopia had disregarded human rights. There had indeed been political assassinations and widespread violence. But it would have seemed wiser and more productive to try to work with the new Mengistu government *before* cutting the aid. As it was, the timing of the announcement created the impression that we were reducing aid *because* of Mengistu's rise to power.

Mengistu certainly took it that way and soon retaliated by ordering the closure of all U.S. facilities in the country, except for our diplomatic mission. Thus we lost an important air base and a major tracking station. The U.S. responded by cutting off all military assistance and arms sales to Ethiopia.

Having received a warm reception in Moscow and Havana and a cold shoulder from Washington, Mengistu turned increasingly to the former two. In May, he asked the Soviets for the arms and other military equipment he could no longer obtain from the U.S. The Soviets cautiously agreed and signed an arms agreement with Mengistu.

Needless to say, none of this was to the liking of Siad Barre, the Somali chief of state. Somalia, Ethiopia's traditional enemy, had irredentist claims on those parts of the Ogaden desert which lie in Ethiopia and had counted on Soviet and Cuban support in asserting those claims. Now, here were those trusted allies courting his enemy, and starting in May even to supply him with arms. Siad Barre protested strongly to both Moscow and Havana, but to no avail.

The Soviets and Cubans actually tried to keep a foot in each camp. In March, Castro visited Mogadiscio and Addis Ababa in an attempt to act as peacemaker between the two. According to Castro, Siad Barre gave assurances that he would not attack Ethiopia.[2]

But Siad Barre was not to be put off so easily. Whatever he may have said to Castro, he continued preparations for an invasion of Ethiopia—and made little effort to hide them. In the June 13 edition of *Afrique-Asie* (Paris), he openly stated that the duty of the leader of Somalia was clear: to reunify the Somali state by any means at his disposal, i.e., to take the Ogaden by force if necessary.[3] The Ethiopians surely interpreted this as a declaration of hostilities.

Just at this tense juncture, with both sides poised for war, the U.S. bumbled its way into the situation with all the finesse of a water buffalo. Perceiving that the Soviets and Cubans would not support his efforts to reclaim the Ogaden, Siad Barre had begun casting about for new patrons. He found one in the White House. On June 11, President Carter indicated the U.S. would "aggressively challenge" the Soviet Union for influence in Somalia and a number of other countries.[4] Encouraged, Siad Barre then asked the U.S. for arms.

That the U.S. wished to lure Siad Barre from the Soviet camp was perfectly understandable—merely part of the international game. But given the explosive state of relations in the Horn, the U.S. ought to have proceeded with extreme caution, making it clear to Siad Barre that while he would find a welcome in the Western camp, the U.S. was no more willing than the Soviets and Cubans had been to support an invasion of Ethiopia. In the final analysis, a war in the Horn of Africa was in no one's interest. Secretary Vance perceived the danger. He subsequently wrote:

We approached our relations with Somalia with caution, for there was growing probability that the regime in Mogadiscio would send its army into Ethiopia to attempt to seize the Ogaden. If we become too closely linked with Somalia, we would find ourselves inadvertently on the wrong side of one of Africa's most cherished principles—the territorial integrity of the postcolonial states. In addition, aggression against Ethiopia would provide in African eyes the same justification for Soviet and Cuban military presence in Ethiopia as South African intervention in Angola in 1975 had done.
... I recommended to the president that we refuse to supply even defensive military equipment or to permit our allies and friends to transfer U.S. arms to Somalia until the Ogaden affair was settled.[5]

Again Vance believed that the president agreed with his recommendation. But as was so often the case, whether the president agreed with the recommendation or not, he did not follow the course of action it called for. As Vance himself reported:

In mid-June, the Somali Ambassador met with President Carter with an urgent new request from Siad Barre for military assistance. The president replied that it would be difficult for us to provide military assistance, but we would see whether our allies could help Somalia maintain its defensive strength. The Somalis interpreted this as a "forthcoming attitude" and on July 9 made a specific request for arms. After considerable discussion, we concluded that "in principle" we would help other countries to meet Somalia's needs for defensive equipment. The Somalis were informed of this decision in mid-July.[6]

This was a strange way to approach our relations with Somalia cautiously. Only days after Siad Barre had practically announced his intention to invade Ethiopia, the U.S. went against Vance's recommendations. The arms commitment was all the encouragement Siad Barre needed. Almost immediately, on July 17, Somali troops crossed the border in force.

Vance recognized the causal relationship between our "forthcoming attitude" and the Somali invasion. "The Somalis had not been able to resist the temptation," he noted dryly.[7]

Richard Moose, our assistant secretary of state for African affairs, called in the Somali ambassador on August 4 and told him that although we had agreed in principle to provide arms to Somalia, the invasion might impede fulfillment of that commitment. That meeting was private. The public impression was still that we would provide the arms.

The Soviets and Cubans, of course, thought that the U.S. was behind the Somali invasion. They had watched as Siad Barre approached us for assurances of support, and only days later poured Somali troops across the border. Obviously, they concluded, the U.S. was using Somalia to undermine the leftist government in Addis Ababa, which had closed down its bases.

In discussing the matter with Brzezinski a short time later, Soviet Ambassador Anatoly Dobrynin confirmed that his superiors in Moscow were convinced of such a conspiracy.[8] Castro was convinced of it too. When I met with him in June 1978, he was still angry about it. "By saying you would give Siad Barre arms," he said, "you helped touch off the war, and since you obviously would have been delighted if Somalia had won and ousted Mengistu, it is difficult not to believe that you did it deliberately."[9]

I did not believe there were any such sinister motives behind U.S. actions in the Horn and I told Castro so. If we had helped provoke the war, I said, it had been inadvertently. At the same time, I had to acknowledge to myself that had I been sitting in Castro's chair, I would have been just as convinced as he of Washington's ulterior motives. And in politics, one reacts not to reality but to one's perception of reality.

Siad Barre had thrown twelve mechanized brigades and 250 tanks against Ethiopia. Disorganized and poorly led, Ethiopia's forces at first retreated in disorder. As Somali forces penetrated deeper into Ethiopia, however, their supply lines lengthened and serious logistical problems arose. Ethiopian forces, moreover, began to rally and put up increasing resistance. By the end of October, the Somali offensive had stalled.

At that point, Siad Barre made a fatal mistake. Between July and November, both Moscow and Havana had urged an end to hostilities, and both, wishing to maintain positions in Somalia as well as Ethiopia, had been decidedly restrained in their support for Ethiopia. The Soviets had provided only limited amounts of military aid; Cuba had sent only a few medical personnel and military advisers. But on November 13, apparently hoping to persuade the U.S. and other Western states to come to his assistance, Siad Barre expelled all Soviet personnel and canceled Moscow's rights to maintain a base at Berbera. He also broke diplomatic relations with Havana and tossed out all Cuban personnel. Perhaps even more infuriating to the Soviets than the Somali action itself was a message from the People's Republic of China to Siad Barre congratulating him for expelling the Soviets.[10]

The U.S. applauded also, but remained unpersuaded that it ought to provide military aid. Hence, the principal result of Siad Barre's November 13 actions was to remove the reason for Soviet and Cuban restraint. With no further reason to worry about maintaining a position in Somalia, the Soviets went full tilt in support of Ethiopia. Ethiopia desperately needed their assistance, for on November 22, Siad Barre renewed his offensive, this time pointing his attack at the city of Harar. As in August, Somalia again seemed on the verge of winning. Addis Ababa pleaded for increased Soviet logistical support and for Cuban troops. In late December, it began to receive both. By February 1978, as many as 15,000 Cuban soldiers had arrived in Ethiopia. Together with the badly mauled remnants of the Ethiopian army, they launched a counteroffensive which soon had the Somalis reeling back toward their own border. The tide had turned. From that point forward, it was clear that Somalia would lose the war.

Concern grew in Washington that the Cuban-Ethiopian surge would not stop at the Somali frontier, but, rather, would roll all the way to the Indian Ocean, leaving Somalia an occupied country. There was also concern that the Cubans would help Mengistu wipe out Eritrean secessionists—concern because now that the U.S. and

Ethiopia were no longer allies, we had done a 180-degree turn. From supporting the central government's position, we had come around to voicing support for the aspirations of the Eritrean people. Making this shift was probably the right thing to do, but clearly the new position was dictated by realpolitik rather than any moral concern for the independence of Eritrea.

The Cubans and Ethiopians assured us that they had no intention of penetrating Somali territory, and in the event, they did halt at the frontier—after chasing the last Somali soldier back across it. The Cubans also assured us privately that they did not intend to become involved in the fighting in Eritrea. Like us, they had reversed themselves on the Eritrean question. Having once supported the secessionists, they now backed the central government's efforts to maintain Ethiopia's territorial integrity. At least, however, the Cubans also stressed the need for a negotiated solution and for some kind of semiautonomous status for Eritrea within the Ethiopian state. And they refused to be drawn into fighting against the rebels they had once backed.

Back in Washington, the Soviet and Cuban involvement in the war with Somalia produced sharp divisions within the Carter administration. The Department of State tended to see the intervention not as part of a broad strategy of encroachment, but rather as a Soviet effort to take advantage of a target of opportunity resulting from a local conflict. Thus, the damage was perceived as limited and probably reparable. Secretary Vance's recommendation was that we work with our European allies and with the African states to end hostilities and negotiate solutions to the broader regional issues—thus closing off the target of opportunity to the Soviets.[11]

Brzezinski, however, inevitably saw the intervention as part of an aggressive and probably premeditated Soviet strategy, which was incompatible with détente. He wanted to respond by sending a carrier task force to the waters off the Horn. It would have taken no part in the fighting, Brzezinski insisted later; rather, its presence alone would have demonstrated our seriousness of purpose.[12]

It is difficult to agree with Brzezinski's reasoning. The presence of an inactive carrier would not have helped the Somalis in the slightest, and rather than showing U.S. resolve, it might have opened us to ridicule. One can imagine the headlines around the world: CARRIER STEAMS HELPLESSLY OFFSHORE WHILE ON LAND CUBAN-ETHIOPIAN FORCES CONTINUE TO PUMMEL SOMALIS.

If we were going to affect the military situation in the Horn after the Soviet and Cuban intervention, we had to stand ready to send a lot more than a carrier task force; it would have taken a major U.S. military commitment, and not even Brzezinski was willing to go that far. Afterward, nonetheless, he was to suggest that all the Carter administration's subsequent foreign-policy failures could be traced back to its failure to heed his advice on this one issue. As he put it: "SALT lies buried in the sands of the Ogaden."[13]

But SALT was buried less by the sands of the Ogaden than by Brzezinski's irresponsible rhetoric and his loose-cannon approach to foreign policy. In his book, Brzezinski acknowledges the existence of unanimous agreement within the Carter administration that there should be "no direct linkage between Soviet and Cuban actions in the Horn and bilateral activities involving either country and the United States."[14] Yet in a press conference on March 1, 1978, Brzezinski gave just the opposite impression, suggesting that while *we* did not impose linkages between SALT and the situation in the Horn, Soviet actions might make them unavoidable.[15]

Given the moment, and the way the remark was phrased, it could only lead to misinterpretation and unwanted speculation. The press the next day reported Brzezinski to have advocated a policy of linkage—exactly what the administration had wished to avoid. And since in addressing a congressional committee on the same day Secretary Vance stuck to the policy line and denied any linkage between SALT and the situation in the Horn, the impression inevitably created was that the administration was sharply divided.

Brzezinski's analysis of events in the Horn had many weaknesses, but perhaps the greatest was his failure to consider the genesis of the problem. He seems to have focused on it only after the die was more or less cast, and never to have asked himself how we got to that point. For example, in February 1978, he believed it imperative that we prevent a close association between Ethiopia and the Soviet Union. Yet by then the U.S. could do very little to prevent such an association. Sending a carrier task force, as he proposed, would certainly have had no effect. Earlier, on the other hand, we might have done a good deal. If denying the Soviets an opening to Ethiopia was important, why had we cut off aid to Ethiopia so hurriedly after Mengistu came to power? We knew he inclined toward Marxism. Did we not think that denying aid might push him irrevocably in Moscow's direction? Our stated policy had been to keep our lines open to Mengistu, but we failed utterly to do that. All such considerations, however, are missing from Brzezinski's reflections. Moreover, it was Somalia's invasion of Ethiopia that raised real problems for us. Had there been no war, there would have been no need for Cuban troops or large-scale infusions of Soviet equipment. Yet, as we have seen, we played a key role in starting the war.

The Soviets and the Cubans were convinced the U.S. was behind the invasion. They had already lost one ally in the Horn (Somalia) through defection; they saw no reason to stand aside and lose another to external aggression. Further, they doubtless reasoned that letting us win this victory in the Horn on the cheap might lead to misinterpretation on our part concerning *their* lack of will. Thus, they reacted to what they perceived to be an aggressive move of ours. Brzezinski in turn saw the Soviet reaction as proof that they were testing *us*. His subsequent portrayal of Soviet and Cuban actions in the Horn as showing contempt for détente had a most deleterious effect on the prospects for SALT and for broader improvement of relations with both the Soviet Union and Cuba.

Brzezinski's portrayal of the situation also did our own country a disservice by giving the impression that we had been bested, when in fact, despite our bumbling, we had come out not too badly. Cuba and Ethiopia honored their assurances to us and did not invade Somali territory. Somalia's national integrity remained intact. As Cyrus Vance later described Brzezinski's reaction: "We were shooting ourselves in the foot. By casting the complex Horn situation in East-West terms, and by setting impossible objectives for U.S. policy —elimination of Soviet and Cuban influence in Ethiopia—we were creating a perception that we were defeated when, in fact, we were achieving a successful outcome."[16]

Brzezinski feared leaving either friends or allies with the impression of passivity on our part. The concern was sensible; the conduct to which it led was not. To be sure, a great power should not be passive in the face of events which affect its interests. But it need not always react with military force. The important thing is that it act intelligently and in the manner best calculated to advance its objectives. Military measures may sometimes be appropriate, but often diplomacy is a better instrument: to exercise effective diplomacy is not to be passive. The situation in the Horn well illustrates the point. The U.S. ought to have concentrated on diplomatic efforts to defuse the situation, rather than, as we did, adding fuel to the fire.

None of this is to say that the Soviets and Cubans did not bear their full share of the responsibility. After all, had they not armed Somalia to the teeth while it was still their ally, it could not have attacked Ethiopia even with an expression of support from us. And just as we could have taken the initiative in mounting a diplomatic peace-keeping effort, so also could they. But to say that the Soviets and Cubans might have behaved more responsibly cannot be much comfort to us. The day that we expect more responsible behavior from them than from our own government is the day we will no longer have any claim to moral leadership in the world.

With the arrival of Cuban troops in Ethiopia, the freeze on the normalization process which Brzezinski had announced on November 16 of the previous year hardened into a rigid refusal to contemplate even minor steps forward until those troops were withdrawn. The whole idea of a step-by-step process based on reciprocity was shelved for good.

Shaba II

In March 1977, as we have seen, the Katanganese had invaded Shaba province in Zaire, but they had been repelled by a joint Zairean-Moroccan force. Now, in May 1978, they tried again, this time crossing through Zambia to launch their attack.

Almost immediately, Castro called in the chief of the U.S. interests section in Havana, Lyle Lane, and told him that Cuba was not only *not* behind the invasion, but wanted it turned off as quickly as possible. Cuba, he said, had received reports in April that the Katanganese were planning such an invasion. He had tried unsuccessfully to stop them. These incursions by the Katanganese, he went on, created a threat to Angola's security. The best thing for all concerned would be to get them back across the border and disarm them. If there were ways in which Cuba and the U.S. could cooperate in defusing the situation, he concluded, Cuba stood ready to help.

Lane, of course, reported Castro's overture to the department by cable. It was read with much interest, and in due course the secretary of state instructed me to reply by asking Lane to thank Castro and to say we would let him know if we saw ways in which we might take him up on his offer of help. I, together with members of the Shaba crisis force in the department's operations center, then began compiling a list of things we might ask the Cubans to do, when the time came.

Unfortunately, our positive response was quickly overtaken by events. The cable from Havana reporting Castro's demarche leaked to the press. On May 19, the *New York Times* reported that Castro had said he wasn't behind the invasion and had offered to help stop it. This report infuriated the NSC. True to form, Brzezinski had interpreted the Katanganese invasion in an East-West context. The Soviets and Cubans, he apparently believed, were again testing us. He wanted a show of force on our part. The U.S. was just announcing that it would participate in a French and Belgian mission to rescue by air the Europeans trapped in Shaba province, and the NSC and White House wanted to portray this as a decisive response on our part to a Soviet and Cuban thrust in Africa. It would be, in effect, Brzezinski's show of force, his "carrier task force." But how could it appear to be a response to the Soviets and Cubans if we let stand Castro's statement that he too was against the invasion and was prepared to cooperate with us in ending it? The NSC and White House solved that problem easily enough by ignoring Castro's statement and insisting that we had stacks of evidence to prove Castro was indeed behind the invasion.

In fact, we had nothing of the sort. I had seen all the reports to which the NSC referred. On their basis, one might reasonably have concluded that the Angolan government knew of the Katanganese plans to invade and had done little to stop them. One might also have concluded that perhaps in the past the Cubans had helped to train and arm the Katanganese. There was no credible evidence, however, that they had encouraged the invasion or in any way supported it. Such allegations appeared in a few third-hand and rather inconsistent intelligence reports. No self-respecting analyst would have based his conclusions on those. Secretary Vance's assessment was similar to mine. As he put it: "We did have some ambiguous, and, as it turned out, not very good intelligence to this effect."[17]

The White House and NSC, however, continued to insist that the evidence was "overwhelming." At one point, on the basis of a single and obviously unreliable report, they had Tom Reston, the department's spokesman, say in the noon briefing that we were receiving new evidence to confirm the old. Such unfounded statements put many of us in a quandary. For example, I was called by a friend who worked on the staff of the Senate Foreign Relations Committee. "You must have seen these reports the NSC keeps talking about," he said. "What can you say about them? Do they convince you the Cubans were behind this?"

What was I to say? I thought the NSC's position on the matter to be outright rubbish. But as a Foreign Service officer serving at the pleasure of the president, I could not openly take issue with the views of my superiors. Neither was I going to lie for them. I took the bureaucratic way out, telling my friend on the committee that I did not wish to comment at all. He understood immediately that my refusal meant that I did not agree with the NSC's statements but did not wish to say so.

He laughed and said, "You're the fourth person I've called about this, and you're also the fourth person to say 'No comment.'"

Shortly thereafter, the Senate Foreign Relations Committee asked to see the evidence. Rather than finding it "overwhelming," the committee found it "circumstantial and by no means conclusive," and said so publicly. John Sparkman, the committee chairman, said the Carter administration had failed to produce convincing evidence that the Cubans were still involved in training and arming the Katanganese, let alone in encouraging them to invade Shaba province.[18]

Meanwhile, President Carter had retreated somewhat from earlier allegations that the Cubans were behind the invasion. In a statement on May 25, the president continued to blame the Cubans and Angolans, but the nature of their responsibility was now watered down. Rather than being accused of encouraging the Katanganese, they were now simply accused of having done nothing to restrain the invaders. But the president phrased even this lesser charge in a way that can only be described as less than straightforward. "We believe," he said, "that Cuba had known of the Katanga plan to invade and obviously did nothing to restrain them from crossing the frontier."[19]

Not once did Carter mention that Castro had *told* us he had found out about the invasion plans and had tried to stop them. Not until June 15, after Castro himself had publicly mentioned informing us of these reports, did Carter acknowledge that Castro had "told one of our diplomats" of knowing of the invasion plans. He added rather lamely that Cuba could have done a lot more to stop the invasion if it had wanted to.[20]

The statement that the Cubans could have done a lot more to stop the invasion was of course a far cry from our earlier claims, first that they were behind it, and then that they had made no effort at all to stop it. This definitely had not been Jimmy Carter's finest, or most truthful, hour.

The timing of the president's renewed attack was particularly unfortunate, for Secretary Vance was scheduled to meet secretly in New York on the evening of May 25 with Carlos Rafael Rodríguez, a vice-president of the Cuban Council of State. Vance hoped at least to begin getting the process of improving relations—which had been derailed since the previous November 16—back on track. Position papers had been prepared for him on the key issues in disagreement, and his intention was to have a frank but constructive exchange with Rodríguez about those disagreements.

The NSC and White House were of course aware of Vance's scheduled May 25 meeting with Rodríguez. They had to have known also that the president's statement of that date in which he, in effect, again called Castro a liar, could not but poison the atmosphere for the meeting. They went ahead with the attack anyhow. Worse, though Vance was too much of a gentleman ever to complain of it publicly, the fact was that the NSC did not even inform him of what it had written for the president to say that day. The impression left on the Cubans was of an uncoordinated, if not bifurcated, style of government. If they were puzzled and inclined to ask which was the real American policy, one could not blame them.[21] I wasn't certain either.

Castro laid the blame at Brzezinski's door rather than Carter's. Carter, he said, had been misled. For his part, he would be ready to meet with Carter at any time to straighten out this and other misunderstandings.[22] Carter never replied.

Should we have called Castro a liar and accused him of complicity on the basis of such flimsy evidence without even testing his expressed willingness to help defuse the situation? To my mind, there is only one possible answer to that question. It does not take much imagination to see ways in which we could have made good use of Castro's offer. Might we not, for example, have suggested that he and Neto, the Angolan president, issue a public appeal to the Katanganese to withdraw from Shaba province immediately, failing which, they (the Katanganese) would be subject to arrest and imprisonment if they returned to Angola?

Perhaps Castro would have refused, but my own sense of things, based on the tone of his conversation with Lane and my own conversations with Cuban diplomats in Washington, was that he might well have agreed. At least we would have tested him. Nor was there any reason we could not have asked for Castro's cooperation and also assisted the French and Belgian rescue mission. The two things were by no means mutually exclusive.

That Castro was sincere about defusing Katanganese troublemaking is suggested by the fact that Cuban forces shortly thereafter did cooperate with the Angolans in disarming the Katanganese, moving them away from the border areas, and incorporating them into the regular Angolan army—disbanding the separate units in which they had previously operated. Further, Cuba was instrumental in easing tensions and eventually in bringing about a rapprochement between Angola and Zaire. As Vice-President Rodríguez put it to me in a conversation in 1982: "The real security threat Angola faces is in the south, from South Africa; neither we nor the Angolans want any trouble in the north, with Zaire."

Nor was this the only helpful action taken by the Cubans in Africa. Also in 1978, they urged the South West African People's Organization (SWAPO) to accept the proposals for a Namibian settlement put forward by the Western contact group (the U.S., France, Great Britain, West Germany, and Belgium). Acceptance of the proposals was blocked by South African, not Cuban, intransigence.

In the Rhodesian problem also, the Cubans kept hands off and played a constructive role. Some in the Carter administration were willing to bet that Cuban troops would appear next in Rhodesia. Instead, Castro supported the Lancaster House agreements, which led to elections and to an independent state, Zimbabwe. Moreover, he continued his support even after his preferred candidate, Joshua Nkomo, lost the elections.

In an assessment paper in early 1979, I tried to put in a balanced paragraph noting that while certain Cuban actions in Africa were objectionable, others had actually contributed to peaceful solutions and had been helpful to us. This pointed up the fact, I went on, that our interests did not always clash. Sometimes there might even be common ground. U.S. diplomacy should take advantage of those circumstances and seek to engage the Cubans in responsible peace-keeping efforts whenever possible. It might, I noted, have been better to have done so in the case of Shaba II.

The paragraph was of course deleted by the NSC. "We aren't interested in your so-called balanced assessment," the council representative told me. "We want to emphasize that the Soviets and the Cubans are the aggressors." He might have added "whether they always are or not."

Trying to score such propaganda points against the other side has its dangers. It unnecessarily raises some tempers and encourages bellicose tendencies. The Carter administration talked so often and in such alarmist terms about the Cubans in Africa—Brzezinski delightedly referring to them as Soviet Hessians—that various members of Congress began to demand that something be done. In mid-1978, some legislators wanted to pass a resolution calling on the administration to close the U.S. interests section in Havana. Of course, the administration had no intention of doing this. It found itself trapped by its own rhetoric, for in scoring its propaganda points, it had ignored a cardinal rule of politics: one's rhetoric must raise only an appropriate level of concern. The Carter-Brzezinski audience expected that actions would follow the tough talk. When none did, Carter was labeled a wimp.

The administration had also spoken with many, often discordant, voices about the conflicts in Africa. A policy line would be developed and the president would assure Secretary of State Vance that he supported it. Vance would stick to the agreed position, but Brzezinski would say something quite different and the president would not correct him. Other voices within the administration would then pop up with third and fourth interpretations. It was not a style to inspire confidence. Yet, it was the style which prevailed all through the Carter years in the White House. With a different cast of characters, it would carry over into the Reagan presidency.

6

The Cubans Try
to Revive the Process
1978

I was scheduled to be in Havana in June 1978 for an orientation and inspection visit to our interests section. The timing, I thought, was unfortunate. One of my principal aims was to iron out with Cuban officials some of the problems that Cuban regulations were causing in our efforts to maintain and supply the interests section. With the dust still unsettled from the shouting match over Shaba II, I could hardly expect them to be in a receptive mood. Postponement was difficult, however, because of various meetings coming up in Washington, and, I reasoned, was probably pointless anyway, since one shouting match might quickly follow another. So I went ahead with the trip. To my surprise, I was received cordially by the Cubans, who heard me out and promised to make every effort to find solutions. Further, I was told as soon as I arrived that I would probably be received by a "major Cuban leader," i.e., Fidel Castro, at some point during my stay.

Meeting Castro was something I had long looked forward to. During my first tour in Havana, I had been too junior for any direct dealings with him. We rubbed shoulders a couple of times at huge diplomatic receptions, but I had never had a chance to talk to him. Nonetheless, having read most of his speeches and analyzed all his major decisions over a period of two decades, I felt I knew something of the man's mind. Castro was an adversary, an old and familiar adversary, but certainly a fascinating one. One need not agree with anything Castro has said or done since he came to power to recognize that he is one of the most interesting political figures to stride about the world stage in the last half of the twentieth century.

On the day before I returned to the U.S., I went to Central Committee headquarters to meet with Castro. I went alone. Castro, accompanied only by an aide who took notes, greeted me at the door and escorted me to a sofa. He offered me a cigar, which I accepted gratefully. Obviously amused by our physical resemblance and mutual penchant for cigars, he asked how long I had worn a beard.

For some ten years, I answered, adding that I had grown it in Moscow and that Tsar Nicholas II, not Fidel Castro, was the model.

"You have chosen a strange role model," Castro quipped. "Even had he not been deposed, Nicholas II would have been remembered by history as a rather mediocre and not overly bright tsar."

"True enough," I replied. "I copy the beard, not the man behind it."

Castro laughed and remarked that the Russians must have loved having a new tsarist beard in their midst. Changing the subject, he said he understood I had been in Havana with the U.S. embassy in the years just prior to our break in relations.

I nodded, and wanting to make it clear that I did not accept the Cuban myth that our severance of relations had been unprovoked and a simple reflection of U.S. hostility toward the Cuban Revolution, I added that I had been taking notes the night he gave the speech that led to the break in relations.

Castro did not argue the point; rather, pausing in reflection, he blew cigar smoke at the ceiling. (So did I.) Finally, speaking slowly and with great deliberation, he said, "Yes, I must acknowledge that I may have had some responsibility for our first divorce—I as well as the United States. I came to power with some preconceived ideas about the United States and about Cuba's relationship with her. In retrospect, I can see a number of things I wish I had done differently. We would not in any event have ended up as close friends. The U.S. had dominated us too long. The Cuban Revolution was determined to end that domination. There was, then, an inherent conflict of interests. Still, even adversaries find it useful to maintain bridges between them. Perhaps I burned some of those bridges precipitately; there were times when I may have been more abrupt, more aggressive, than was called for by the situation. We were all younger then;

we made the mistakes of youth. And we were not the only ones making mistakes. The United States made many also in its dealings with us."

At that point, Castro's mood abruptly changed from detached reflection to barely controlled anger. While he may have had some responsibility for our earlier disagreements, he went on, that had certainly *not* been the case in our recent dispute over Cuba's alleged role in the invasion of Shaba province. He had come to us in good faith and offered assistance, he said. In response, the U.S. had insulted him and rejected his offer. This time the responsibility for the misunderstanding was solely ours.

I replied that rarely was anything *solely* the fault of either one side or the other. In any event, I went on, how we recovered, how we now handled the situation, was more important than who was responsible. Misunderstandings inevitably occurred between nations, but if both were sensible, they recognized that it was in their mutual interests to continue efforts to resolve the problems between them. That was certainly the case now in U.S.-Cuban relations.

Castro agreed. For his part, he said, he was ready to expand the dialogue with the U.S. We could not agree on everything or resolve all the problems between us, but there were a number of areas in which we could make rapid progress. He was ready to sit at the negotiating table when we were. Castro added that he had been especially puzzled by U.S. efforts to make him the scapegoat for Shaba II, since only days before he had "received a positive signal from the U.S. regarding an expanded dialogue."

Castro looked at me expectantly, obviously interested to see how I would reply. I was mystified, but tried not to show it. I hoped my blank look would pass as "inscrutable" and my silence as "discreet." I waited a long moment and then answered with the cliché that he would always find the U.S. ready to meet him halfway in a constructive dialogue (something I wished were true).

Castro and his aide exchanged glances, but Castro quickly went on to conclude the conversation on that theme by requesting that I transmit to my government his sincerest wishes for a new era of pragmatism in our relationship.

Castro had made his point. I stayed another hour or so, talking with him of the early days of the Revolution and current events in the Horn of Africa. All the while, however, I was asking myself what "positive signal" we had given him.

Upon my return to Washington, I went directly to the office of Viron "Pete" Vaky, who had replaced Todman as assistant secretary of state for American republics affairs. Vaky was a calm, straightforward, and thoroughly competent professional with decades of experience in Latin America.

I reported my conversation with Castro and specifically asked if he had any idea what Castro had meant by a "positive signal."

Vaky smiled slightly and said he'd look into it for me. A few days later, he called me back to his office. He was not yet at liberty to tell me the whole story, he said, but I would doubtless be filled in during the next few days. Meanwhile, he could say that Castro had suggested a series of confidential talks. A preliminary contact and two subsequent rounds of talks had already been held; a third and expanded round would be held shortly in Atlanta.

Vaky apologized for having been unable to inform me of all this sooner, especially in view of the awkward moment it had caused me with Castro. The NSC, however, had wanted the whole matter closely held. He could now tell me that the Cubans had raised the question of the possible release of political prisoners. He would need my help in shepherding this question through the bureaucracy with maximum discretion. I would also shortly be asked to draft a series of briefing papers in preparation for the August meeting in Atlanta.

This was welcome news, but why had I been brought in so late? Was I not the department's expert on Cuba? Did it make any sense, then, to have held these meetings without even telling me?

No, probably not, but such things happen all the time. In an effort to avoid leaks, information is sometimes restricted to a handful of senior officials. This is unfortunate, but in leak-prone Washington, understandable. The problem comes when those few top officials make decisions without consulting anyone else, for usually the experts have been cut out of the process and the senior officials are flying blind. In this particular case, no harm had been done. In other instances, however—the Bay of Pigs, for example—the results have been disastrous.

During the weeks that followed, I was gradually filled in by Peter Tarnoff, the director of the Executive Secretariat and Vance's right-hand man, and by Undersecretary of State David A. Newsom, who had conducted the first two rounds of talks. The picture was as follows.

Castro had made an overture through Bernardo Benes, an exiled

Cuban banker. Benes had gone to the White House and passed on Castro's suggestion that the two sides talk behind closed doors so as to avoid the speculation and media hype that often accompanies discussions through normal channels. Benes's message had been referred to the NSC, which, though not particularly receptive to the idea, had decided at least to explore it. Hence, in May, David Aaron, Brzezinski's deputy, met in a New York hotel with José Luis Padrón, a trusted confidant of Fidel's and soon to become minister of tourism.

From what I could glean, the NSC's only interest was in determining whether or not the Cubans would withdraw from Africa. On that score, Padrón had given Aaron little cause for optimism. He had, however, raised the matter of the several thousand Cuban political prisoners. President Carter had indicated an interest in their release, he noted. Castro might be willing to oblige, provided the U.S. would take those who did not wish to remain in Cuba following their release.

Apparently the NSC was unenthusiastic, but it could hardly turn the subject down cold since the prisoner release was a stated U.S. objective. The Cubans were told that we would negotiate it—but the Department of State, not the NSC, would do the negotiating. The department, in turn, was instructed to open contacts on the matter, but to keep it in strictest confidence. Undersecretary Newsom himself conducted the talks, meeting with Padrón in New York and later in the privacy of his own home in Washington. Newsom and Padrón made progress on the prisoner-release idea. They also established a rapid and direct communications channel that later proved invaluable in emergency situations and in getting messages directly to Castro or other senior Cuban leaders.

A less measurable but nonetheless valuable result of the Newsom-Padrón talks lay in the personal confidence that developed between officials on both sides. Years later, after the Carter administration had ended and Newsom had retired, Padrón still spoke warmly of him. "When during our meeting at his home, Ambassador Newsom himself served our drinks and his wife served dinner, our preconceived ideas about the arrogance of all American officials went out the window," Padrón once told me.

Like Newsom, those of us who later dealt with Padrón came to have confidence in his integrity and in that of his assistants. We might disagree strongly, and we might withhold certain facts or calculations from one another, but I cannot think of a single instance in which

Padrón and his colleagues lied to us, or we to them. Together, we developed something to build on—a foundation of confidence. Unfortunately, we never got beyond the foundation.

Newsom had worked under severe restraints. Having concluded that the Cubans were not disposed to negotiate the withdrawal of their troops from Africa, the NSC instructed the Department of State to discuss political prisoners with the Cubans, *but neither to raise nor discuss with them any other matter, whether bilateral or multilateral in nature.* This had proved increasingly difficult and awkward. Other issues kept cropping up. The Cuban side would mention some minor misunderstanding that needed clearing up. Newsom, to his discomfort, would have to say he had no instructions to discuss it. More than anything else, this limitation made the American side appear very narrow. Bowing to logic, the NSC agreed to a round of expanded talks. Aaron would join Newsom in discussing a range of issues with the Cubans at a meeting to be held in Atlanta in August 1978. It was for this meeting that I was asked to prepare briefing papers.

As I moved more deeply into the process, I realized that the NSC and the Department of State viewed these talks very differently. From Secretary of State Vance on down, State saw them as positive, dynamic, and open-ended. They offered an opportunity to address the problems between us. The NSC's perception, on the other hand, was essentially negative and static. We would listen to (but not hear) the other side only as the price we had to pay to reiterate our refusal to take any additional steps toward improving relations until Castro withdrew his troops from Africa.

In fairness, it should be said that the NSC's negativism was not entirely gratuitous. There could have been damaging domestic political repercussions from appearing to deal with an unrepentant Castro. Hence, any discussions with the Cubans had to be approached cautiously. Even so, demanding Cuban withdrawal from Africa as a precondition was as unrealistic as would have been Cuban insistence on our withdrawal from Guantánamo. We had to begin with less sweeping, more feasible, steps, and to realize that achieving our major objectives was likely to be a long-term process. *Any* progress in that direction was worth while. Unfortunately, the negative NSC view was to prevail. It conditioned the Atlanta meeting and all subsequent rounds of talks until the very last one, in September 1980. As we shall see in Chapter 8, only at that last meeting, from which the NSC was excluded, did we finally make progress. By then it was too late.

If the U.S. side was divided in its approach to the talks, the Cubans were not. Castro's objective and strategy were clear: to resuscitate the normalization process. This was the best chance the two sides had had in almost twenty years to reach a *modus vivendi*.[1] Brzezinski's knee-jerk opposition, plus disagreements and misunderstandings over Africa, had halted the step-by-step process begun in March 1977. Very well, Castro reasoned, he would resuscitate it. Well before the May 1978 shouting match over Shaba II, the Cubans had carefully reviewed U.S. policy statements in search of a major concern they might readily address.[2] President Carter had always said human rights ranked high on the list of things we wished to accomplish in our opening to Cuba. The Department of State, moreover, had just published a Cuban GIST paper—a brief résumé of U.S. goals, meant to inform the general public. This document set forth three major U.S. goals: (1) the moderation of Cuban foreign policy—most importantly, the withdrawal of Cuban troops from Africa; (2) compensation for U.S. citizens whose goods and properties had been nationalized by the Cuban government; and (3) the enhancement of human rights in Cuba, especially the liberation of political prisoners.

The first two were complex issues which would obviously take time to work out. The third, however, was something the Cubans could handle right away. In putting forward the prisoner release as a concession, the Cubans did not seek a *quid pro quo*. However, since they hoped for normalization, they obviously expected some response.[3] In this they were to be disappointed. Newsom could discuss only the prisoners. Nor did that change in Atlanta. At one point in early August, I suggested that a small *quid* be put forward at Atlanta, to maintain some semblance of reciprocity. Why not, for example, lift the prohibition on the sale of medicines to Cuba? The idea was promptly shot down by the NSC. There were to be *no* steps on our side.

As good as the NSC's word, the meeting in Atlanta accomplished nothing. Meanwhile, however, we had made progress toward settling details of the prisoner issue—how many people we would accept for entry and under what circumstances. During Newsom's conversations with Padrón, it had become clear that the first step was to develop more precise data on how many prisoners wished to come, how many family members they would bring with them, and other details which could be obtained only from the prisoners themselves. The Cubans invited us to prepare a questionnaire, which we quickly

Wayne Smith talking to Fidel Castro in the latter's office.

(Facing page) The former Cuban capitol, now housing the Academy of Sciences.

The first American diplomats to visit Cuba in sixteen years begin negotiations with the Cubans on maritime boundaries, in April 1977. The American delegation is on the right. From right to left, its members are Wayne Smith, Culver Gleysteen, Stephanie Van Reigersberg, Terrence Todman, Rozanne Ridgway, Frank Willis (hidden behind Ridgway), and Robert Hodgson, with his hand under his chin. The Cuban delegation is on the left. Pelegrín Torras is second from left.

The former American embassy building, Havana, now housing the U.S. interests section.

Preparing for dinner customers at the Bodeguita del Medio.

The Havana waterfront. The U.S. interests-section building is
farthest right on the point.

The fighting in front of the interests section, May 1980. The bus has just disgorged progovernment attackers armed with clubs and chains, and the man in the foreground has run out from under the canopy to challenge them. The main group of several hundred ex-prisoners is out of view to the right.

During the fighting, Vice-Consul Bob Hagen gestures to someone through our shattered front window.

A partial view of the fighting on the steps a few seconds after the busloads of progovernment attackers arrived. The attackers at lower right are beating a man on the ground with chains.

An hour or so after the fighting, police cars cordon off the interests section.

Roxanna and Melinda Smith share a laugh with Fidel Castro and Antonio Nuñez Jiménez, vice-minister of culture, at a cookout given by Nuñez Jiménez in May 1982.

Wayne Smith with Fidel Castro at the cookout given by Nuñez Jiménez in May 1982.

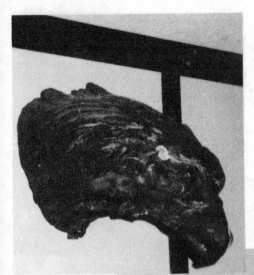

The head of the eagle that once stood atop the *Maine* monument, Havana. The head now hangs in the U.S. interests section.

Atop the *Maine* monument, twisted bolts that once held in place the American eagle.

did. They must have distributed it the day they received it. In an amazingly short period of time, completed questionnaires flowed back, eventually thousands of them. As we read them, one thing became apparent: most of the respondents had already been released from prison. Only about a third were still behind bars. In some cases, questionnaires were filled out by men and women released five or even ten years previously. We mentioned this by phone to our inter-locutors in Havana. Their response was that even though those in question were indeed free, all had been imprisoned for political crimes and none wished to be integrated into Cuba's new socialist system. They wished to leave. The Cuban government assumed that in keeping with our professed interest in freedom of egress, we would wish to take them.

No, we explained in a series of conversations, that was not exactly the case. While we believed in freedom of departure, the capacity of the U.S. to absorb political dissidents from around the world was limited. In the present situation, our first priority had to be for those still incarcerated. Political prisoners would be defined as those in prison on August 1, 1978; those released prior to that date would be defined as ex-prisoners. We intended to request Congress to autho-rize admission of a large enough number, under the Refugee Act, to include all political prisoners who wished to come, plus their families. After the prisoners had been taken care of we would deal with an undetermined number of ex-prisoners.

The Cubans accepted this arrangement without argument, noting that 2,500 was probably a good estimate of how many prisoners would elect to come to the United States. They intended to release all but a few Batista war criminals and dangerous cases,* or about 5,000 in all. Approximately half might wish to leave Cuba. That squared with our calculations. We had been rather surprised to note that only about half of the questionnaire respondents had said they wanted to come to the U.S.

Next came the modalities, the mechanics of getting the prisoners out and over to the U.S. Here we ran into a roadblock in the person of Attorney General Griffin Bell, who seemed to oppose the whole idea. Part of Bell's opposition doubtless had to do with his belief that

---

*In the event, it did not work out that way. Some of the prisoners the Cubans failed to release were neither Batista war criminals (those held for war crimes against the Fidelistas during the Revolution) nor dangerous cases.

we were already overburdened by refugees from Southeast Asia. But he seemed also to resent the fact that an immigration matter (his turf) had been negotiated by others. Whatever the case, he demonstrated a profound ignorance of what was involved. On one occasion, for example, he said he saw no reason to allow Castro to empty his jails of pickpockets and send them all to us. When it was carefully explained to him that we were talking about *political* prisoners, not common felons, Bell responded that he would be willing to admit any prisoners still held from the Bay of Pigs invasion. Once more, we carefully explained the facts. Most members of Brigade 2506 taken prisoner at the Bay of Pigs had long ago been returned to the U.S. in exchange for tractors. The U.S. now wished to bring about the release of several thousand *other* prisoners as quickly as possible. If we could accept refugees from Vietnam, Cambodia, and the Soviet Union itself, why not from Cuba?

The attorney general was unmoved. He did not say he would refuse to admit the released prisoners; rather, he imposed such cumbersome and unrealistic screening procedures that processing them would have taken ten to twenty years. Insisting that he would review every case and make the final decision personally, Bell sent a team of FBI agents, officials of the Immigration and Naturalization Service (INS), and Department of State consular officers to Havana in October 1978 to do the preliminary screening of some fifty political prisoners and their families. The screening team took some two weeks, and another two weeks passed before Attorney General Bell acted on their recommendation. Not until November did this first group of released political prisoners fly to Miami.

Those of us in State who believed in the prisoner-release program could only pull our hair in exasperation and plead with the Department of Justice to adopt more streamlined procedures. We were powerless, however, against the obduracy of the attorney general, President Carter's friend and appointee. If he was to be turned around, the White House would have to take a hand. The president had said he attached high priority to the release of Cuban political prisoners. Now, because of the attorney general's foot-dragging, the whole release program was in danger of collapse. One would have expected the president to instruct his attorney general to cooperate. But if not for the storm of criticism that hit the administration after the arrival of the first released prisoners in November, Bell might have continued to obstruct the program. Antonio Cuesta turned things around. A famous and respected figure in Miami, Cuesta had been captured in 1966 while leading a commando raid against Cuba. Encountering a superior force and having fought until he was out of ammunition, Cuesta, who had vowed never to be taken alive, had tried to kill himself by detonating a grenade. He had been blinded by the explosion and suffered near-fatal injuries, but to his chagrin, he had survived, and was sentenced to thirty years in prison. Released in August 1978 after twelve years behind bars, he arrived in Miami in November to a hero's welcome. No sooner was he off the plane than he delivered a broadside against the attorney general for delaying the release of other prisoners. "We prisoners saw Carter as a champion of human rights," he declared. "Now it looks as though [the Department of] Justice is ruining what Carter had achieved."[4]

Cuesta was especially critical of Bell's personal review of every case. At the present pace of processing, Cuesta concluded, many long-suffering prisoners would die of old age before the attorney general got around to them.

The *New York Times,* the *Washington Post,* the *Miami Herald,* and a number of other major dailies joined the fray with editorials urging Attorney General Bell to speed up the process. As the *Washington Post* pointedly summed it up: "By urging Mr. Castro again and again to free these people, with the understanding that most of them want to come to the United States, President Carter has in effect invited them here. The least his administration can now do is to let them in with as little red tape as possible."[5]

The logic of such advice was unassailable, and in the face of it, the attorney general relented. He asked Congress for a quota of refugees large enough to accommodate all those prisoners who wanted to come, and more importantly, he agreed to accelerate the admissions process. He would no longer review each case; rather, special teams would be rotated in Havana to interview the former prisoners and their families and determine their eligibility for entry on the spot.

With this shift by the Department of Justice, we were able to agree to process the former prisoners as fast as the Cubans released them. They had been speaking of releasing at the rate of four hundred per month; very well, we said, our special teams would be prepared to process up to that number per month.

Meanwhile, Castro had begun a dialogue with the Cuban-American community. When we had reached preliminary agreement with the Cubans on the prisoner release and entry program back in August, Castro had wanted to make some announcement to that effect. He clearly assumed that Carter would see merit in doing so, and would seek credit for his human-rights policies. The prisoner release was evidence that his opening to Cuba was bearing fruit. The expectation that the White House would want to make a public announcement was fully shared by those of us in the Department of State who knew of the Newsom-Padrón talks. We reckoned without the NSC, however, which, as in the case of the war in the Horn of Africa, chose to see the glass as half empty. We had achieved one of the president's highest-priority objectives in Cuba, but the only objective in which the NSC had any interest was Cuban withdrawal from Africa. As we hadn't achieved that, the NSC apparently considered the talks a waste of time and did not wish to acknowledge them publicly. To my astonishment, therefore, and to the bewilderment of the Cubans, word came down from the NSC that there would be no public announcement of a U.S.-Cuban agreement; indeed, we were not to indicate that we had even been in touch with the Cubans on the matter. The Cubans were told we wished the talks to remain confidential.

The released prisoners and their families would shortly begin to arrive in the United States. Since their arrival obviously couldn't be kept secret, we would have to say something. The NSC instructed us to say, when the time came, that the U.S. government welcomed the release of these prisoners, but that we had not negotiated for it and did not know what had prompted it!

In other words, the president's human-rights policies were to be given no credit at all. I remember thinking at the time that with political advisers like these, however well intentioned, Carter wasn't likely to make it into a second term.

The only reason I ever heard for our refusal to take public credit was that the NSC—and, according to the NSC, the president—feared that acknowledgment of our talks with the Cubans might send the wrong signals to countries whose cooperation we sought in opposing Cuban activities in Africa. If that was the rationale, it was thin indeed. Few if any of those countries would not have applauded us for bringing about the release of Cuban political prisoners. Nor was there any reason we could not have informed our friends and allies that we were discussing other matters with the Cubans. When one has sharp disagreements with another government, confidential exchanges of views are perfectly normal. All we had to say to interested governments was that we were discussing our various disagreements in private with a view to avoiding new collisions. No one would have raised an eyebrow. Most would have thought it an obvious and sensible way to proceed.

The Cubans remained puzzled at American reticence, but, not surprisingly, decided to make some hay of their own with the Cuban-American community. They asked if we had any objections to their announcing the decision to release prisoners as a gesture to the exiles. Foolishly, in my view, we answered that we had no objections. I suppose the White House was relieved. Castro had provided a ready-made explanation that in no way involved the administration.

Accordingly, in a press conference on September 6, 1978, Castro invited representatives of the Cuban-American community to come to Havana for a dialogue. One of the things to be discussed, he said, was his intention to release large numbers of political prisoners and to permit them to join their families in the United States. Another matter for discussion was the expansion of exiles' visits to families still in Cuba.

The irrepressible Bernardo Benes and a number of other leaders of the Cuban-American community immediately set up a committee to talk to Castro. This came to be called the Committee of 75 (simply because at a certain point it had seventy-five members). The more intransigent members of the community would of course have nothing to do with the committee. They vowed never to join in a dialogue with Castro; rather, their motto was "War to the death" (though, to be sure, they intended to wage the war from the comfort and safety of their homes in Miami). As far as they were concerned, anyone who would sit down at a table with Castro had to be a Communist sympathizer. They attacked Benes and the rest of the Committee of 75 in those terms. Several committee members were set upon and beaten. The lives of others were threatened, and one was in fact murdered. Benes's bank was picketed, and an unsuccessful boycott was mounted against it.

Despite such opposition, the Committee of 75 flew to Havana in November for a marathon meeting with Castro, and returned again in December to sign an agreement with him under which he pledged to release four hundred prisoners a month and to vastly increase the number of Cuban-Americans permitted to return every month to visit families on the island.

Castro's dialogue with the Committee of 75, and the fact that the first prisoners arriving from Havana in November were escorted by Bernardo Benes and other members of the committee, naturally led the Cuban-American community to assume that the prisoner release was something worked out between themselves and Castro. It appeared to be a gesture on Castro's part to *them*, not at all a result of Carter's human-rights policies. Therefore, instead of feeling gratitude to Carter for his role in the liberation of their loved ones, they felt only irritation at his attorney general for delaying their entry.

The MIG-23 Affair

Even as we discussed the prisoners with the Cubans during the summer of 1978, another irritant arose. Intelligence reports indicated the Soviets had provided the Cuban air force with a squadron of MIG-23s. This was confirmed in the fall and quickly became a public issue.

Cuba had for some time been modernizing and upgrading its weapons systems. It had, for example, replaced an outmoded fleet of patrol boats with new Soviet Komar missile patrol boats. It had acquired new armored personnel carriers and tanks, and would shortly receive conventional diesel-powered submarines. Until the arrival of the MIG-23s, however, none of the new acquisitions approached violation of the 1962 Kennedy-Khrushchev understanding. In the case of the MIG-23, there was some doubt. The problem was not simply that the MIG-23 was a considerably more powerful weapon than the MIG-21, until then the most advanced aircraft in the Cuban air force. That in itself might not have had relevance in terms of the 1962 understanding. What *did* concern us was the fact that one particular model of the MIG-23 was capable of carrying nuclear devices. Even worse, distinguishing that model from those that were not nuclear-capable was virtually impossible except from quite close up—closer than our overhead cameras could zoom in.

Of course, even if the MIG-23s had been nuclear-capable, they would have posed no threat without nuclear weapons to carry. We had confidence in our ability to detect such devices. Among other things, we had highly sensitive radiation sensors. The maintenance of nuclear weapons, moreover, leaves telltale "tracks." We had detected none of these in Cuba. Even so, had the Soviets sent Cuba the nuclear-capable MIG-23, we would have considered their action provocative *in intent* and a probable violation of the 1962 understanding. The Carter administration, like those which preceded it, meant to enforce that understanding. This was made clear to the Soviets and Cubans in diplomatic conversations.

Over several weeks, we received assurances from both the Soviets and the Cubans that the nuclear-capable model had not been added to the Cuban air force and would not be; neither, they said, were any nuclear weapons on the island, as we should well know. A concerted intelligence effort tended to confirm these assertions. We got some close-up aerial shots of the new planes and from these and other means determined that they were *not* the nuclear-capable model.

Inevitably, some in the American body politic argued that nuclear-capable or not, the MIG-23s violated the 1962 understanding and we should demand their withdrawal. Some of the MIG-23s were fighter-bombers, the argument ran, with a longer range than the IL-28 bombers whose withdrawal we had insisted upon in 1962.

This argument had a surface logic, but it crumbled on closer examination. First, as Ray Garthoff has pointed out in his excellent article on the subject in the *Political Science Quarterly*,[6] the IL-28 became an issue in 1962 not so much because of its capability as an offensive weapon (which was all along questionable), but because the U.S. had made a public commitment to have it withdrawn. The MIG-21 was a more potent aircraft than the IL-28, yet we never defined it as an offensive weapon. Over the years, squadrons of MIG-21s, fighter-bombers as well as fighters, had been provided to the Cuban air force. The U.S. had raised no objection.

Second, one must evaluate weapons systems in a rather narrow time frame, comparing them with other *existing* systems and counter-systems. In 1947 the Soviets might have considered squadrons of U.S. B-17s positioned near their borders a serious threat. Today, they would be a tourist attraction. Whatever our judgments about the IL-28 in 1962, the more sophisticated weaponry of 1978 had rendered it, like the B-17, obsolete. Comparing the MIG-23 and the IL-28, then, was really like comparing the prices of apples in years separated by two decades. In 1978 a plane whose range barely reached up to Jacksonville, Florida, was not much of a threat—unless it could carry nuclear weapons. The Department of State finally realized that, and in January 1979 issued a calm statement which ended the mini-flap.

As Ray Garthoff has speculated, the purpose of many American conservatives in questioning the introduction of the MIG-23s probably had less to do with the aircraft themselves than with the desire to block the signing of a new SALT agreement. Even if they could not prove their case, they reasoned, challenging the introduction of these aircraft was worth doing if it raised new doubts about Soviet adherence to international agreements. How much damage they actually did to the prospects for SALT II is impossible to gauge. Probably not much. Garthoff viewed the whole MIG-23 affair as "a minor tempest in the domestic political scene."

Perhaps. It contributed, however, to an incident which did have serious consequences for U.S.-Cuban relations. By November 1978, Castro was probably reconciled to the fact that his effort to revive the normalization process would not pay immediate dividends. The U.S. applauded his release of political prisoners, but offered nothing in return. The U.S. delegation had stonewalled both in Atlanta and in a follow-up meeting in Cuernavaca, Mexico. To every Cuban proposal, the U.S. replied that perhaps *when* Cuban troops were out of Africa, the U.S. would consider additional steps forward. Obviously, the U.S. was playing an all-or-nothing game. Still, Castro reasoned, at least the two sides were talking again, and at a relatively high level. He saw enough value in that to be willing to continue the exercise and this time to participate directly. Hence, at the end of the meeting in Cuernavaca in October, Padrón suggested a subsequent meeting in Havana, indicating that he had carried the exchange as far as he could. If the Americans wanted to discuss such substantive and highly charged issues as the Cuban presence in Africa, they would have to talk to Castro himself.

The American delegation of course promised to report the invitation, but in fact there was little enthusiasm for it among the delegation members, and much less among those to whom they reported back in Washington. The few in the Department of State who had known about the meetings had thought them a good idea, but had understood that for progress to be made, some give on both sides, ours as well as theirs, would be necessary. It was now clear that this was not to be. Further talks, then, were regarded as probably futile. Everything else being equal, the invitation would have been politely declined. There was, however, a new consideration. When we began the opening to Cuba in 1977, a number of Americans were being held in Cuban prisons on political grounds; I had visited some of them during my first trip back to Cuba in April 1977. By November 1978, all of them had been released save four. With Cuban prisoners being released in droves, the Carter administration wanted to make a special effort to get these four Americans out. Peter Tarnoff, on the secretary of state's instructions, mentioned the matter to Padrón and expressed the hope that if an American delegation went to Havana, they might be able to bring these four men home with them.

Padrón promised to raise the question with Castro. A few days later, he called back. There could be no promises, he said, but Castro would discuss the matter.

The president did not wish to send as high-level a group as had gone to Atlanta and Cuernavaca. Instead of Undersecretary of State Newsom and David Aaron, therefore, Peter Tarnoff and Bob Pastor, the NSC's Latin American adviser, were instructed to fly down secretly, accompanied only by an interpreter. They were to go in a plane large enough to carry four additional passengers.

I had tremendous respect and admiration for these four remaining Americans and there were few things I wanted more than to see them freed. Even so, I had to recognize that they were not, strictly speaking, prisoners of conscience. All had been convicted of espionage or of counterrevolutionary activity.

Larry Lunt, fifty-five, a ranch owner at the time of the Revolution, might have left Cuba along with thousands of other Americans, but the CIA had recruited him to remain. He had done so, and had been apprehended and sentenced to thirty years in prison after the missile crisis.

Everett Jackson, thirty-eight, had tried to take pictures of missile sites from a small plane in 1969. His plane forced down, he had parachuted to safety. He had been sentenced to thirty years.

Juan Tur, sixty-one, born in the U.S. of Cuban parents, had lived most of his adult life in Cuba. He had become involved in counterrevolutionary activity in the early 1960s. Arrested in 1966, he too had been sentenced to thirty years.

Claudio Morales, forty-eight, a Puerto Rican, had been given twenty years in 1966 for smuggling people out of the country—a counterrevolutionary crime.

None of this, of course, meant that we should try any less energetically to free them. On the contrary, all had been acting on principles and convictions we shared. But it did mean that the Cubans were not likely to see any reason to pardon them unless Cuba would somehow benefit from that act. Putting myself in the place of the Cubans, I would have seen little likelihood of any such benefit, given the position of the U.S. So I was not optimistic that Tarnoff and Pastor would have a full plane on the way home.

Any small hope that Castro would return the four died with the joint U.S.-British air and naval maneuvers held in mid-November right off the northern coast of Cuba. We gave the Cubans no notification of these maneuvers. Their first warning came as Cuban radar screens showed a large fleet approaching. Also, in what the U.S. later insisted was a coincidence, on almost the same day, we resumed SR-71 reconnaissance overflights. Not knowing what to expect, and given all the bellicose talk in the U.S. occasioned by the MIG-23 crisis, the Cubans assumed the worst. They went to full mobilization and war alert. Only several days later, after having been informed by us through diplomatic channels that these were only maneuvers, did they demobilize.

The next time I saw Sánchez-Parodi, he spread his hands and asked simply, "Why?"

I told him what I had been told to say: these were routine maneuvers planned long in advance and conducted in international waters; we were not required to notify the Cubans and had seen no reason to do so.

I said it, but I myself was not convinced. Routine maneuvers! With that kind of force virtually within sight of the Cuban coast? I wondered how routine we would have considered the movements of a major Soviet fleet suddenly spotted a short distance from Puerto Rico and headed straight for the island at flank speed.

Why had the decision to go ahead with the maneuvers not been the subject of consultations among the NSC, the Department of State, and the Pentagon? As far as I know, State was not even informed, let alone consulted. Perhaps some minor official in, say, the department's Bureau of Politico-Military Affairs was told about the maneuvers. If so, he informed no one else, and, indeed, this was not a matter to be transmitted through such routine channels. It should have been raised and discussed at a relatively high level, for its possible consequences were obvious. At the very least, Undersecretary of State Newsom should have been consulted. But he had not been, nor had I.

Furious, I called the liaison officer in the Pentagon to ask why there had been no prior consultations with the Office of Cuban Affairs. His reply was essentially the same as the one I was told to give to Sánchez-Parodi a few days later: the maneuvers were routine. He insisted the Department of State had been informed "through channels," though he could not specify what channels had been used.

In any event, he said, the Atlantic Sea Command in Norfolk had on November 8 issued a public notice that the maneuvers were to be held. Further, the maneuvers had been carried out with the full approval of the NSC; of that he was certain.

Shortly after my conversation with the Pentagon representative, I saw Bob Pastor, the NSC's Latin American adviser, in the hallway and asked if the NSC had indeed given its approval to the maneuvers. He replied that, yes, the NSC had approved them as a matter of routine. He had assumed that State had approved them as well. "If State objected," he asked, "why didn't someone over there say so before the thing got going? After all, everyone knew about them; there was even a notice in the press."

I took strong issue with the assertion that "everyone knew about them." Upon investigation, I determined that something *had* appeared in the press—in a local Norfolk newspaper which no one in the Department of State would ever have had occasion to see.

I was never able to establish to my own satisfaction whether the absence of consultations resulted from a bureaucratic lapse, or from something more calculated. Of course, it may just have been one of those things that fell between the cracks. But it is also possible that the NSC and the Pentagon made a point of not flagging the matter for State's attention because they knew we would raise objections.

Whatever the case, the results were the same. With the maneuvers, any chance of bringing home the four Americans disappeared. It was this episode also, one of Castro's aides told me subsequently, that led Castro to view the Carter administration's responses as hopelessly capricious.

"It was difficult for us to understand why you had responded to a positive overture with a punitive threat," the aide commented. "We in effect made a unilateral concession [i.e., the release of the prisoners]; you answered by holding maneuvers off our coast. It was as though you wished to punish us for acceding to your wishes. And that you chose to do so just at the moment you were asking us for still another concession, the release of the four Americans, puzzled us further. It is difficult to deal with another government when there is no clear causal relationship between your actions and its responses."

Castro was furious, but kept his anger in check. When Tarnoff and Pastor arrived in Havana in early December for their secret meeting, Castro protested the maneuvers in strong terms, but was cordial and hospitable to the two emissaries. Needless to say, the meeting produced nothing. Castro was in no mood to make any further concessions. In the wake of the November maneuvers, he understood fully that his effort to resuscitate the process we had begun in March 1977 had failed. The U.S. had spoken of a process based on reciprocity, but had so lost touch with that concept that it was as likely to respond with sticks as with carrots to his concessions.

If some in Washington had thought the maneuvers might frighten Castro into withdrawing from Africa, they were proved wrong. He insisted more emphatically than ever that a withdrawal of Cuban forces could occur only as changes in the security situation in Angola and Ethiopia made that possible. He had no intention of negotiating the matter with the United States.

As for the four American political prisoners—no, he said, he could not simply release them. He did, however, hint at a trade. Cuban public opinion might be more receptive to the release of the Americans if Washington freed four Puerto Rican independence leaders, including Lolita Leblón and two companions who had shot up the U.S. Congress in March 1954 and had been in prison ever since.

Tarnoff and Pastor said they would report this suggestion to President Carter. The meeting then broke up, and the two returned home —in a plane with four empty seats.

As 1978 came to a close, U.S.-Cuban relations were almost as strained as they had been before Carter took office—and worse was to come.

7

Growing Problems
1979

Shortly after the new year began, Pete Vaky asked me over lunch if I would like to be chief of mission in Havana. Lyle Lane was to be transferred in the summer and I was in line to replace him.

I didn't have to think twice. Of course I wanted to go. I had prepared myself to return to Cuba ever since 1961, and I wanted this job more than any other in the Foreign Service.

Roxanna was equally pleased. It would be novel, she said, to take our two children to live in the city where our marriage had begun.

Glad though we were to be going, we were under no illusions that this would be an easy or pleasant assignment. The atmosphere between the two countries was too strained to permit such hopes. Still, as Roxanna put it, "It couldn't be more strained now than the last time we were there."

The Impact of Events in Grenada

The atmosphere was not helped any by Maurice Bishop's March 13 seizure of power in Grenada. No one wasted tears on the leader he deposed, the tyrannical and bizarre Sir Eric Gairy, who literally had spent more time worrying about flying saucers than about the welfare of his people. In fact, he was at the United Nations talking about flying saucers at the time of the coup. But while nobody mourned the old government, many in Washington raised eyebrows at the new one, for its leader, Maurice Bishop, was known to be close to Fidel Castro. There was no evidence that the Cubans had engineered or even encouraged the March 13 coup. They did, however, immediately declare solidarity with the new government and offer it military assistance. That was reason enough for Washington to show prudent concern, but surely no cause for alarm. Grenada, a tiny little island of some 100,000 souls, posed no danger to the United States. Even to suggest that it might was demeaning, I thought. Nor could Grenada threaten its neighbors, unless the U.S. fleet gave it dispensation to do so. Of course we wished to limit Cuban influence, just as Havana wished to increase it. But the hard fact was that we held the overwhelming military and political advantage in the region. We also held the strongest economic cards. If we couldn't play them in such a way as to limit Cuban influence and enhance our own, we weren't worthy of calling ourselves a great power.

The National Security Council, unfortunately, did not take such a sanguine view; rather, its reaction, as colorfully put by one of its officers a few nights after the coup, was that events in Grenada meant "a Cuban octopus is loose in the Caribbean." It was time to ring the alarm bells, and ring them we did. In overreacting we made matters worse.

Without question, Bishop was a Marxist and admired the Cuban Revolution. From the outset, he was paranoiac in his belief that the United States would not permit him to retain power, that it would move forcibly to oust him and possibly return Sir Eric Gairy to office —a conviction nurtured by the fact that the latter established residence in the U.S. after the coup. On the other side of the ledger, Bishop was a genuinely popular figure, supported by the great majority of Grenadians. He was practical enough to see that antagonizing the U.S. needlessly would be foolhardy, and that he needed an economic relationship with us. U.S. tourism and exports to the U.S. market were the island's principal sources of hard currency.

What we needed was a calm and steady policy which would reassure Bishop that we had no hostile intentions toward him, would bring our economic leverage to bear in a constructive way, and would subtly remind Bishop that there were limits to how far he could go in his relationship with Cuba without exciting U.S. concern and bringing on consequences not favorable to his interests. It was above all a situation in which our demarches had to be carefully phrased so as not to offend national sensitivities.

171

That was the kind of policy we needed. It was the exact opposite of what we did. For beginners, we had our ambassador deliver a poorly worded admonition to Bishop which was almost certain to be misinterpreted. *Any* improvement in relations between Grenada and Cuba, our ambassador was instructed to say, would be taken as a matter of great concern by the U.S.

Bishop of course took that to mean that anything he did with respect to Cuba—even the simple establishment of diplomatic relations—might be seized upon by the U.S. as a pretext to move against him. Thus, instead of reassuring Bishop, we further excited his suspicions. Instead of being respectful of nationalist sentiment, we offended it.

Nor could we blame the NSC for the clumsy wording of the instruction cable sent to our ambassador. The NSC may have set the alarmist tone, but the cable was drafted in the Department of State and even approved by the Office of Cuban Affairs. I was away when it was presented for clearance; another officer signed in my absence. When I returned the next day and read over the instructions then already on the way to our ambassador, I went through the ceiling. First I chewed out the officer who had approved them. Then I called the ARA front office to see if we could not amend them. No luck there. Everyone else was reasonably happy with the instructions, I was told; anyway, they already had NSC approval; it was therefore too late to change them.

We could hardly have gotten off to a worse start with Bishop, but in fact the beginning accurately presaged what was to come. Instead of trying to engage Bishop, the U.S. adopted an increasingly hostile attitude toward him, rarely exchanging views through diplomatic channels and after a time refusing to discuss anything at all. Instead of using our economic leverage, we withheld it. Bishop, for example, requested that we assist in the construction of a major new airport which he hoped would stimulate increased tourism. We flatly refused. Such rigidity may have made us feel tough, but I could not see that it accomplished anything in policy terms—other than to push Bishop even closer to the Cubans. The Cubans were happy enough to step in and help build the airport.

Nicaragua

Grenada was not the only new problem disturbing U.S.-Cuban relations. Inevitably, there was fallout also from the civil war raging in

Nicaragua. Not that the rebellion there was of Cuba's making either. Clearly, it was a spontaneous movement sparked by the Nicaraguan people's disgust with Somoza and his corrupt, arbitrary rule.

The Carter administration had no sympathy for Somoza, but feared Nicaragua might turn to the left if the Sandinistas, the principal armed revolutionary group, gained control.

With a sinking sense of *déjà vu*, I watched us repeat in Nicaragua our Cuban mistakes of twenty years earlier. Conceptually, we understood in 1978 as in 1958 that our best course was to encourage moderate forces to fill the developing power vacuum. The Carter administration *said* that was what it intended to do, but like the Eisenhower administration, failed utterly to carry through. In mid-1978, the Carter administration did, with the full backing of the OAS, launch a negotiating process carried on by an international mediation panel. Some progress was made in the search for a moderate solution, but crucial mistakes in the Carter White House derailed the process. First, in June 1978, against the advice of the Department of State, Carter sent Somoza a letter commending him for considering certain steps toward greater respect for human rights. Such congratulations were decidedly premature. None of the steps had actually been taken —and most never were. Worse, the letter concluded by inviting Somoza to continue discussing his constructive actions with the U.S. ambassador. Somoza of course interpreted the letter as a sign that U.S. favor continued and that we would not insist on his relinquishing power.

After the June letter, only a firm show of determination by the Carter administration might have convinced Somoza to step down sooner rather than later. But when in the fall of 1978 push came to shove in the negotiating process, the administration failed to shove. By October, the international mediation panel, which was headed by my old office companion from Havana, Bill Bowdler, together with the Nicaraguan Frente Amplio de Oposición (Broad Opposition Front), or FAO, had worked out a peace plan. Somoza was to resign and turn power over to a government of national unity including representatives of all sixteen opposition groups—the Sandinistas being only one of the sixteen. A constituent assembly would be named to organize elections, which would be held at the end of 1981. The National Guard was to be reorganized, but, significantly, not disbanded. The Sandinistas were understandably unhappy with the proposal, for it left them at a disadvantage. But at that point, the other opposition groups far outnumbered the Sandinistas. Whatever the latter thought of the plan, it could have worked if Somoza had resigned and given it a chance. Somoza, however, would have resigned only under U.S. pressure. But the U.S. failed to press him, and allowed the whole negotiating process to collapse. From that point forward, we really had no policy in Nicaragua. We simply drifted.

With a peaceful solution ruled out, Somoza's opponents turned to armed struggle. The civil war escalated in intensity, and it became clear that those with arms in hand would have the inside track to power once it was over. That meant the Sandinistas, for they were the principal armed group.

By failing to throw its weight decisively behind the peace plan, the Carter administration not only lost its best chance of bringing about a satisfactory solution in Nicaragua but also increased the chances that the Sandinistas would end up in power—exactly what we did *not* want. Alfonso Robelo (then a leader of the FAO and now a leader of the Nicaraguan *contras*) summed it up as follows:

If at that moment, in October, November, December of 1978, they [the U.S.] had been ready to put pressure on Somoza, like saying, "Okay, forget it, you're not going to have a sanctuary in the States . . ." things of this nature or other things they can do, Somoza would have stepped down and a different thing would have happened. We lost the best opportunity we had at that time. . . . After that, the Broad Opposition Front was left with nothing and the only people who had initiative were those in the violent mode, the FSLN [i.e., the Sandinistas].[1]

The Carter administration acted against the advice of our most informed senior diplomats. Both Pete Vaky and Bill Bowdler urged that we encourage Somoza to resign. Bowdler especially knew what the consequences would be if we waited too long. He remembered Cuba. But both were ignored.

Why? For a variety of reasons, some reflecting misjudgment; others, however mistaken, based on solid moral principles. For one thing, by the time negotiations had reached the crucial point, the NSC, inexplicably, had convinced itself that Somoza could survive the crisis. While we might not like him, the council reasoned, it would be foolish and probably futile to pressure him. The NSC's Latin American adviser asked me in September 1978 if I agreed with Pete Vaky that Somoza could not last. When I replied that I did, that in my view Somoza was finished, whether his final demise came in two months or two years, the adviser replied that both Vaky and I were dead wrong. "The problem with all of you," he said, "is that you see this as a replay of Cuba in 1958. But it isn't. The Cuban army wouldn't fight; the National Guard will, and since it will, Somoza will be able to hang on."

I pointed out that the Cuban army had fought for a time also, but had quickly become demoralized and quit. The Guard was better led, so the process might take longer, but it too would lose heart as it realized it was fighting the Nicaraguan people as a whole. That was the crucial point, I concluded. Somoza could not indefinitely defy the united will of his own people now that a significant number of them were armed.

I argued to no avail—as had Vaky, Bowdler, and others. Until it was far too late, the NSC went on expecting Somoza to survive. Even in June 1979, only a month before Somoza's final defeat, the NSC's Latin American adviser was still predicting that he would weather the storm.[2]

In addition, some in the Department of State were opposed on moral grounds to pressuring Somoza out. For example, Tony Lake, director of the department's policy planning staff, took such a position, and influenced Secretary of State Vance in that direction. Lake was a dedicated and highly principled officer whose views were never capriciously voiced. He felt that since President Carter's policy was not to intervene in the internal affairs of smaller countries, we ought to follow that policy under all circumstances. We could not intervene in Nicaragua under one set of circumstances, but then say we couldn't do so in, say, Guatemala or the Philippines under others. Lake also argued that the business of removing other governments carried with it practical as well as moral liabilities. For example, in the eyes of the rest of the world, U.S. involvement in the 1963 assassination of President Ngo Dinh Diem in Vietnam saddled us with responsibility for the outcome of the Vietnamese imbroglio.

I respected the intellectual integrity behind this position, but I thought it failed to come to grips with the real situation we faced. When, as in Cuba in 1958 and Nicaragua in 1978, a dictator's survival depends upon the perception of continued U.S. support, the U.S. intervenes no more by withdrawing that support than by continuing it. Either way, its actions have a decisive effect on the outcome. What is important in such cases is to choose the alternative that best serves U.S. objectives. In this case, the choice was clear: to get Somoza out while time remained to bring in a moderate transitional government.

And we certainly did not have the assassination of Somoza in view; rather, it was a matter of showing him that since he had lost the support of his people, he would receive no further U.S. backing, and would be well advised to resign in favor of a transitional government while he still could.

There was also a pragmatic consideration behind our inactivity— a consideration that played a role in Lake's argument. Somoza had powerful friends in Congress, among them Charles Wilson of Texas, a member of the House Appropriations Committee, and John Murphy of New York, who as chairman of the House Merchant Marine Committee could have jammed up implementing legislation for the Panama Canal treaties. They and others threatened to mount efforts to block key pieces of legislation, such as foreign aid and the canal treaties, if the administration pressured their old pal Somoza. This threatened opposition was probably not decisive in itself. The administration doubtless calculated that it could be overcome. But since for other reasons the administration was reluctant to pressure Somoza anyway, the attitude of his friends in Congress may have tipped the scales toward inaction.

For a mix of reasons, then, we did nothing. With negotiations paralyzed, the fighting grew steadily more intense during the first half of 1979. This was neither a bloodless coup nor a comic-opera revolution. It was a full-scale civil war with heavy fighting all over the country, great destruction, and high loss of life. Somoza soon lost the upper hand. Despite desperate measures such as the indiscriminate bombing and shelling of heavily populated areas, he was on the ropes by the middle of June 1979.

Only in late June did we attempt to get a handle on the situation. Our new ambassador in Managua, Larry Pezzullo, was sent in to tell Somoza that we expected him to resign. Bill Bowdler meanwhile helped to hammer out a last-minute agreement between the opposition and the authorities regarding modalities for a transitional government. Our aim was the same in June and July 1979 as it had been in the fall of 1978—to avoid a Sandinista-dominated government. But what might have worked the previous year would not hold together now. It was too late. The Sandinistas had grown too strong and gained too much momentum.

Zbigniew Brzezinski also got into the act. A meeting of OAS foreign ministers took up the Nicaraguan situation in late June. The Department of State wanted the OAS to call for a cease fire, followed by Somoza's resignation in favor of a transitional government. Brzezinski, however, insisted that Vance also propose the creation of an OAS peace-keeping force to move into Nicaragua as soon as Somoza left. The area specialists knew that this proposal would not fly, that Latin American governments, always sensitive to anything smacking of armed intervention, would never accept it. Vaky, Bowdler, and Pezzullo all warned against it. Brzezinski wasn't listening. Neither was President Carter. Vance was ordered to propose the peace force —with predictable results: the U.S. suffered a humiliating defeat. Not a single country backed us.

The Latin Americans put forward their own resolution, which was along the lines of the original Department of State proposal. It called for Somoza's resignation and for a transitional government to hold elections "soon."

Somoza finally gave up and flew out of Nicaragua on July 17, 1979. A few days later, a new coalition government, which included several parties and persuasions, assumed power. Theoretically, it was not dominated by the Sandinistas, but they clearly held the principal levers of power. Shortly they would use those levers to move aside the other components of the coalition. Faced with the live prospect of a Sandinista-controlled government, the Carter administration had two broad options: it could launch a preemptive military operation to prevent the Sandinistas from consolidating their position; or it could try through a mix of dialogue, economic inducements, and diplomatic admonitions to preserve pluralism and bring the Sandinistas around. The first option would have carried a very high cost in world opprobrium and damage to our hemispheric relations. Only if we had concluded that the Sandinista government was intolerable would it have made sense to pay such a price. The Carter administration had not reached that conclusion and therefore accepted the second option. It viewed with concern the Sandinistas' Marxist proclivities and their close ties to Havana, but it hoped to place limits on both.

Back to Havana

As the Somoza regime collapsed in Nicaragua, the Smith family packed for Havana. I well understood that the situation in Nicaragua would add to the formidable list of disagreements between our two countries. On the other hand, it seemed to me that it might also point up the need for a closer dialogue with the Cubans. If we wished to

177

limit Cuban-Nicaraguan ties, we would need to seek Cuban restraint. We could only succeed by convincing both the Cubans and Nicaraguans that restraint served their interests better than adventurism. Effective diplomacy would be essential, and I counted myself lucky to be taking up my new job at such a challenging moment.

Secretary of State Vance was also upbeat. When I went to say good-bye, he underscored his desire to revitalize a dialogue with the Cubans—a dialogue which he said was now more important than ever. He encouraged me to work at it from Havana, while from Washington he would make new efforts to get our Cuba policy back on track. I left his office feeling that with his support I might be able to accomplish something worth while during my tour in Havana. I have no doubt that Vance was sincere. So was I. But quite soon, his good intentions—and mine—were to be overwhelmed by a wave of adverse circumstances.

Roxanna and I couldn't retrace our 1958 route to Havana. The ferry no longer ran from Key West. Absurdly, the usual way to fly to Cuba from the U.S. by scheduled airline was through either Mexico City or Toronto. We thought it would be cheaper and more convenient to charter a small plane in Miami. That proved a wise decision in more ways than one. Tom Cooper, the owner of a small charter company, had a taste for Cuban food and the floor show at the Tropicana. "I'll pilot the plane myself and take my wife Jerrie along," he'd said. "We'll get you there without even a bump."

He was as good as his word. We had a smooth flight on a beautiful day, and by the time we landed in Havana, Tom and I had found we were kindred spirits. Had we flown through Toronto instead, an enduring friendship might not have been formed.

Once arrived in Havana, we moved right into the old ambassador's residence. Lyle Lane and his wife gave a huge reception that first night to introduce us to the diplomatic corps. It was a gesture I much appreciated, for I had to get to know as many of my diplomatic colleagues as possible before the Sixth Non-Aligned Summit Conference, scheduled in a month's time. The interests section would be responsible for reporting what happened at the conference, and as corridor bargaining at such affairs is more significant that what is said on the floor, we could not do a good job simply by listening to the speeches.

Most Third World countries were sending delegates to the conference. Few would confide in us, representing as we did a so-called imperialist power. Their embassies in Havana, however, would also know what was going on, and these diplomats would be more likely to confide in us, being colleagues. So it would be up to us to find out as much as we could from them. That is the sort of thing a diplomat normally does.

I concentrated that evening on sizing up the other diplomats in town, especially the ambassadors of the key Third World countries, such as India, Yugoslavia, Nigeria, and Algeria. I found them a highly professional, serious group, and also downright friendly. Several even invited me to come around for a rundown on what they expected to happen at the conference. By the end of the evening, I had begun to relax and to have more confidence that the interests section would be able to handle its reporting chores creditably.

The first month in Havana was a time of feverish activity. The original interests-section staff, all who had served under Lyle Lane, were leaving Havana; some had already left. An entirely new team was coming in—just before a major international conference. For at least a few days, the Havana interests section would be one of the major reporting centers in the U.S. Foreign Service—with no one on the staff who had been at post more than two months. Many of my colleagues in the diplomatic corps expressed puzzlement over this strange and illogical way to proceed. One asked, "Why would your government do such a thing? Is it a calculated test of your mettle, or is it that your government believes an entirely new staff will provide a fresher, more objective view of the conference?"

In fact, it was neither. The transfer cycle in the Foreign Service is a game of musical chairs. If anyone in the cycle fails to move on time, the whole game breaks down. Lyle Lane had to leave Havana by late July because he had been appointed ambassador to Uruguay and had to be in Washington during August and September for his consultations and confirmation hearing. If he missed that time window, he might be delayed as much as six months in arriving at his new post. The rest of his staff also had to get to their new assignments or risk losing them. In short, transfer takes on a momentum of its own in which all sorts of rational priorities are simply ignored.

Getting my own feet on the ground and making sure the others on the staff were aboard and knew their jobs took up all my time during that first month. Roxanna's was taken up with getting us settled into the residence and getting the children into school. Our daughter Melinda, then seventeen, was to go to boarding school in

Fort Lauderdale. Sanford, twelve, would go into the sixth grade at the International School in Havana. The school had an interesting history. Before the revolution there had of course been many private schools in Havana: parochial schools, exclusive schools for the upper classes, and several for the various foreign communities. The school most used by the American and British communities was Ruston Academy. All these institutions had been closed as part of the great egalitarian process after 1959. This created a hardship for the diplomatic corps. Diplomats serving in Havana during the early 1960s had either to send their children to schools abroad, or subject them to the Marxist-Leninist indoctrination that soon became an integral part of the Cuban educational system.

The French were the first, in 1963, authorized to reestablish a foreign-language school. Then, in 1965, Penny Powers, an indomitable British woman who had once worked at Ruston Academy, convinced the Cubans that an English-language school was needed as well. Given the use of a small house and permitted to hire English-speaking Cuban teachers, Miss Powers opened with only twenty students. By 1979, the school had almost a hundred, mostly the children of English-speaking diplomats—British, Canadian, Nigerian, Indian, Jamaican, and now American.

The school did the best it could with limited resources, and at least through the sixth grade managed to provide quality education. It suffered most from cramped quarters, a tiny library, insufficient laboratory equipment, and the lack of a playground or any sports facilities. Roxanna and I tried to help out by opening the residence grounds. Once or twice a week our lawns were covered with children playing soccer and softball and the pool was filled with others taking swimming lessons. On those days, there was more laughter and joy in the air than the old place had heard in a long time.

We in the English-speaking community in Havana owed a great deal to Miss Powers. Without her, there would have been no school. It was a source of great satisfaction to all of us when upon her retirement she received the Order of the British Empire.

More on Nicaragua

One of my first reporting cables from Havana covered Castro's speech on the anniversary of his July 26, 1953, attack on the Moncada barracks. The Sandinistas had newly triumphed in Nicaragua, and several of their leaders sat on the speaker's platform behind Castro.

Remembering the Castro of old, I expected a fiery performance—one in which he would call on Nicaragua to follow Cuba's example in the struggle against Yankee imperialism. But times had changed, and so had Castro. His speech was moderate in tone, and rather than urging Nicaragua to accept the Cuban model, he said it should construct its own. Each revolution responded to distinct national conditions and idiosyncrasies, Castro noted; hence, the Nicaraguan Revolution would develop along lines quite different from those of the Cuban Revolution. That was as it should be, Castro said.

Nor did he urge the Nicaraguans to defy the United States; rather, he seemed to want an accommodation between the two, and he even congratulated the U.S. for saying it would give aid to the new government. The U.S., he said, apparently had learned from its mistakes. "They are not making the same errors in dealing with Nicaragua that they made in dealing with us," Castro concluded.

I noted all this in my cable to the Department of State and described it as an encouraging sign. Castro might of course have been feigning moderation, but that in itself would have been a marked change from his confrontational style of the 1960s.

As the months went by, we learned that Castro was indeed advising the Sandinistas to proceed slowly and pragmatically. At least for the time being, he cautioned, Nicaragua needed a mixed economy, a pluralist system, and good relations with the Church. Further, he urged the Sandinistas not to make his mistake; they should not burn their bridges to the U.S.[3]

In a conversation with me in early 1980, Castro confirmed that he was giving such advice to the Nicaraguans. That did not mean they would follow it. As one of Castro's aides put it as we left his office: "The Sandinistas may sometimes be as reluctant to take that kind of counsel at their age and at this stage in their revolution as the *comandante* [i.e., Castro] might have been at the same stage in his."

The Carter administration tried to deal realistically with the new government in Managua. From the beginning, however, the relationship was troubled. The administration's efforts to use economic assistance to our political advantage ran up against a cadre of hostile congressmen who blocked the enabling legislation. Only after almost a year of acrimonious debate did the aid bill finally pass. So many slurs and aggressive statements were made about the Nicaraguan government during the debate that our ambassador in Managua, Larry Pezzullo, felt that our relationship with the Nicaraguans might have been harmed more by the process of getting the aid than the aid itself could ever enhance it.

The Soviet-Brigade Crisis

Nicaragua would remain a contentious issue, but for a few weeks it was overshadowed by a crisis largely of our own making. I got news of it with my coffee at six thirty on the morning of August 31. I was up early because I had an important meeting at the Foreign Ministry.

Frank Taylor of the *London Daily Telegraph* was already at the breakfast table when I came down. An old friend from Moscow days, Frank was in Havana to cover the Non-Aligned Summit Conference. He had come out to the residence for a late dinner the previous evening and stayed overnight.

"What's this about a Soviet brigade?" he asked as I poured my coffee.

I had not turned on the Voice of America that morning. Startled, I asked what he meant.

"BBC says Senator Frank Church made a statement last night claiming there is a Soviet brigade in Cuba and the U.S. will insist on its removal," Frank explained.

Bloody hell, I thought to myself. The morning's appointment at the Foreign Ministry concerned that very brigade. On August 29, I had received a confidential cable from the department instructing me to express to the Cubans our concern over the brigade's presence and to suggest that it be withdrawn. I had immediately asked to be received by an officer of the Foreign Ministry. When twenty-four hours passed and my urgent request had not been answered, I called again to insist.

The duty officer at the Foreign Ministry asked if it couldn't wait a few days; at the moment, he said, everyone was frantically busy with last-minute arrangements for the Summit.

No, I replied, it couldn't wait. This was an urgent matter of great importance to both countries. The duty officer called back in the afternoon to say Vice-Minister Pelegrín Torras would receive me early the next morning.

Now it might be too late for the meeting with Pelegrín Torras to accomplish anything. Why, I wondered, had no one told me Senator Church intended to go public? (Only later did I learn that Vance thought he had dissuaded Church from making a statement. Church's announcement had taken the department by surprise also.)

Growing Problems, 1979

The August 29 cable had not been my introduction to the subject. Reports of a Soviet brigade in Cuba had stirred excitement in Washington even before I left for Havana, though I must say I never understood why. The whole affair struck me from the beginning as a great noise over nothing. After all, there was nothing new about the presence of Soviet military personnel in Cuba. At the time of the 1962 missile crisis, some twenty thousand Soviet troops had been there. Their removal had not been part of the 1962 understanding. We were worried about missiles and IL-28 bombers, not conventional ground forces. But the mission of the troops had been to protect the bombers and the missiles; once those were withdrawn, most of the troops left as well. Over the years that followed, American intelligence efforts focused hardly at all on the troops that remained. The standard reference in intelligence briefings suggested that there were some 3,000 to 5,000 Soviet military personnel in Cuba, mostly in an advisory capacity. Then, in the spring of 1978 came reports that some were part of an organized unit. That did not strike me as anything to lose sleep over, *provided* it was a conventional unit, as all evidence indicated.

A coordinated report issued by the intelligence community on July 12 tended to play the matter down; it confirmed the presence of a unit, but drew no conclusions as to its size or mission. Further, whatever was there had clearly been there all along, for the same reports which spoke of the possible presence of a brigade also emphasized that there had been no recent Soviet troop arrivals in significant numbers.

Sen. Richard Stone of Florida had asked me to come by for a farewell chat early in the morning of July 17. As I entered the waiting room, two army majors were just leaving his office. I recognized one as being from the Defense Intelligence Agency and had a sudden premonition as to why they were there: to leak the July 12 report to the senator. I was right. As I went in, I could see the senator was upset.

"What's this I hear about a Soviet brigade in Cuba?" he asked. "Is it true? If so, it means there's a Soviet base there and that is intolerable. President Carter assured me he would never permit the establishment of Soviet bases anywhere in this hemisphere."

I pointed out that so far the reports were fragmentary and unconfirmed. Even if there was some kind of unit there, I went on, a conventional infantry or armored unit would pose no threat. As for

183

the matter of a base, I was sure the president had been thinking of Soviet bases to service offensive weapons systems of some kind, not of a barracks to house a small Soviet ground unit.

Stone was not be be persuaded. If this was a base, he repeated, he would expect the president to live up to his promise.

A bit later that same day, Stone raised the matter of the brigade at a Foreign Relations Committee hearing on SALT II, asking government witnesses such as CIA Director Stansfield Turner and Secretary of Defense Harold Brown whether or not a Soviet unit had been discovered in Cuba.

Surprisingly, in view of the intelligence community's July 12 report, Turner, Brown, and others denied that we had discovered anything new in Cuba. It was true that the unit was not new. But since we had not previously been aware of its presence, and in our public statements had spoken only of Soviet *advisers*, it was misleading to suggest we had found nothing new in the situation. I wondered why Brown and Turner had not been more forthright in their replies. On the basis of their assurances, Senator Church that same afternoon issued a committee statement (which Stone refused to sign) that "apart from a military group that has been advising the Cuban Armed Forces for 15 years or more, our intelligence does not warrant the conclusion that there are any other significant military forces in Cuba."[4]

The rest of the committee could say what they wished; Stone wasn't buying it. He fired off a letter to President Carter asking for a written response to the question he had put to Turner and Brown in the committee hearing: What about that brigade?

Stone had indicated to me that he intended to write such a letter, and I assumed Carter would refer it to the Secretary of State. Hence, on July 18 I sent an informal note to alert his staff and suggest that any response to Stone be low-keyed and not deny the possibility that a Soviet unit of some kind might be present in Cuba.

For the next two days, I was out of play, packing to leave for Havana. On the night of July 20, with my car packed and ready to head south, I went by the department for final good-byes to friends. While I was there, someone showed me a draft letter to Senator Stone which had been prepared for Vance's signature in reply to the query which, sure enough, Stone had sent to the president (and which had in turn been referred to the secretary of state). The language of the draft reply was similar to that used by Brown and

Turner at the July 17 Foreign Relations Committee hearing. It simply denied that there was any evidence of a base or of any significant change in the Soviet military presence in Cuba.

I expressed concern to the staff officer who had shown me the draft. Weren't we needlessly putting the secretary of state out on a limb, and the rest of the administration with him? Why appear to be denying reports of a Soviet unit in Cuba? The intelligence community might the next day conclude that a brigade was indeed there, and then it would look as if Vance had been trying to hide the truth. Would it not be better to acknowledge that a Soviet unit might be there, and then go on to say that while small numbers of conventional ground forces posed no threat to the U.S., we would take all measures necessary to make certain they not become a menace to us or any of Cuba's other neighbors?

"Sure, it might be better to say that," the staff officer acknowledged, "but how can we? We have to go with the intelligence community's assessment, and this is it. And this version has already been cleared with others in the cabinet. We can't just rewrite it."

I said I knew it would be difficult to change at this point, but I thought he ought to try. He said he would see what he could do. That was the end of it. We said our good-byes, and a few minutes later I was crossing Memorial Bridge on my way to Miami.

As I had heard no more about the matter until the August 29 cable came, instructing me to discuss it with the Cubans, I had allowed myself to believe it had been dealt with quietly and satisfactorily. Foolish hope. I subsequently learned that on August 27 the intelligence community had indeed changed its assessment. As I had feared, the secretary of state was left on a limb. Fearing the new assessment would leak to the press, he gave instructions that congressional leaders should be briefed on a confidential basis.

Senator Church was understandably upset over the administration's reversal, which left him on a limb as well—in the midst of a life-or-death election campaign. He called Vance on August 30 to ask if a public statement would soon be made. When Vance said no, Church asked if Vance would object if he—Church—made one. Vance replied that it would be harmful, but that the decision was up to Church. Vance thought Church would remain silent,[5] but that same evening, Church informed the press of the brigade's presence and demanded its removal.

The rest of the story is well known. Having first tried to avoid the issue simply by denying it, and then having allowed others to set the tone of our public reaction, the administration tried to regain the initiative by taking a tough stance. Both Secretary of State Vance and President Carter went on record as saying the status quo was unacceptable,[6] thus suggesting that we would insist on the brigade's withdrawal even at risk of military confrontation. Others in the administration suggested ominously that the Soviets were testing us in Cuba and we would have to respond or lose credibility.

From Havana, I sent a cable warning that we should not repeat the assertion that the status quo was unacceptable unless we really meant it. Whatever Soviet inclinations might be, I wrote, the Cubans definitely would not agree to withdrawal of the brigade, and in this instance the Soviets were unlikely to ignore Cuban views. Hence, I concluded, we could only change the status quo at risk of a global confrontation reminiscent of the 1962 missile crisis. Unless we were willing to accept that risk, we shouldn't say the status quo was unacceptable, for our bluff would almost certainly be called and we would then end up looking like a paper tiger.

To their credit, both the president and the secretary of state subsequently acknowledged that the brigade crisis had been poorly handled and that their own statements had added to the problem. Meanwhile, however, we went ahead—raising the issue with the Soviets, urging them to remove part of the brigade or at least to modify its command structure and armaments. Why we ever thought the Soviets might help us out of this public-relations problem we had created for ourselves I never understood. Predictably, they refused.

The status quo turned out to be acceptable after all, but not before the administration had done tremendous harm to its own credibility and to important American priorities. SALT II was shelved and détente was dealt a mortal blow. The brouhaha over the brigade also left another festering scar on relations between the U.S. and Cuba— as if there weren't enough of them already. The Cubans were convinced we had known all along that the brigade was there and had simply dredged up the matter in a transparent effort to undermine Cuba's image just prior to the Sixth Non-Aligned Summit Conference. They saw the episode as clear evidence of bad faith on our part. The U.S., on the other hand, saw it as reaffirmation of the Cuban-Soviet military tie at a time when we were increasingly concerned over Cuban foreign policy in the region.

In only one small way did the misunderstanding prove useful. It will be recalled that I was not received by Vice-Minister Pelegrín Torras to discuss the matter until August 31. Even then his reply was totally noncommital. He simply heard me out and then replied politely that this was really none of our business but he would report my demarche to his superiors.

Meanwhile, on August 28, Undersecretary of State David Newsom had discussed the issue with the Soviet chargé d'affaires in Washington. A long-standing Cuban complaint was that the U.S. always tried to handle problems in Cuba by talking to the Soviets. In this instance also, they initially charged that we had opened the question with the Soviets first. I was having lunch with one of Castro's aides the day this view was first articulated, however, and so had a chance to shoot it down in the launching stage. I pointed out that had I been received on August 29, the day I requested the appointment, we would have been able to discuss the issue with the Cubans and the Soviets at about the same time, which was what the Department of State had intended. The Cuban side, I noted, could not in fairness fault the U.S. for its own delay of almost forty-eight hours in receiving me. Further, I pointed out, had I been able to discuss the matter with them before it became a public issue, there was a slim chance that we might have been able to defuse it. I was there as a channel between the two governments, I concluded; they ought to make better use of the channel.

The Cubans seemed to take my admonition to heart. They dropped their charge that we had ignored them, and a few days later Fidel Castro called me in to discuss his upcoming trip to the UN General Assembly. Clearly, he was letting me know that he had received my message and that henceforth I would be used as the channel to the U.S. government. From that point forward, I always had ready access to senior levels of the Cuban government.

The Non-Aligned Summit

For months, the U.S. had fretted that Cuba would use its position as host to push the Non-Aligned Movement (NAM) in a more radical direction. Our concerns were shared by the more moderate members of NAM, such as India, Nigeria, Tanzania, and Yugoslavia. Marshal Tito of Yugoslavia had broken free of Soviet domination at great cost and risk to his country and was determined that the NAM, which he had helped found, should not fall under the same domination. Yet, that seemed to be what the Cubans were working for. Ever since the

1973 Non-Aligned Summit Conference in Algiers, Castro had pushed the idea of a natural alliance between the socialist countries and the Third World. The bourgeois imperialist states were the enemies of both, he reasoned, and the enemies of one's enemies ought to become one's friends.

As Cuba prepared for the Summit, our fears grew. The draft Cuban position papers sought to have the natural-alliance theory incorporated as official NAM doctrine. As an Indian diplomat put it, "Cuba wants the NAM consciously to tilt toward Moscow."

There was great excitement as the Summit opened on September 3. Most observers, myself included, expected a dramatic clash between the radicals led by Castro, and the moderates led by Tito. As Castro began his opening speech, our expectations seemed on the way to fulfillment. Furious over what he believed to be U.S. efforts to sabotage the Summit by manufacturing the brigade crisis, Castro gave the U.S. a tongue-lashing and seemed to be warming up for a thundering radical philippic. His remarks about the U.S. were so pointed that I felt compelled to get up and walk out of the conference hall—something I would have to do many times during the next three years. A worried protocol officer awaited me in the anteroom. "We have already called for your car," he said; "please follow me. We'll make you as comfortable as possible until it arrives. And may I say I'm terrible sorry you'll be leaving us."

I almost burst out laughing. The Cubans had obviously expected me to walk out and were prepared. Suddenly the whole thing seemed to take on some of the aspects of a parlor game. "Don't concern yourself, Juan," I replied; "we all have our parts to play."

Meanwhile, back in the conference hall, Castro's speech had taken an unexpected turn. He did not once mention the natural-alliance theory, nor did he, as expected, challenge the moderates. Quite the contrary. Having blistered the U.S., he turned to the need for unity within the NAM. At one point he assured the delegates: "We will work with all member countries—without exception—to achieve our aims and to implement the agreements that are adopted. We will be patient, prudent, flexible, calm. Cuba will observe these norms throughout the years in which it presides over the Movement. I declare this categorically."[7] This passage was greeted by long and enthusiastic applause. The delegates sensed that there was to be no open clash and appreciated it. In the days that followed, their intuition proved correct. Castro backed away from extremism.

Why had Castro altered course? My assessment was that in push-ing the natural-alliance idea and other radical positions during the months leading up to the conference, Castro had concluded that resistance to them in the NAM was simply too strong—and that the costs to him, in terms of the leadership position he craved, were out of all proportion to the possible gains. Pragmatically, he decided to pull in his horns.

The Summit ran on for some six days, concluding in the wee hours of the morning on September 9. On balance, the results were better than we had dared hope. There was no tilt toward Moscow. Another concern had been that the more radical Arab states, angry at Egypt for signing the Camp David accords, would succeed in having Egypt expelled from the movement. That did not happen. The Egyptian delegation was subjected to a good deal of verbal abuse, but their country's position in the organization came through virtually unal-tered. The radicals managed only to get a resolution calling for a review of Egypt's credentials after the end of a year. It was apparent that nothing would come of that—and nothing did.

On these and other issues, the moderates more than held their own. We had reason to be pleased. Washington, however, was still shell-shocked over the brigade embarrassment and in no mood for bal-anced assessments. I think the only conference event that penetrated the consciousness of observers back home was Castro's fiery opening speech. For months afterward, official assessments continued to speak of the "radicalization" of the NAM that Castro supposedly had ac-complished during the Summit.

Baseball Games and Amphibious Exercises

I had arrived in Havana hoping I could help to mend fences between Washington and Havana. Yet within weeks of my arrival, animosity between the two had reached new levels of intensity. In part, this had to do with our embarrassment over our own mishandling of the Soviet brigade issue. Governments are never so inclined to huff and puff as when they have just made fools of themselves. Washington's increased concern was not entirely without substance, however. Cas-tro was now chairman of the NAM and had recently acquired new allies in the hemisphere—Grenada and Nicaragua. These successes, it was feared, might presage a new assertiveness on Castro's part, which would have worrisome long-term implications. For example, they might encourage a return to the confrontational tactics of the

1960s. The Sandinista victory, after all, had in a sense vindicated the guerrilla warfare advocated by Castro during that earlier period.

Long accustomed to expressing its concern over situations in the Caribbean by sending gunboats, Washington followed the pattern in this instance. Major new air and naval maneuvers were to be staged just off the Cuban coast in October, culminating in a mock amphibious landing at the Guantánamo naval base.

I thought we were overreacting. Havana's relationship with the new revolutionary regimes in Grenada and Nicaragua did alter the regional equation in ways the U.S. could not, in prudence, ignore. I agreed that we should impress upon the Cubans our determination to defend our interests and protect our friends. We might usefully have told both the Cubans and the Nicaraguans privately that we would not tolerate interference on their part in El Salvador, where guerillas were trying to overthrow the government; that if we caught them at it, we would retaliate. I disagreed strongly, however, that we should try to make our point with air and naval maneuvers. The Cubans would not be intimidated by such demonstrations in the least. They had played this game for almost twenty years—for so long that it was deeply ingrained in them to respond to our threats with defiance. Hence, military maneuvers were likely to make the Cubans nastier and more intractable than ever, without producing any compensating gains.

Further, measures so strongly reminiscent of earlier gunboat diplomacy could not but offend other Latin American countries, even those made nervous by Cuba's new alliances in the region. Friends such as Costa Rica, the Dominican Republic, and Honduras, for example, relied on U.S. assurances of support in the face of their more powerful neighbor, Cuba. Their natural inclination was to support us, but given the history of U.S. interventions in the region, not even they could endorse the landing of marines.

In sum, it seemed to me that we could accomplish more with diplomacy than with military demonstrations. The Cubans would not accede to threats, but they might respond to calm reminders that if relations between us were to improve, both sides had to behave prudently and take the other's security interests into account. It was worth a try anyway. Had it not worked, we would always have had military options as the next resort. But to wave our swords before first trying serious diplomacy, and to wave them without really having any intention of using them, did not strike me as the best way to proceed.

But proceed we did. On October 17, 1979, some 1,800 fleet marines staged an amphibious assault at the Guantánamo naval base; they then remained for a month for further maneuvers.

The landings at Guantánamo provided one amusing footnote. As marines stormed ashore at one end of the island, baseball teams from a number of countries, including the U.S., were playing the amateur world series at the other. When the American team came onto the field, "The Star-Spangled Banner" was played, and the Cuban crowd stood in silent respect. A Cuban in the stands quipped to me at the time: "You can't raise your flag over us by force, but you can through baseball."

The American team played with heart, but, I must sadly report, lost two straight games to the Cubans.

Release of American Political Prisoners

There was only one other bright spot after the Non-Aligned Summit Conference. On September 17, the Cubans released the four remaining American political prisoners—Larry Lunt, Everett Jackson, Juan Tur, and Claudio Morales.

As mentioned in the preceding chapter, Castro had hinted that he would release the four if the U.S. first released four Puerto Rican nationalists. There was never any written agreement to that effect, nor even a verbal understanding sealed with a handshake. Given the circumstances under which Castro had suggested the exchange, however, it seemed to me the Cubans were honor bound to free the Americans if we paroled the Puerto Ricans—and there was a good deal of sentiment in the U.S. favoring parole. All four Puerto Ricans had been behind bars more than twenty-five years. All were now elderly and seemed unlikely to cause further problems. Why not let them spend their last years with their families? If we could thereby bring about the release of the four Americans, so much the better.

Before leaving Washington, I had written several memoranda strongly urging the parole. I continued to push for it in cables from Havana, and to argue that we did not need a formal agreement with Castro on this matter; his word would be enough.

On September 7, the Puerto Ricans were released. I halfway expected a call from the Cubans that same day regarding the four Americans. No call. Nine days later I was beginning to ask myself if I had been wrong. Might the Cubans beg off on grounds that there had been no signed accord? Fortunately not. On September 16, José Luis Padrón called to say the Americans were being moved from the prison to a transient facility in the Miramar district. "You can pick them up there tomorrow," he said; "they're all yours."

Seeing the four of them walk into the interests section the next morning was a tremendous thrill for all of us. Ever since I had visited the prisons in 1960 and seen the difficult conditions under which the Americans were confined, bringing about the release of every last American political prisoner had been a burning personal objective. Larry Lunt's case, moreover, had been familiar to me since I worked on the Cuban Desk back in 1964. Now, fifteen years later, he was free at last. If I was moved, one can imagine the joy and relief of the prisoners themselves. "My God," said Juan Tur with a tremor in his voice, "there were times when I never expected I'd live to see this day."

A van waited to take the four to the Varadero airport, where they were to be picked up by an American Lear jet. We had only to issue them passports and get them on their way. The moment was so special, however, that I thought it should not pass without a few champagne toasts. Our consular officer, Jay Baker, had put the champagne on ice the day before, and while the passports were being typed up, we uncorked it. That almost proved to be a serious mistake on my part. I simply hadn't stopped to think that the four of them had not had a drop of spirits in over ten years. By the time we had gone through the third glass of champagne, they had become a bit unsteady on their feet, and one had begun to assert rather belligerently that he'd like to go back and tell one of the prison guards what he thought of him. I suddenly had a horrifying vision of their departure being marred or even postponed by some champagne-induced incident. I needn't have worried. These were disciplined and strong-willed men. All put down their glasses after the third. Larry Lunt spoke for the rest. "Thanks very much," he said. "It was a nice touch, but we'd better wait until we get to the other side."

I watched their van until it passed the *Maine* monument. Knowing they would be back with their families that evening meant more to me than anything that happened during the next three years in Havana.

The Soviet Invasion of Afghanistan

Neither the baseball games nor the release of prisoners brought about any easing of tensions between the two governments. Rather, U.S.-Cuban relations took a further downturn with the Soviet invasion of Afghanistan in December 1979. This was, to be sure, a brazen act of aggression which deserved our strongest condemnation. Our outrage, however, should have been directed at Moscow and only peripherally at Havana. Soviet tanks, after all, had rolled into Afghanistan, not Cuban tanks. And while the Cubans did not publicly condemn the Soviet action, privately they deplored it. How could they not? With Cuba in the chair of the Non-Aligned Movement, the Soviet Union had invaded a founding member of that movement and had not even bothered to inform, let alone consult with, its Caribbean ally. Cuba had been made to look foolish. Further, the invasion undercut several important Cuban objectives. For example, Castro had hoped to use Cuba's three-year chairmanship of the NAM to consolidate a preeminent and enduring leadership position. Because of the invasion, and his association with its perpetrator, however, he spent the three years fending off challenges to his non-aligned credentials.

By invading a member in good standing of the NAM, moreover, the Soviet Union cut the ground from under the argument that there was a natural alliance between the Third World and the socialist camp. And if there were no such natural alliance, Castro's position within the NAM became more vulnerable to attack.

Cuba was also seeking a seat on the UN Security Council, and until the invasion of Afghanistan, had seemed certain to win one. After that, however, sentiment turned against Cuba, and it eventually lost the Security Council seat to Colombia by a very close vote.

The cause of these setbacks was not lost on the Cubans. Not a single Cuban official publicly endorsed the invasion for almost a year, nor did any do so privately. Quite the opposite. Virtually every Cuban official with whom I spoke in the weeks after the invasion made a critical comment, albeit in a discreet fashion.

Given Cuba's economic dependence on the Soviet Union, an open split between Havana and Moscow was not to be expected. Even so, Cuba might have protected its non-aligned credentials more effectively by abstaining on the UN resolution which condemned the invasion. Instead, Cuba cast its ballot against the resolution on January 14, 1980. In a lengthy explanation of the vote Cuba's ambassador to the UN, Raúl Roa, Jr., said the resolution placed Cuba in a historical dilemma. Given a long list of U.S. aggressions against Cuba (which he proceeded to enumerate), the latter was not going to be placed in the position of voting with the U.S. and against the Soviet Union. This was a rather convoluted way of saying that while Cuba did not support the Soviet action, neither would it join other nations in condemning it.

Cuba's interests would have been better served by abstention. Its vote in support of the Soviet Union gave the U.S. an exploitable opening. We might have called attention to the limitations on Cuba's freedom of action pointed up by this failure to condemn an invasion which it suggested it deplored. Our friends in the NAM could also have used it in questioning the validity of Cuba's non-alignment.

At the same time, however, it did *not* serve our purposes to ignore the differences that in fact clearly existed between the Cuban and Soviet positions. On the contrary, we should have emphasized them and tried to drive the wedge between Moscow and Havana a bit deeper. Instead, Washington pretended that Soviet and Cuban views coincided, and reacted with the same hostility toward Havana as toward Moscow. Rather than exacerbating the differences between the Soviet Union and Cuba, this approach tended to mute them. And rather than pointing out that even some of Moscow's allies had reservations about its actions, we seemed intent on proving that they unanimously agreed.

Life in Havana

As we settled into life in Havana during the last months of 1979, Roxanna and I were surprised at how little the face of the city had changed. It was shabbier than we remembered it. Most buildings seemed to need a coat of paint and a bit of sprucing up. Many of the mansions stood silent and empty, their owners having long since departed for Miami.

The stores where we had once shopped were now run by the government, and one needed a ration book to make purchases. But they were still there, as were the apartment buildings where we had lived, and most of our favorite restaurants. Within two weeks we could find our way around the city as though we had never been away. Told that El Colmão was still open, we set off one night to find it. It was on an obscure side street in a part of city we had not revisited, but we went to it like homing pigeons. It was as lively as ever. The authentic flamenco music had been tropicalized over the years and the food was not very good, but the patrons more than made up for these shortcomings with their spirit. They sang; they danced on the tables; they laughed boisterously. Turning to a man at the table next to us, I remarked that they all seemed to be having a good time.

"*Por Dios, hombre,*" he shouted back, "we've all been on our good behavior since you came in. You ought to see us when we really let loose!"

I found their exuberance refreshing and reassuring. It was like looking through a window and seeing that the Cuban soul was intact.

El Colmao, however, was only a small corner of spice in a city that had lost, or suppressed, much of its zing. In the old days, the streets had throbbed with music and life. In 1979, we had a sense of grayness as we walked around town. In fairness, however, one has to admit that if Havana is not the city of lights it once was, it is probably better off without some of those "lights"—the rampant corruption, prostitution, and crime-controlled gambling of the old days. All are now but memories.

There were a lot of other changes we had to admire. Before the Revolution, there was not a single public beach within a bus ride of Havana. Unless one had the money to belong to a club or private beach, one had to swim off the sea wall. Now, all beaches were open to the public.

One saw no beggars in the Havana of 1979, nor any of the poverty and misery which abound in so many other Latin American cities. In Cuba, the basic needs have been provided to all. Everyone is guaranteed enough to eat, adequate clothing, access to education, medical care, and a place to live. The diet is monotonous, and one may have to stand in line to buy food; some of the housing remains substandard. Still, that no one goes hungry or homeless is no small achievement.

The Cuban people have of course paid a high price in political and civil liberties. There is little freedom of expression and no freedom of the press at all. It is a command society, which still holds political prisoners, some of them under deplorable conditions. Further, while the Revolution has provided the basic needs of all, it has not fulfilled its promise of a higher standard of living for the society as a whole. Cuba was, after all, an urban, middle-class society with a relatively high standard of living even before the Revolution. That standard of living has fallen somewhat. Everyone has enough, yes, and the 15 or 20 percent formerly comprising the bottom social strata live better than they did before the Revolution. The majority of Cubans, however, are less well off materially. More food, clothing, consumer goods, and entertainment were available to them before 1959 than now.

Cuban government officials who are candid enough to admit this argue that the situation is temporary. The Revolution, they insist, is channeling resources to build an economic infrastructure that in time *will* provide the promised better way of life to all, and one in which goods will be equitably distributed.

Maybe, but after twenty-five years, one has to wonder. The most to be said at this point is that the verdict of history is still out. Meanwhile, though the balance sheet is mixed, the Revolution has enough gains to its credit—and its promise of a better future is credible enough—so that most Cubans continue to support it. There is some disgruntlement (as the Mariel exodus was to make clear), but only on the part of a minority. After three years in Cuba, I came away in no doubt that Castro could easily win a fair and honest election. The majority is still with him. The U.S. government deludes itself in choosing to believe otherwise.

8

The Year of Mariel
1980

At the moment of Castro's triumph, events turned against him. Until the Non-Aligned Summit Conference, everything had gone his way. His interventions in Africa may have irritated the U.S., but on balance they had raised his stock in the Third World. After years of isolation, he at last had two allies in this hemisphere—Grenada and Nicaragua. His relations with Moscow were probably more harmonious than they had ever been. And, most importantly, he had just realized his fondest dream by becoming chairman of the Non-Aligned Movement.

Even the weather smiled. A hurricane moving toward the island held off until the day after the Summit before striking a glancing blow, which put the airfield under two feet of water. Had it struck a day or two earlier, the Summit would have been disrupted and hundreds of delegates stranded. Juan Meléndez, the Foreign Ministry's chief of protocol, crowed over Cuban luck at a diplomatic reception a few evenings later. "You see, Smith," he said in high good spirits, "the gods are on our side."

He spoke too soon. Before the year was out, a plague of new problems descended on the island. The Soviet Union's invasion of Afghanistan in December of 1979 fatally undercut several of Castro's most dearly held foreign-policy objectives. Also, 1979 was not a good year economically. By December, the island was feeling the pinch.

Crops were poor. Sugar production was down, and, worse, the world price had plummeted. Cubans were asked to make new sacrifices. Food rationing was tightened and new austerity measures were imposed. That such steps were necessary two decades after the Revolution had promised a new and better life for all was most demoralizing. Why sacrifice, some workers must have asked themselves, if sacrifice led only to more sacrifice? Absenteeism increased and worker productivity declined.

The Visits of the Exiles

Adding to internal disgruntlement, and hence to Castro's problems, were the visits to Cuba of some hundred thousand Cuban-Americans —the exiles—in the space of just over a year. We had pressed exiles' visiting rights since our first talks with the Cuban government back in 1977. At first Havana resisted the idea, but after a few successful test runs in 1978—in which Cuban-Americans were first flown to Mexico or Jamaica and from there back to Cuba—Castro decided it was feasible. During his dialogue with the Committee of 75 in late 1978, Castro promised to step up these visits, and in early 1979 he began to do so. The U.S., meanwhile, urged him to allow the visiting exiles to fly directly from Miami to Havana, hoping not only that this would be cheaper and more convenient but also that American travel agencies and airlines might thus have a share of the action. Castro acquiesced, provided Cubana aircraft could also participate in the service. By the early summer of 1979, the deluge had begun. Sometimes as many as five or six large jets a day disgorged passengers from Miami.

The U.S. had urged Castro to permit exiles to visit, but had not urged so many visits so fast. That was Castro's own idea. He was doubtless motivated in part by a wish to improve his standing with the Cuban exile community. His principal goal, however, was financial. The exiles, after all, returned with dollars in hand. The more who came back, the greater the Cuban government's earnings. To induce them to leave their dollars behind, the Cuban government opened special stores where the visitors could buy for their families in Cuba such items as fans, TV sets, radios, and other appliances— for dollars. It also charged exaggerated prices for air fares and hotel accommodations.

The plan was successful. Cuba earned over $100 million from exile visits in 1979 and 1980. But there was a cost: unrest among the Cuban population. At a time when most Cubans were asked to tighten their belts and face more years of hard work for little return, relatives from Miami and New Jersey were flooding back into the country with tales of the good life in the U.S. To hear them tell it, everyone had a mansion, three cars, an unlimited number of TV sets, and more food than anyone could eat. Life was easy! More and more Cuban citizens began to yearn for a piece of that vision. Pressures for emigration inexorably increased.

Disagreements over Immigration

For its part, the Cuban government was willing to permit tens of thousands of its citizens to leave. Many already had exit permits, though by no means all who wished to leave could do so. Many— especially military-age males—were refused. The problem was that there was no place for them to go. Few other countries, the U.S. included, accepted more than a trickle of Cuban immigrants. In the absence of normal emigration channels, growing numbers of Cubans forced their way into embassies in Havana seeking political asylum —not because they had political difficulties, but because they wanted to leave the country in search of a better life (just as did the Mexicans, Haitians, and West Indians who were also arriving in the U.S. in droves). Cubans were refused visas by most Latin American embassies, but those who broke in and asked for asylum almost always received it, and the embassy in question would then try to get them safe conduct out of the country. If the Cuban government refused to grant it, those seeking asylum—usually called asylees—simply remained as "house guests" of the particular embassy for an indefinite period. In December 1979, almost a hundred of these asylees languished in the various Latin American embassies in Havana. More than fifteen of them were living in the Venezuelan ambassador's residence. Roxanna and I had Christmas Eve dinner there in 1979. In the midst of a really sumptuous meal, the ambassador urged his guests not to feel guilty about taking second helpings. "The boys over there in the garage" (i.e., his asylees) had two turkeys and a ham of their own, he assured us, for the Venezuelan embassy didn't serve leftovers to asylees.

Cubans in growing numbers were also stealing boats to get across the Straits of Florida. This was particularly galling to the Cuban government, for while the U.S. accepted without question all Cubans who arrived by small boat, in most cases it would not have given these same people immigrant visas if they had applied at the interests section in Havana. To the Cubans, we thus appeared to be encouraging illegal departures even as we restricted legal means of entry. Cuban officials approached me on several occasions in late 1979 and early 1980 to urge discussions about establishing a normal flow of immigration between Cuba and the U.S. I reported each demarche and recommended that we respond affirmatively, but we never agreed to hold such talks.

Our failure to process the political prisoners as rapidly as we had promised also aroused Cuban suspicions. We had agreed to handle four hundred every month, plus their families. Between January and July 1979, however, sixty a month was our top. The cause was bureaucratic lethargy and ineptitude, not calculated foot-dragging. Name checks back in Washington took an inordinate amount of time, and keeping teams of INS officers in Havana steadily on the job proved impossible even though the officers themselves worked efficiently and often into the night. The problem was that the teams were rotated periodically, and sometimes gaps of several days occurred between the departure of one team and the arrival of another.

These were real difficulties, but as far as the Cubans were concerned, our snail's pace was part of a plan. We had gotten them to begin releasing political prisoners by promising to remove them as fast as they were freed. Instead, the Cubans believed, we were deliberately delaying the process, thus causing hundreds of prisoners to stack up in Havana. "You hope thus to create a core of dissidents," one official said accusingly in August, adding that since we weren't living up to our part of the bargain, Cuba would be justified in halting the prisoner-release program altogether.

Our processing rate improved after July. One month we cleared over 300 prisoners, and the rate rarely dropped below 250. We still weren't doing all we had promised, but the Cubans could see we were making a concerted effort. They remained suspicious, but stopped threatening to halt the program.

Maritime Hijacking

On October 24, 1979, a new and even more urgent problem arose—one which contributed directly to the decision the following year to permit a sealift from Mariel. On that day, several Cuban citizens overpowered the captain and crew of a scow, the *GH-41*, and forced them to sail to Florida. Stealing a boat was one thing, hijacking it another. The latter placed lives at risk. One might feel great sympathy for those desperate enough to commit such an act, but the fact remained that hijacking, whether of a boat or a plane, was an act of terrorism.

U.S. authorities did not so treat the case of the *GH-41*, however. The hijackers were not arrested or even detained; they were immediately paroled into the country. No effort was made to investigate the case.

The next day I was called to the Foreign Ministry and handed a note protesting the inaction of U.S. authorities. Cuba, the note pointed out, continued to respect the anti-hijacking agreement: it detained and prosecuted aerial hijackers. Did U.S. law-enforcement agencies not intend to do the same with boat hijackers? If not, Cuba would have to reconsider its own position.

The Cuban diplomat who handed me the note urged that I emphasize the gravity of this case. "We aren't asking you to return the hijackers to Cuba," he said. "We understand that wouldn't be politically feasible, and it isn't necessary anyway. What is necessary is that your government reaffirm its intention to uphold the law with respect to hijackings. That will help to discourage what might become a very dangerous practice."

Returning to the interests section, I cabled the text of the Cuban note to Washington, along with a recommendation that we issue a statement condemning maritime hijacking and warning that anyone who arrived at our shores as the result of such an act would be prosecuted to the extent of the law. I fully expected Washington to act quickly on my recommendation. After all, we *did* deplore hijacking, didn't we?

I was to be surprised. The Department of State responded neither to my cable nor to the Cuban note. My follow-up cables also disappeared into the Washington void.

Eventually, I did receive a message from the department, explaining that the hijackers of the *GH-41* had not been prosecuted because they had not entered our waters under their own steam. How *had* they arrived? Why, they had been towed in by the Coast Guard! One can imagine the derision with which the Cubans greeted this explanation. "In other words," noted a Cuban diplomat, "an agency of your government towed the boat in, and now your government says it can't prosecute *because* that agency towed it in. Wouldn't it be simpler just to say, 'We arranged things to avoid prosecution'?"

That was not true, of course. We had towed in the *GH-41* because the vessel was in trouble, *not* to avoid prosecuting its hijackers. But the Cubans would never believe that. In their place, I wouldn't have believed it either.

In January 1980, I had a chance to state my case at an interagency meeting in Washington. An American plane had been hijacked to Cuba. Plane and passengers were returned safely, but there had been some hairy moments. A few days later, the Federal Aviation Administration hosted a symposium to discuss how we might better handle aerial hijackings and assure continued Cuban cooperation in dealing with the hijackers. I was brought up from Havana to state my views. To an audience of some 150 representatives of interested agencies, including the FBI and the Department of Justice, I said that continued Cuban cooperation with respect to aerial hijackings could be assured only if we discouraged maritime hijackings. It was a case of tit for tat. If we failed to take a stand on the one, it would be unreasonable to expect continued Cuban cooperation on the other.

After my talk, a number of people from the Department of Justice expressed support. Something had to be done about these boat hijackings they agreed. I returned to Havana encouraged and naively expecting the Department of Justice to move into action. In fact, it moved not at all.

After the first hijacking in October, four additional boat hijackings occurred prior to the Mariel sealift. At least two were serious episodes involving a real danger to the captain and crew. On February 16, 1980, sixteen Cubans, seven of whom were armed, took control of the *Lisette*, a Liberian freighter, and forced it to sail to Florida. All sixteen were immediately paroled into the country; there was no criminal investigation and no attempt at prosecution. The same was true in the case of three Cubans armed with knives and handguns who on February 25, 1980, resorted to violence in forcing the captain of the fishing boat *Lucero* to sail to the United States.

Each hijacking prompted another Cuban protest note. Each note was sent up accompanied by several cables from me urging action. The Cuban notes, and, I suppose, my own cables, became increasingly shrill. Certainly I began to lose patience after a clear warning from Vice-President Carlos Rafael Rodríguez failed to convince Washington that we had a serious problem on our hands. Called in by Rodríguez on February 19, after the hijacking of the *Lisette*, I was left in no doubt that the Cubans would take retaliatory actions unless we soon clarified our position on maritime hijacking. "I hope, Smith, that you are emphasizing to your government the gravity with which mine views this situation," Rodríguez began. He went on to say: "There are those in the Cuban government who have come to see this as something of a litmus test of U.S. intentions. They note that U.S. officials continue to describe Cuba as an island prison even while they ignore our requests for a normal flow of immigration. They note also that you welcome anyone who arrives by small boat, even hijackers, at the same time that you restrict the issuance of visas. All this looks to them like a deliberate effort to create problems for us by encouraging illegal departures accompanied by violence. So far, we have been patient. Despite your failure even to reply to our notes, we have continued to cooperate in deterring aerial hijackings. But our patience is running out. Unless your government responds soon, we may have to take measures of our own, and those measures could include the opening of a new Camarioca. If your government wants people in small boats, we can give you more than you bargained for."

I reported Rodríguez's remarks to Washington and added my own appeals for action. It was as if I had fed it all into some great inscrutable receptacle from which no response ever came.

Castro himself publicly repeated the warning in a speech on March 8 to the Federation of Cuban Women. Referring to the inaction of U.S. authorities, he said: ". . . they encourage illegal departures, the hijacking of boats, even receiving as heroes those who hijack boats. . . . We have asked them to take measures . . . and we hope they do. If not, we would then have to take our own measures. We have reminded them that we once opened Camarioca. . . . We hope we don't have to take such measures again."[1]

Castro's remarks went into the same receptacle that had swallowed Rodríguez's private admonition. I began to despair. I did not interpret the warnings of Rodríguez and Castro to mean that the Cuban government was actively preparing for a new sealift; rather, such a move would be a last resort, to be made only if we failed to act. But when we still had not acted by the end of March, time was running out.

What had happened back in Washington? Was everyone asleep? Not quite. The White House and the Department of State vaguely grasped that we faced a problem. But both failed to comprehend its nature and magnitude, and perhaps for that reason neither succeeded in convincing the Department of Justice, the responsible agency, of the need to act.

I was later able to reconstruct the way things played out in Washington. In October 1979 the first Cuban protest note, together with my cable recommending an anti-hijacking statement, were referred to the Department of State's Bureau of Legal Affairs. There they remained untouched in someone's in-box until February. At that point, the issue was transferred for action to the Department of Justice. After the hijacking of the *Lucero* in late February, the Department of State called the matter to President Carter's attention. He responded with a note which said: "We should restrict these maritime hijackings by law if possible; use public warnings, and cooperate with Cuba."

Thus armed with clear instructions from the president, State called Justice to urge an action program. Philip Heymann, the assistant attorney general, said he was unfamiliar with the problem but would look into it.

He had not done so by mid-March, however, when State called to remind him of its—and the president's—concerns. Obviously trying to throw the ball back to State, Heymann asked the latter to outline those concerns in writing. Robert Owens, of State's Bureau of Legal Affairs, complied, sending a letter to Heymann on March 24 urging a maximum effort to discourage hijackings.

Clearly unwilling to take action, but not wanting to say so, Justice responded with the oldest dilatory tactic in the book: it asked for information it already had. After all, the Coast Guard, INS, Customs, and the FBI—the agencies that had dealt with hijackings, with the admission of the perpetrators and whether or not to prosecute them —were all part of the Department of Justice. If anyone had complete files on the subject, Justice did. Nevertheless, on March 28, James S. Reynolds, of Justice's Criminal Division, said in a letter to State: "As I continue to explore what contribution the Department of Justice can make to the solution of this matter of mutual concern, I believe it would be helpful to determine the number of hijackings which have occurred . . . as well as general details about each incident." The letter then went on to request a list of hijackings, with dates, kinds of vessels involved, and a description of each incident.

Myles Frechette, the director of Cuban affairs in the Department of State, sent me a copy of the Reynolds letter as proof that "the wheels were grinding." Myles seemed to expect that I would be pleased. I wasn't. I was appalled. I found it outrageous that five months after my urgent recommendation for an anti-hijacking statement, and almost three weeks after Castro's public warning about the possibility of a new sealift, Justice played dumb. I fired back a bitter letter to Myles suggesting that the department accuse Reynolds of gross incompetence and tell him what he could do with his request for information. Then, swallowing my anger, I had the interests section compile and send in all the information Reynolds had requested. It did not the slightest bit of good, of course. Justice remained as inactive as before.

Only two points can be made in Justice's defense. The first is that because of the intense anti-Castro sentiment in Miami, Justice feared that obtaining a conviction for hijacking would not be possible in a Miami court. That fear was well founded, as we were to see in December 1980, when at long last (and after it was too late to prevent the Mariel sealift) one hijacking case—that of the *Victoria de Girón*, which had been seized on July 10, 1980— was finally brought to trial. Even though the evidence was overwhelming, the federal judge threw out the case on grounds that escaping to freedom was no crime. That of course missed the point. Escaping to freedom was not a crime, but using force against a boat crew was. The judge refused to listen. Having stated his ruling, he came down from the bench and joined a loud and unseemly celebration in the courtroom. It was not American law's finest hour.

But the fact that prosecution would be difficult in Miami did not in any way relieve the Department of Justice of the obligation, the duty, to try. Had it really wished to press the matter, it could have prosecuted in every case, and when the impossibility of obtaining a fair trial in Miami became clear, it could have asked for a change of venue. At the very least, it could have issued the sort of statement I had been asking for since October 1979—condemning hijackings and indicating our intention to try everyone involved in such incidents. Promising conviction was beyond the power of the Department of Justice, but promising to uphold the law was not. It did not even do that. Had such as statement been issued prior to the Mariel operation, it might have made a difference. But no statement was issued until July 1980, and by then of course it was far too late.

In Justice's defense, second, was the fact that State never clearly indicated that failure to deal with the issue might result in a new

Camarioca. Even though he was writing after Castro's March 8 speech, for example, Robert Owens did not even mention the possibility of such a sealift in his March 24 letter to Philip Heymann. Nor, so far as I have been able to determine, did other officials at State warn their counterparts at Justice. Perhaps this was not just an oversight. Even Department of State officers who ought to have known better were strangely complacent right up to the start of the sealift. On April 3, for example, an interagency meeting was convened by the department's Bureau of Refugee Affairs. Participants were asked whether the U.S. should take seriously Castro's threats to open a new Camarioca, and, if so, whether it should prepare to handle a massive new wave of refugees.

The majority of those at the meeting answered no to both questions. Strangely, they did not even relate the possibility of a new sealift to the maritime-hijacking issue; rather, the consensus was that the Cubans would be placated by our accelerated processing of political prisoners. So nothing was done to prepare for a new Camarioca. That this was the wildest kind of wishful thinking became apparent a few days later at the Peruvian embassy.

The Peruvian Embassy Affair

If the U.S. performance in all this was less than brilliant, so was that of the Cubans. Our own bumbling helped to create an explosive atmosphere, but a gross miscalculation on Castro's part caused it to go bang.

Whatever else may be said of him, Castro's political instincts are usually pretty good. In the spring and summer of 1980, however, those instincts seemed not to be working and Castro not to be himself. At the few diplomatic receptions he attended, he appeared drawn and preoccupied. It was not difficult to understand why. Not only did he face maddening internal and international problems—the most difficult in over a decade—but on January 11, 1980, he had suffered a grievous personal loss. Celia Sánchez died of a tragic illness. His secretary and confidante since his days in the Sierra Maestra —and some said also his mistress—Celia Sánchez had occupied a place in his life that transcended any single role. Totally devoted to him, she was probably the only person in the world he fully trusted. As some Cubans put it, Celia Sánchez was Castro's gyroscope. After she died, he lost his equilibrium for a time, until he could learn to walk without her. For months after her death, his decisions reflected a certain irrationality—and none more so than the decision to remove the guards at the Peruvian embassy.

On April 1, a group of Cubans who wished to leave the country crashed through the gates of the Peruvian embassy in a bus, seeking asylum. They were not armed, but guards on both sides of the gate opened fire, and one of the guards was killed in the cross fire.

Castro was already in high dudgeon over the asylee problem. This latest incident drove him up the wall. One of his aides told me later: "When we informed the *comandante* of the policeman's death, his face turned deep red. I have never seen him so angry."

Castro's subsequent action reflected that anger. On the morning of April 4, the Cuban government announced that it would no longer risk the lives of its policemen to prevent people from entering the Peruvian embassy. The Peruvians had refused to keep such people out, so the Cuban government felt no further obligation in the matter. As *Granma** put it that day: "We cannot protect embassies that do not participate in their own protection."

Removing the guards was a calculated gamble. I spoke to a number of Cuban officials about it at a reception the evening of April 4. Since they all took precisely the same line, I assumed they were repeating something out of an official briefing paper. The decision to remove the guards was a master stroke, they said; it would put a stop to all this asylum nonsense. Dozens of people would doubtless enter the compound. That would show the Peruvian diplomats the error of their ways. They wouldn't be able to work with all those Cubans on their hands. Eventually, they would have to either ask the Cuban government to remove the asylees, or eject them themselves. They would henceforth think twice before sheltering more asylees. So would other Latin American embassies.

One of the Cuban officials wanted to bet me five pesos that not more than several hundred people, and probably considerably fewer, would take advantage of the guards' absence to go in. I said I wouldn't take his money. On April 5, however, it seemed that he might have won his bet. Cubans who wished to leave could not believe their government was sincere. An unusual number of pedestrians milled about near the embassy that morning. A few entered the compound, but most hung back, waiting to see what would happen.

---

*The official organ of the Cuban Communist party, and Cuba's principal newspaper.

Encouraged by police inaction, the crowd became bolder as the afternoon wore on. After Castro came by and calmly assured those inside that they would indeed be allowed to leave the country, the trickle into the embassy became a stream. The stream became a flood the next day, following an announcement by the Ministry of Interior confirming that those who entered the Peruvian embassy after the removal of the guards would be free to emigrate to any country that would accept them. Further, they would be allowed to return to their homes to pack their belongings. Within hours after the statement became public, the embassy was inundated by a human tidal wave. By the night of April 6, almost ten thousand people were inside. They sat on the roof and in trees, and crammed every square foot of the compound (roughly the size of a city block). Other thousands converged from all over the island. Trains and buses disgorged passengers, usually with cardboard suitcases in hand, who headed straight for the Peruvian embassy. When on April 7 the compound was filled to capacity, a police cordon was thrown around it to keep new arrivals out. Fights erupted between police and those still trying to get in. From inside, those who had already made it jeered at police and shouted encouragement to those trying to break through. Castro again came to have a look, and according to newsmen who were there at the time, was shaken by what he saw. He may at that point have realized that he had miscalculated. A great tear had suddenly appeared in his orderly, regimented socialist society.

The Cuban government was taken aback. Why, I have never understood. It had been apparent that not all Cubans were enchanted with the system, and it should have been obvious that in a population of ten million, there would be thousands who would take advantage of an opportunity to get out. It should have been obvious, but it had not been. The Cuban government was shocked. I found that somewhat comforting. If we were capable of deluding ourselves, so were they.

The urgent question now facing the angry, frustrated, and near-panicky Cuban leaders was how to get out of the mess they themselves had created. They first began a campaign of invective against the ten thousand, describing them as the dregs of society—delinquents, parasites, and homosexuals. Castro borrowed a term from Engels to describe them: *lumpen,* a word he pronounced with the utmost scorn. But vilifying the people inside the embassy did nothing to solve the problem.

The simplest solution, of course, would have been for Peru to accept all ten thousand. To encourage this, Cuban authorities stressed that all were free to go; Peru had only to arrange transportation. Peru, however, was not about to cooperate. It eventually flew a few planeloads to Lima, but with much of its own citizenry in poverty, Peru was in no position to accept ten thousand Cubans. Hence, in a statement on April 6, the Peruvian government washed its hands of the matter. The UN high commissioner for refugees, not the Peruvian government, the statement read, would be responsible for arrangements to remove the Cubans inside the compound to any country that would accept them.

The Cuban government committed another error. It issued a statement that any Cuban who wished to leave was free to travel, provided only that he or she had a visa from the country of destination. With respect to those inside the Peruvian embassy, the statement was categorical: "They are free to return to their homes and to leave and enter the embassy as many times as they wish. The Cuban authorities will not take any measure against them. They may also travel to Peru or any other country which grants them a visa. This is their affair and that of the country willing to take them."

By attaching no conditions of any kind and emphasizing that transportation was a matter of no concern to them, the Cubans left themselves wide open. They probably did not expect many takers and were therefore surprised when the Costa Rican president, Rodrigo Carazo, responded on April 13 by offering to fly all ten thousand to his country. A refugee center would be set up so that international agencies could screen them and arrange for their resettlement elsewhere.

The Cubans could not have been enthusiastic. This offer might let Jimmy Carter off the hook, and they were determined not to allow that to happen. Cuban leaders were still furious over Carter's statement on April 9 in which he had ripped into Cuba as a Soviet puppet and a police state and had then added: "We see the hunger of many people on that island to escape political deprivation of freedom and also economic diversity. Our hearts go out to the almost 10,000 freedom-loving Cubans who entered a temporarily opened gate at the Peruvian Embassy just within this week."

The Cubans were looking for a way to make him eat his words, and were already toying with the idea of permitting a sealift. Still, they had now stated flatly that those inside the compound could go to any country they wished, and how they got there was their affair. To reject the Costa Rican proposal outright would have been brazenly contradictory. So the Cubans decided to go along with it and see what happened. They issued travel documents to those inside the Peruvian compound, and on April 16 flights to San José, Costa Rica, began.

Washington breathed a sigh of relief. From the U.S. standpoint, the Costa Rican airlift was ideal. The U.S. would not be inconvenienced by a wave of refugees; rather, at our own measured pace, we would be able to take them out of the Costa Rican center. Meanwhile, by interviewing arriving refugees and playing up their reasons for leaving Cuba, we could embarrass Castro day after day at no cost to ourselves.

The Costa Rican airlift was all to our advantage, none to Castro's. He had probably suspected that would be the case. If he had any doubts, they were certainly dispelled as he watched the way the first arrivals were handled in San José. They were greeted by President Carazo himself and by a battery of Western newsmen. The dozens of refugees interviewed on radio and TV were encouraged to talk about food shortages, restrictions on freedom of expression, and other negative aspects of Cuban life.

One would have expected nothing else. It was all part of the game. Had the shoe been on the other foot, the Cubans would have behaved the same way. But as Castro watched in Havana, he doubtless decided it was time to shift the venue of the game and impose some penalties on the other side. He had not wished to retract the earlier statement, but now he saw he had no choice. On April 18, the airlift was terminated. According to *Granma* that day, a center in San José was unnecessary. Departing Cubans could fly directly to any country willing to receive them. Further, *Granma* went on, the U.S. and Costa Rica had cooked up the idea of a refugee center for purely demagogic and propagandistic purposes. Cuba would play their game no longer.[2]

The Mariel Sealift

Clearly, permitting a sealift was an option Castro had all along held in the back of his mind. He has not revealed exactly when he decided to exercise it, but probably the decision came after the establishment of the Costa Rican airlift. Going ahead with the airlift would have made no sense if he had already fully made up his mind to do the other. That he wanted to keep the option very much alive, however, is suggested by the fact that when Napoleón Vilabóa, a Cuban exile from the old Committee of 75, was in Havana about April 12, he was assured that those inside the Peruvian embassy could be taken out by small boat. He returned to Miami with the news. Other members of the exile community had doubts about its authenticity, however, and as long as there was an air bridge to San José, a sealift seemed pointless. But on April 18, the airlift was closed. That same day, several exiles in Miami received calls from Havana confirming Vilabóa's story. The *Granma* editorial of April 18 also carried a broad hint that the plug was about to be pulled. "To travel to the U.S., there is no need to make a stop in Costa Rica," it noted. "It costs less and is quicker to travel directly to Key West, some 90 miles away."

My own guess is that the final decision to initiate the Mariel operation was taken in a meeting of senior leaders on the evening of April 17. One can imagine the scene. Those around the table were doubtless tired, angry, and feeling hemmed in. Obviously they had to close down the San José air bridge; it was turning into a public-relations disaster. But how then to extricate themselves from the mess at the Peruvian embassy?

"Look," one of the leaders must have said, "we've been telling the Americans for months that unless they publicly condemned boat hijackings, we would open a new Camarioca. They ignored us. They didn't even answer our notes. So what are we waiting for? Let's send all those people in the compound up to Key West in small boats!"

"Yes," others would have chimed in, "the Americans not only ignored our warnings but have taken unfair advantage of our present difficulties. When Jimmy Carter said his heart went out to the people in the compound, it was a cheap propaganda shot. But since he says he feels so deeply for them, let's give them to him."

Castro would then have stroked his beard and said, "Yes, let's do that. But why stop with the ten thousand? There are thousands of others who want to go. Unless we take the offensive, the Americans will continue to incite them; they'll go on encouraging boat hijackings and illegal departures. Let's demonstrate once and for all that we can hit them with more people in small boats than they ever wanted to see. Maybe that will shut them up. First we'll tell the Cubans in Miami to remove the ten thousand by boat. Then we'll let them pick up anyone else who wants to go. That way, we'll stick it to the Americans, get rid of our own malcontents, and demonstrate that participation in this Revolution is voluntary."

The meeting would then have adjourned amidst a chorus of approvals. The next day, April 18, the calls were made to Miami. On April 19, the first two boats arrived in Mariel, and by April 21, Napoleón Vilabóa was headed south with a fleet of boats. The Mariel exodus was on.

Meanwhile, the Cuban government had taken a series of measures to demonstrate the Cuban people's repudiation of the "traitors" who were leaving. *Granma* scathingly denounced them as worms (*gusanos*) and said it was clear that those signing up to leave were either social misfits or lazy parasites. Cuba was better off without them, *Granma* proclaimed daily.

On April 19, the day the first boats arrived in Mariel, hundreds of thousands of shouting Cubans marched past the Peruvian embassy with placards and chants proclaiming loyalty to the Revolution and hatred of the "worms" inside. No clashes occurred between the marchers and the "worms," but that may have been only because a strong cordon of police around the compound kept the two groups apart. Away from the compound, plenty of violence erupted. Orders had gone out to the local Committees for the Defense of the Revolution (the famous block committees, known as CDRs) to demonstrate disdain for those who wanted to abandon the country. Several of the Peruvian-compound refugees who had returned home to pack their things were beaten up by neighbors.

As the Mariel exodus went into high gear, such incidents multiplied. Notices were posted instructing Cubans who wished to leave to register with the Cuban Immigration Service. Long lines formed immediately, and just as quickly became the targets for hecklers sent by the CDRs to show "disdain." The antagonism did not always stop at heckling. Fights, sometimes block-long melees, broke out between prospective emigrants and hecklers. Too, as the former registered, their local CDRs were immediately notified. Usually, by the time they returned home, a reception committee was waiting. They would be pelted with eggs, made to wear signs saying "I am a worm," and sometimes forced to run a gauntlet of jeering neighbors. In many cases, they were beaten up, and in at least one or two cases they were beaten to death. Always, the homes of those departing were painted with aerosol cans: "Traitors live here" and "Worms inside" were among the milder terms of abuse.

Nor were the demonstrations of "disdain" confined to the victims' neighborhoods. They were subjected to the same kind of harassment and humiliation at their places of employment—and at schools. That was the cruelest of all. Children whose parents had registered to depart were often pointed out by teachers and then set upon by classmates who made their lives a living horror.

Rare are the nations without shameful episodes in their past. The U.S. has its share. The degradation of would-be emigrants was certainly such a blot on Cuba's history. No thoughtful Cuban should be able to look back on what happened during those spring and summer months of 1980 without a deep sense of wrong.

If the streets of Havana were filled with hatred, by May the port of Mariel was filled with boats. Thousands had arrived—so many that Cuban teams assigned to process and load emigrants could not fill them fast enough. Instead of picking up passengers and returning to the U.S. within a few hours, as the first boats had been able to do, boats now had to wait in the harbor for days, and then for weeks. And the character of their human cargo changed. The first few boats had taken back refugees from the Peruvian compound and families registered with Immigration. As time went on, however, more and more passengers of another kind were thrown aboard. In a typical case, the captain of a boat with a capacity for, say, forty passengers would present a list of the forty people for whom family members in Miami had sent the boat. But Cuban Immigration would reply that he could take back only ten of those he had come for. The other thirty passengers would be chosen by the Cuban government.

Who were these other passengers? Sometimes they were simply people who had applied to leave but for whom no one had sent a boat. Often, however, they were men and women who had been in trouble with the law. Several thousand were criminals actually serving time in prison. Castro admitted as much when, in a speech on June 14, 1980, he crowed over sending his "chicken thieves" to the U.S.

Some Americans were puzzled when Castro subsequently denied sending any *criminales* to the U.S., but he was actually not contradicting himself. In Spanish, a *criminal* is one convicted of a felony; those convicted of misdemeanors (such as chicken theft) are *delinquentes*. Castro's contention has always been that he sent the former

213

but not the latter. The contention does not bear close scrutiny, however; many of those packed onto the boats by the Cuban government were criminals by anyone's definition.

Why did the Cuban government deliberately include such people? One reason was pure orneriness. Mariel, after all, was an outburst of anger and frustration. In their rage, many Cuban leaders wanted nothing so much as to rub Jimmy Carter's face in the mess, which, rationally or not, they believed he had helped bring on them.

Another reason was to give credence to Castro's claim that those departing were the dregs of society. Who but the dregs, Castro wished to suggest, would want to leave such a wonderful revolution? But those who saw the refugees arriving in Key West during the first days of the exodus recognized that these were *not* the parasites and degenerates Castro made them out to be. Most were perfectly normal, respectable people. Seeking to turn this perception, Castro added to the flow several thousand people who *were* misfits.

The Carter administration handled the sealift no better than the events leading up to it. For one thing, it had made no preparations to receive any refugees, despite Castro's warning and despite the extremely volatile situation that had existed in Cuba since April 1. It was unprepared, and it took an inordinate length of time to get organized to handle the flood.

For another, the administration seemed unable to decide what to do—whether to greet the refugees with open arms or to blow them out of the water. On April 23, at the same time that Coast Guard vessels were providing assistance to boats headed for Cuba, Department of State spokesmen warned that such trips were illegal, that violators would be arrested and their boats seized.[3] On May 5, President Carter was affirming that we would greet the refugees with open arms.[4] But ten days later, U.S. officials again threatened strong action against boat owners who brought refugees back from Cuba;[5] that hardly sounded like an open-arms policy.

And then, in the middle of all this, the administration announced that in May, new air and naval maneuvers would be held at the Guantánamo Naval Base—as if that might somehow frighten Castro into changing course. The faith of American officials in the efficacy of military maneuvers is truly puzzling. Except in a narrow range of situations—and this was not one of them—military maneuvers are among the least effective and least imaginative devices one can resort to in international politics. In this case, the announcement played right into Castro's hands, giving him a wonderfully convenient external threat to rally the Cuban people against and to divert their attention from the turmoil at home. Taking full advantage of the opening, he immediately warned that Cuba was about to be attacked and called for mass rallies and marches to demonstrate the determination of its people to fight.

I fired off a series of cables urging that the maneuvers be canceled. Since they obviously helped Castro more than they threatened him or dissuaded him, I noted, I could not for the life of me fathom why we wanted to go ahead with them. Several U.S. embassies in Central America supported me, noting that the governments to which they were accredited opposed the maneuvers and would issue critical public statements if we went through with them. Washington wanted no quarrel with our allies in the region at such a crucial moment and so reversed itself. It canceled the maneuvers, with the explanation that our naval vessels could be put to better use saving lives in the Straits of Florida—lives endangered by Castro's unauthorized and unsafe sealift.

With the maneuvers thus out of the way, I thought there might be some chance of negotiating an end to the sealift. I had been on the Cuban Desk back in 1965 when we had convinced Castro to replace the Camarioca sealift with an orderly departure process. In some ways, prospects were better in 1980 than they had been in 1965. Castro had initiated Camarioca without any prior expression of interest in establishing a normal flow of emigration. Yet, he had quickly closed down the sealift in return for a normal emigration process. This time, Cuban officials had been urging such a process long before the Mariel operation began.

There would have to be a sweetener, however. The Cubans had long complained that the U.S. never wanted to discuss issues of interest and concern to Cuba; rather, it always wanted to stop at matters of interest to the U.S. Vice-Minister of Foreign Relations Ricardo Alarcón had emphasized Cuba's unhappiness on that score in a May conversation with me. "If we ever get back to negotiating anything," he had said, "it will have to be on the basis of a step-by-step process based on reciprocity—the same kind of process the U.S. itself suggested back in 1977. We aren't going to sit down with you to talk about stopping the Mariel operation and then have that be the end of it."

If we were to have any chance of getting the sealift closed down and an orderly departure system instituted in its place, we would have to present the negotiations for bringing about such a system as just the start of a dialogue that would then carry us, issue by issue, to the discussion of all the other problems between us.

I suggested such a tit-for-tat approach to Washington, and at least in the Department of State, it seemed to win acceptance. Hence, when I was informed that Peter Tarnoff and Bob Pastor would be coming in June for a round of confidential talks, I was optimistic. To reassure myself further, I flew to Washington to review the bidding with Tarnoff. Once I had read the position paper he had prepared for the talks, I felt tremendously encouraged. It took a tough stance, as it should have, demanding that the Cubans suspend the sealift and offering them no *quid pro quo* for doing so. But the all-important "step-by-step" formula was there. Negotiations on immigration were described as simply the start of a continuing dialogue.

I returned to Havana confident that we could reach some agreement with the Cubans. When Tarnoff and Pastor arrived a week later, however, the position paper had been drastically altered, and the tactic we had agreed upon dispensed with. Now we were simply to demand that the Cubans close down the sealift. Period. Nothing was said about eventually going on to discuss other issues.

Aghast, I asked Tarnoff what had happened to the original paper. He shrugged his shoulders. "The NSC reworked it," he said.

Bob Pastor nodded. "We thought the other approach was too soft," he explained.

I strongly disagreed and said so. It wasn't soft, it was realistic. Without something to suggest a willingness to move beyond the immediate problem, the present talks were doomed before they began. "If this is the best position you could come up with," I concluded, "you should have stayed home; this will be a wasted trip."

I was correct. The talks lasted an hour or so, but for all practical purposes were over in the first ten minutes. As soon as the Cubans realized that we had come only to demand suspension of the sealift, they tuned us out.

Tarnoff and Pastor flew home the next morning with the Mariel operation still booming. Three more months would pass before, in September, we made the kind of proposal the NSC had rejected in June. Thereupon, the sealift was suspended. That might also have been the result in June, and had it been, 100,000 fewer Cuban refugees would have come to the U.S.

The Incident at the U.S. Interests Section

Meanwhile, we at the interests section had an urgent problem of our own. On May 2, a full-scale riot had erupted in front of our building, and some 450 Cubans had sought refuge inside.

To understand what happened that day, we must go back to the summer of 1978. At that time we had defined "prisoners" as those released after August 1, 1978, and "ex-prisoners" as those released prior to that date. We had said that only after we had processed the prisoners could we begin to take ex-prisoners. As a result, some who had been released only days or weeks before the cut-off date—sometimes with the understanding that they could emigrate—were left in limbo. Without regular employment, homes, or often even ration cards, they had lived from hand to mouth for almost two years, waiting for us to document them for entry into the U.S. By March 1980, their wait seemed near an end. The program for political prisoners was winding down. Only a few prisoners and their families remained to be processed. Knowing this, the ex-prisoners had been coming by the interests section with increasing frequency to ask when their turn would come. We responded that we had sought authorization to begin processing them and expected a favorable answer at any time. The Department of State did not let us down. In late April, it promised to have the authorization in our hands by the beginning of May. The ex-prisoners were informed of this and assured that interviewing would begin as soon as possible.

We were closed on May Day, a holiday in all socialist countries. Castro addressed a massive rally that day, whipping the crowd to a frenzy with his scathing denunciation of the "worms."

When we arrived at the interests section on May 2, we found a crowd of some eight hundred ex-prisoners gathered outside, plus the usual fifty or sixty visa applicants lined up at the front door. "We have come to hear that the program for ex-prisoners begins today," spokesmen for the eight hundred told the marine guard.

In fact, the authorization cable *had* arrived. We were ready to begin interviews. I realized, however, that with people who wanted to leave being assaulted in the streets, it was exceedingly dangerous to have this crowd in front of the building.

Vice-Consul Susan Johnson Lamanna normally dealt with the ex-prisoners. I asked her to assure the crowd that the authorization had arrived, and urge them to disperse. The crowd listened to her and cheered the good news, but they refused to disperse. There were shouts for the "chief" to come out, and spokesmen told Susan the crowd was unlikely to break up unless I spoke to them myself. I had not wanted to do that, for I assumed Cuban security officers were filming the whole event from a nearby building and I did not want to give them the opportunity to record a scene which could so easily be misconstrued, or deliberately portrayed, as showing "the chief of the U.S. interests section inciting a mob."

Our first priority, however, had to be to disperse the crowd. They had been there over two hours. It was only a matter of time before the neighborhood CDRs reacted to their presence—or the security forces themselves decided to disperse them. So I put caution aside and went out. A cheer went up as I appeared—which doubtless further irritated watchers on the government's side.

I thanked the ex-prisoners for their patience. Some I knew had been waiting for many months in difficult circumstances. Their wait was almost over, I assured them. All who were registered with the interests section would be called in for interviews, case by case. Of that I gave them my word on behalf of the U.S. government. I then urged them to leave immediately. It was dangerous for them to be there, and, moreover, we could not begin the interviews with such a large crowd outside.

I went back upstairs and watched from my office window. Sure enough, the crowd began to break up and move away. Just when I was beginning to think we were home free, two buses suddenly careened around the corner and disgorged men armed with baseball bats, chains, and machetes. Other armed men—doubtless sent by the CDRs—poured down side streets. Within seconds, the several hundred ex-prisoners had clashed with the government supporters. A furious riot ensued as the two sides battled one another with fists, rocks, bats, and anything else at hand.

A scream of terror had gone up from the women and children in the visa line as the fighting began. As stones whizzed by and men battled all around them, they threw themselves against the glass door, begging the marines to let them in.

At the first sign of trouble, the marines had barred the door. Everything I had learned in the Foreign Service told me it was our duty to keep that door closed—our first concern had to be for the classified files and our own personnel. But that was my official self speaking. As a human being, I was sickened by the idea of refusing sanctuary to women and children. Looking down, I could see that the marine at the door was also torn. He was marine enough to know what the book required, but man enough not to turn his back on terrified women and children. I could read on his face what he was going to do. Even before his hands moved toward the bar, I knew he would open it—and I was glad. "Good boy," I mumbled to myself, deciding then and there that I would pretend I hadn't seen him lift the bar. If I took official notice, I would have to reprimand him, and how could I in good conscience reprimand him for doing something which every fiber of my being had willed him to do? Anyway, what was done was done; it wouldn't be changed by a reprimand.

As the door opened, the families just outside poured in. Out of the corner of my eye, I saw several ex-prisoners break off their fight and also head for the door. I did not wait for more. I had to see to the classified material. Except for some relatively unimportant files in two cabinets in the first-floor visa office, all classified material was stored on the third floor and above. The first floor might now be lost, but if the marines had followed their standing instructions and locked the steel door to the stair well, our classified material could still be protected. My second officer, Timothy Towell, had grabbed his movie camera and was filming the melee below. Shouting for him to make certain all safes on the third and fourth floors were locked, I tore downstairs to make sure the steel door was secured. It was. I then rushed back to the second floor to call the visa office, only half expecting anyone to answer. One of the vice-consuls, E. Webb Spradley, picked up the phone immediately. "Visa office," he answered matter-of-factly.

"How is it down there, Webb? Did someone get the two cabinets locked?" I asked without pausing.

"Sure, boss," he answered. "We locked the cabinets as soon as the alarm went off. There are lots of people coming down the hall, but they all look friendly and we're okay."

Next I called the marine guard stationed in the first-floor hallway next to the elevators. He reported that everyone near him seemed to be safe also. The hallway was quickly filling with strange Cubans, but they all appeared frightened, not menacing. He confirmed that he had locked the elevators in place, as he should have.

"You did fine," I said, "but now unlock one of them and pick me up on the second floor. I've got to get down there."

While I waited, I glanced out the window. The fighting was tapering off as more and more of the ex-prisoners made for what remained of the door. By now, the glass was almost completely gone. Men poured through the gap unimpeded. Out in the street, a group of five or six men lashed at someone on the ground with chains and baseball bats. He seemed to be dead already. We saw several prostrate forms hauled away on stretchers that day, some of them probably dead.

On the steps closer to the building, an ex-prisoner knocked down a government supporter carrying a machete. As the latter groped around on all fours, the ex-prisoner tore his shirt off, jerked the machete away from him, and ran for the door. When later in the day we examined the shirt, we found documents in the pocket which identified its owner as a member of the Cuban government. (The machete now graces my library shelf.)

A minute later, I was downstairs. A mass of people filled the hallway and waiting room. Many of the men were covered with blood, and several seemed badly injured. One of the ex-prisoners was already working on them. "I was a medic in prison," he explained.

Expressing thanks for his help, I promised to return in a minute. Before providing for the wounded, I wanted to see if we had any doors left up front. We did. Most of the plate glass in the reception area was pretty well gone, but the interior door leading from the reception area into the remainder of the building was intact. The last stragglers were just coming through. I ordered the marines to close it tight and to keep someone on guard there at all times.

By now, a vociferous mob surrounded the building. I could see few police, certainly not enough to stop these people if they should decide to rush the building. I went back to the visa office and called the Foreign Ministry to demand protection. No one answered. I tried again with the same result. Seeing an interests-section driver in the hallway, I decided to go to the Foreign Ministry, which was only a few blocks away. I signaled to the driver, who gamely followed me out the front door. An interests-section vehicle was parked at the end of the block, miraculously untouched by the violence that had been raging around it. We started for it, but as I looked over at the crowd, some sudden instinct pulled me forward. I suppose I was so angry that I subconsciously wanted to let off steam. I marched over and halted in front of them. "Who's in charge here?" I demanded.

For a moment, they seemed surprised. No one answered, so I went on: "This is a diplomatic establishment and is not to be violated. You should stay back of this line."

I waved my hand to indicate an imaginary line between me and the crowd, then turned to a policeman and said, "It's your duty to protect that building. See that you do your duty."

He looked at me but said nothing. A few muttered insults rose from the crowd, but no one moved toward me. Obviously tempers were under control. This was not a crowd on the verge of a rampage. With a sense of relief, I walked back across the street to the car. "We may come out of this in one piece," I thought to myself on the way to the Foreign Ministry. There, I was received by Luis García, head of the North American Desk. The message, I was sure, would reach the senior levels of government within minutes. Thumping the desk to emphasize my points, I protested this unprovoked attack on visa applicants and others gathered peacefully outside the interests section. I demanded police protection for our building, which was now surrounded by a mob. The world community would be watching, I concluded; any move against the interests section would brand Cuba as an international scofflaw.

By the time we got back to the building, more police had arrived and a loose cordon had been thrown around it. Even more reassuring, I could see Gen. José Abrahantes, the chief of state security, on the front steps. I walked over to him and explained what had happened. We now had several hundred people inside, I told him, and needed a guarantee of their safety.

"You have it," he assured me. "You can tell them that no harm will come to them. If they will leave peacefully right now, we'll bring buses to the back door and take them safely out of the area. No one will be arrested. Meanwhile, I'll calm things down out here."

I suggested that he ought to disperse the crowd, not simply try to calm it.

"We've already tried," he said; "they won't disperse."

I didn't like the sound of that. I couldn't believe his security forces couldn't disperse the crowd if they wanted to. The longer the crowd stayed, and the larger it grew, the more dangerous our situation. I promised to transmit the general's offer to evacuate by buses at the back door, adding that I didn't think there would be many takers.

As I reentered the building, the full gravity of the situation hit me. The corridor was covered with blood. Some of the wounded still lay along each side, but they were gradually being removed to a makeshift hospital, which our administrative officer, Harold Vickers, and the ex-prisoner medic had set up in an unused complex of offices just off the visa section.

One of the vice-consuls had taken a count. Just over 450 refugees were now inside. Dazed, they huddled together. Children were crying; a number of women moaned softly. The question on every mind obviously was, What will happen to us now?

All eyes turned to me as I asked for quiet. The expression in those eyes was unnerving. It was one of trust and relief, seeming to say, "Here's the chief of the interests section; he'll know what to do and how to take care of us."

Why unnerving? Because in truth I had no more idea than they what to do. I suddenly had the responsibility for 450 lives, and felt very alone and unsure of myself. I couldn't let them see my uncertainty, however, and so, falling back on my training as a Marine Corps drill instructor ("When in doubt, brazen it out"), I tried to strike a confident pose. "Everything is going to be all right," I began. I felt foolish saying it, but as I looked around I could see it was what they needed to hear.

This was all very sad, I went on, but it was done, and now they had to look to the immediate future. No one was going to make them go anywhere they didn't want to go. I then transmitted the offer General Abrahantes had just made. The choice was theirs. Those who wished to leave should gather at the back door. Those who wished to stay were free to do so. I had no idea how we would arrange for their eventual departure or how long it would take. What I could say was that I would not force anyone to leave, and as long as they remained, we would see to their safety and do our best for them. The first step was to get organized—to move all the wounded to the hospital, clean up the corridor, arrange some games for the children, and appoint someone to act as spokesman—at least temporarily. Meanwhile, I would begin negotiations with the Foreign Ministry.

There was a smattering of applause and a few nods of approval. "You can count on us, *Señor Jefe,*" one shouted.

About fifty people decided to leave, some because they had been accidentally caught up in the melee and wanted no part of a dispute with the government, others because they had compelling personal problems. One man explained to me that he had a sick wife and two small children at home. "No matter what happens to me," he said, "I've got to try to get back to them."

The police outside were informed that fifty would be coming out. A bus was brought up to the door and the fifty, shielded by a line of police, were rushed aboard and then whisked away. Several phoned later to report that they had indeed been dropped off unharmed.

About that time, Acting Foreign Minister René Anillo appeared at the front door. He had come, he said, to make sure we had adequate police protection and to see if we needed medical assistance. "We'll send in doctors," he said, "or if there are wounded who need emergency treatment, we'll take them to the hospital, treat them, and then return them unharmed to the interests section."

I thanked him for his offer and said I thought we had one or two in such critical condition that they might indeed need a doctor. I would consult and let him know right away.

"All we ask," he concluded, "is that you make certain those inside have been disarmed. We can't send in our medical personnel otherwise."

I assured him we had already done that. Only one weapon had been found—the machete taken from the attacker on the steps.

In our makeshift hospital, the voluntary medic was doing a superb job. With bandages and disinfectant from our first-aid kit, he had dressed most of the wounds. The wounded were resting as comfortably as possible on mattresses on the floor. For one man, however, the medic could do nothing. The poor fellow made a gurgling sound as he breathed and complained of excruciating pain in his chest.

"I think a broken rib has punctured his lung. Unless we can get him to a hospital, I'm afraid he'll die," the medic told me.

I got down on all fours to talk to the man. "*Chico*, you're in a bad way. We've got to get you to a hospital. We have the guarantee of the Cuban government that you'll be returned here as soon as you're in condition to come back."

No, he said, he preferred to die right there. At least he would be among friends.

I felt torn apart. If I persuaded him to leave and anything happened to him—if the Cubans didn't keep their word—I would have nightmares about it for the rest of my life. But could I let him lie there and die? No, I decided, I could not. In a hospital he at least had a chance; here he had none. I bent back down and insisted. "Please," I said, "you *must* go. If you don't, I'll have your death on my conscience. So, for my sake if not for yours, let me get you to the hospital."

The reasoning was convoluted, I grant, but it worked. "Okay, *Jefe,*" he whispered. "I'll give it a try."

Within a few minutes, we had an ambulance at the door and he was taken out on a stretcher. I called the Foreign Ministry to remind them of the promise that he would be returned. To emphasize their intention to keep that promise, the Foreign Ministry said we could send Vice-Consul Bob Hagen to the hospital with the man. Hagen went and stayed until he was convinced the man was being well treated. He was eventually sent back to us, patched up and in good spirits.

I got back upstairs to find that the Department of State had ordered us to go to zero burn—to burn every shred of classified material in the building. Secretaries, marines, and all those not otherwise occupied, were frantically trundling bags of documents up to the incinerator.

I spent the next few hours reporting to the department what had happened. When I went down to the first floor at about six in the evening, I found a changed atmosphere. The refugees had organized themselves into brigades: one to clean, one to maintain order, one to care for the children, one to look into food supply, and so on. They had the whole area spic and span. The children were playing in the patio, and from the shocked, bewildered crowd of the afternoon, our four hundred house guests had transformed themselves into a smiling, confident-appearing group of people. They were beginning to make friends with the interests-section staff. (One of the young ladies made such good friends with a marine guard that they were married a few months later in Florida.)

The atmosphere was relaxed, even pleasant, despite the jeers and catcalls from a crowd of several hundred still gathered across the street. As I got off the elevator, the refugees greeted me more or less cheerfully. How could I not feel better? With people as resilient as these, I thought to myself, we could come through anything.

Our few K rations and other emergency food items in the basement were distributed. The dinner wasn't much, but enough to stave off hunger pangs.

That first night, we slept where we could. There were only a few mattresses and cushions. Most of the men slept on pieces of cardboard.

The next morning, I went back to the Foreign Ministry to see how we might resolve the problem. The four hundred who remained inside were not likely to come out, I explained to Luis García, head of the North American Desk. They simply did not believe they would be unharmed if they did. Since most were ex-prisoners or visa applicants who would at some point be leaving the country anyway, why not allow them all to go right now? We could bring in special flights for them and have them all out in a few hours. "Don't we have enough problems between us?" I asked. "Surely we don't need another—especially since it is one that can be so quickly and easily resolved."

"Have they all been issued visas or other travel documents?" García asked.

"Some have," I replied, "and I can assure you the rest will be documented by this evening. All you have to do is give the word. I'll get the planes in right away."

"I'll see what I can do," García promised.

I returned to the interests section and called a staff meeting. Reporting my conversation with García, I tried to give it the most optimistic interpretation possible. There was a good chance that we could have all our house guests on the way to the U.S. within twenty-four hours, I concluded, provided our consular and immigration people could get them all documented by sundown. I did not really expect the Cubans to respond that quickly, but I thought they might indeed authorize departures within a few days. Meanwhile, the task of documenting the four hundred was good therapy. The Americans had a specific job to concentrate on, and having travel documents in hand would raise the morale of the refugees.

Harold Vickers scratched his head and squinted across the room at me. "I hope you're right, Chief," he said, "but personally I think these birds are going to be here for a long time. We'd better get used to them."

"Here, Vic," I said with a laugh, "I have such confidence in a quick exit that I'm willing to bet you a whole peso they'll be gone by tomorrow night." I slapped a peso down on the coffee table.

"You're on," Vic said, placing his peso next to mine with a flourish. The meeting then broke up. Consular and immigration officers went down to begin interviewing and documenting the refugees.

Vickers went off to see to their care and feeding. He sent drivers out to scour the markets for bread, jam, and milk—all readily available without ration cards. We found a commercial-size coffee urn down in the old basement cafeteria (which hadn't been used in years) and brought pounds of coffee from our homes. Within a few hours, the refugees were having a decent morning meal. There was even chocolate for the children.

Our spirits were further lifted by gestures of support from other diplomatic missions. That first day, surrounded and isolated as we were, we had felt very much alone. On the afternoon of May 3, however, we heard that the British ambassador, John Ure, with Union Jacks flying, had tried to drive through the crowd to reach us. When turned back, he had gone straight to the Foreign Ministry to warn that Her Majesty's Government was watching events at the interests section closely. Any failure to respect its diplomatic status would be regarded as a most serious matter and would affect relations between London and Havana.

Other diplomatic missions, led by the Swiss ambassador and his wife, quickly came to our assistance with food, bandages, blankets, and clothing. With these supplies, plus the things we could buy on the open market, by May 4 we were beginning to provide normal meals and somewhat more comfortable sleeping accommodations.

By May 4 also it had become apparent that Vickers would win his bet. Our consular and immigration people had performed heroically. Working around the clock on May 3, they had documented not only the four hundred inside, but many of their immediate family members outside the building. All for naught. No call came from the Foreign Ministry and my calls to them went unanswered. Eventually —on May 5 or 6—I was informed by Luis García that my quick and easy solution had been ruled out by the senior levels of the Cuban government. They wanted an end to it as badly as I did, he said, but feared that permitting all four hundred to leave without answering to Cuban authorities would encourage others to crash into diplomatic establishments in large numbers in hopes that they too would be whisked out of the country. The Cuban government did not intend to harass or prosecute any of these people, but they would have to come out and turn themselves over to the Cuban authorities without any guarantees.

"Well, then," I said to García, "we're in for a long siege. Not many of those people will accept those conditions, and in the present atmosphere, I can't say that I blame them."

A long siege it was. Most of the four hundred were with us from May 2 until the latter part of August. The last eleven left the building on September 23. It was a trying summer, but we managed rather nicely, thanks to the interests-section staff. They built four-tier wooden bunk beds in the visa-office waiting room, turning it into a huge dormitory. They installed showers in the basement, handled food supply, laundry, and all sorts of unforeseen problems, such as getting a refugee's false teeth repaired. Francine Bowman, our general services officer, somehow got all the rusted old stoves in the cafeteria working again and reopened it with a ribbon-cutting ceremony as the refugees' dining room. There were tables and benches for only a hundred, so they had to eat in four shifts, but as they were not in a hurry to go anywhere, that inconvenienced no one.

Through it all, the staff was cheerful, cooperative, and, above all, considerate of one another and of our four hundred house guests. I was fortunate—we were all fortunate—to have such co-workers.

The Department of State responded well to our crisis, quickly allotting emergency funds and shipping in by air large quantities of freeze-dried food and medical supplies.

For more than four months, the interests section was closed to the public. A police cordon stretched around the building during that entire time. The American employees, recognized on sight by the police, were allowed to come and go freely. Cuban employees were issued special passes and had to come through at a designated checkpoint. I do not recall any being refused entry, however. Indeed, after the first week or so, the police outside tended to be rather cooperative.

The Cuban government could have placed us in a near-impossible situation simply by disconnecting our water and lights, or by blocking the flow of food into the building, but never did. Rather, the Cubans' approach seemed to be to avoid measures that would further exacerbate the situation, and, instead, to wait patiently for the refugees inside to change their minds.

Anyone walking into the building during those four months would at first have thought it a grim place. Marines in combat gear stood just inside the doors. Windows were boarded up. A barbed-wire entanglement filled the stairway. But all that was erased by the laughter of the children at play and the smiles of the refugees as they went about their daily routine. As the great majority were ex-prisoners, being cooped up inside bothered them not at all. They were accustomed to it. One of them commented to me: "I spent fifteen years in Cuban prisons, *Señor Jefe*. Contrasted with that, being here with you is a pleasure. The food is the best I've had in years. We like your movies, and we all have confidence that you'll get us to the United States soon. Yes, I'm very happy to be here. My only regret is that we are a burden to you and to your staff."

Certainly, there was no sense of hopelessness among the refugees. No one sat staring at the wall. Quite the contrary, with one or two exceptions, they exuded purpose and confidence. They organized a school for the children, and, looking to the day when they would arrive in the U.S., English classes for the adults. They went at their lessons with a passion; choruses of "I am very pleased to meet you" rang through the corridors. We helped out by providing video cassettes and by showing an American movie every evening.

They also staged plays and musical skits, organized card games, played dominoes, and, most of all, read voraciously. After years of being denied books published in the West, they simply absorbed Kurt Vonnegut, John Updike, Gore Vidal, and other relatively recent authors. No matter how many books we brought, there were never enough.

I often wished some young Ph.D. candidate had been with us that summer. He or she could have written a fascinating microcosmic study of an emerging democracy. Not only did our four hundred begin to exercise their right to read what they wished, they also elected their own representatives. For the first week or so, spokesmen and brigade leaders were loosely appointed. During the second week, however, the refugees decided that formal elections ought to be held. They constructed voting booths, nominated candidates, and distributed campaign literature just as if these were national elections. Many had never voted in their lives. They took great pride in doing so now.

That the refugees were thus represented by their own elected leaders was a great convenience to me and to the rest of the interests-section staff. If something needed doing, we had only to confer with the leaders. I met with them several times a week to discuss problems and inform them of any progress in my talks with the Cuban government. The arrangement worked smoothly and to our mutual satisfaction. One might have expected friction to develop between the refugees and the interests-section staff as the weeks passed, but that was not at all the case. If anything, our respect for one another grew into a deep affection. I know that I came to consider the four hundred as one of the finest groups of people in my experience, the kind one would wish to have at one's side in a tight spot.

Our tranquility inside the interests section was not broken even by the gigantic march on May 17. It had been called by the Cuban authorities *before* the May 2 incident, with the purpose, originally, of denouncing the maneuvers at Guantánamo. But with the maneuvers canceled and four hundred refugees inside the building, the May 17 march became virtually a repetition of the one at the Peruvian embassy a month before. Its purpose now was to repudiate those inside. But this march was on a much bigger scale than the one on April 19. Close to a million people passed by the interests section that day.

Anyone looking down from an airplane on our small building engulfed by a shouting, apparently threatening, human sea, might have imagined those inside to be cowering in fear. Nothing of the sort. Inside, all was calm. I had talked to the refugees and staff that morning, urging both to go about their normal routine and pay as little heed as possible to the march. The blinds were to be closed, and except for a few marines assigned to keep an eye on the crowd, no one was to peer out the window, make gestures, or otherwise take notice of the marchers. Nothing would dampen their enthusiasm more, I pointed out, than marching past a building from which there was no sign of life.

We served an unusually good lunch that day, and amused our guests with the video cassette of a TV program the Cuban government had put together to "prove" the May 2 incident had been started by the ex-prisoners after—you guessed it—"they had been incited by a U.S. official." There I was on film, as I had suspected I would be. Actually, the Cuban program was so poorly done that it convinced no one, and was more amusing than irritating. For example, it showed one of the ex-prisoners throwing a rock. This, according to the commentator, was what had started the fighting. This man had thrown a rock at peaceful passers-by and they had simply defended themselves. The only problem was that the ground around the man supposedly casting the first stone was already covered with bricks and rocks. Obviously, his was not the first to be thrown. The refugees always got a laugh out of that scene, and seemed to find the whole cassette wryly amusing. So we showed it to them again on May 17.

The staff had a picnic in my office—cold turkey, ham, and chilled French wine. Inside, we were cool, comfortable, and well fed. Outside, the crowd slogged by in the heat.

Back at our residence, to demonstrate that we were unperturbed by the march and were carrying on as usual, Roxanna hosted a poolside lunch for various members of the diplomatic corps. As they swam and ate, they watched the march on TV.

Not that we were complacent or unprepared for trouble at the office. Tear gas and other defensive weapons were laid out near at hand, and we had gone through drills of defending the building floor by floor all the way to the roof. We were ready for the worst, but none of us thought it would come to that. For one thing, Foreign Minister Malmierca had assured me the previous evening that we would be given all the police protection we needed. And sure enough, by 9 A.M. on May 17, the cordon of police around the building was four ranks thick. The crowd wasn't likely to get in, I reasoned, unless the police had orders to let them through, and I could not see that the Cuban government stood to gain anything by allowing a mob to sack our building.

As I studied through a peephole the hundreds of thousands of faces passing by us the morning of May 17, I was struck by the lack of interest, almost boredom, I read there. Oh yes, people chanted and sang when directly in front of the building—when, in other words, they were on camera—but fifty yards farther up the street, most of them walked along silently and impassively. This was not a crowd thirsting for blood. It was a crowd which for the most part was there because it had been ordered to be.

The day passed without incident in Havana, but not in Miami. The Department of State had insisted that we evacuate several members of the staff and all dependents except Roxanna. Our son, Sanford, and his inseparable friend, David Jordan, son of our public-affairs officer, made the trip up together, David's parents having kindly offered to look after Sanford.

I did not think the evacuation really necessary, but could understand why the department wanted to take no chances. It was indeed better to err on the side of prudence. As it turned out, however, our evacuees were no safer in Miami than they would have been in Havana—perhaps less so. They arrived in the midst of the worst race riots in the city's history. Not only that, but the department had them billeted in a hotel near the rioting. They could see the burning buildings and cars from their rooms. Few ventured outside. Sanford and David did sally forth one afternoon, intending to play video games in an arcade down the street. They were chased back to the hotel by a gang of young toughs. "Some safe haven that was," the evacuees complained upon their return to Havana.

The End of the Crisis

All during the summer of 1980, in private talks with the Cubans, I hammered away at two main points: that continuance of the sealift was damaging Cuba's image abroad and that there could be no improvement at all in relations between us until it was closed down and they had agreed to take back the criminals and other excludables dumped on us in its course. After the failure of the Tarnoff-Pastor mission in June, I redoubled my own efforts, realizing that if anyone was going to persuade the Cubans, it would, by default, have to be me. My strongest argument was that the sealift was causing widespread anger among the American people. "You fellows may have thought you were being nasty to Brzezinski," I pointed out over and over again, "but what you have in fact done is to offend the American people, including many who favored a more normal relationship between us. This has been a terrible miscalculation on your part and you ought to correct it as soon as possible."

At first, the standard Cuban reaction was to scoff. "The miscalculation was on your side," they'd say; "someone in Washington should have answered our notes on maritime hijacking."

As the weeks passed, however, a subtle change crept into the Cubans' attitude. I think they realized that Mariel was turning against them. It had a disruptive impact in the U.S., yes, but at the same time the continuing image of people "voting with their feet" was embarrassing to Cuba. Further, the effect on the economy was severe. With several hundred thousand people actively trying to leave the country, hundreds of thousands of others thinking about it, and the rest of the population involved in "repudiating" the first two groups, not much work got done that summer. Cuba's economic planners must have pleaded that this not go on much longer.

The first sign of a shift was the calling off of the CDRs. No longer were people beaten up in the streets. Rallies to denounce the "worms" were canceled. Increasingly, the government concentrated on getting people back to work.

I also sensed that Cuban anger at us was subsiding, that Cuban officials were no longer looking for ways to offend Washington. It was fortunate that they had mellowed. Otherwise, in early July there might have been an armed conflict. We learned that the Cubans were loading refugees on a major passenger vessel, the *Blue Fire*, and all indications were that she would disgorge over three thousand people onto a Florida beach at just about the time Jimmy Carter was arriving in Miami for what amounted to a campaign appearance. The White House was determined the president would not be so embarrassed. Orders went out to use military force if necessary to prevent the *Blue Fire* from entering port. I was informed later that a frogman team would have been sent in to disable her. Had that failed, destroyers would have blocked the harbor mouth. The Cubans would certainly have reacted with military force of their own. Fortunately, Secretary of State Edmund Muskie (who had replaced Cyrus Vance when the latter resigned over the aborted Iranian hostage-rescue mission) insisted that we talk to the Cubans first. He instructed me to deliver a letter from him to Carlos Rafael Rodríguez and to use that opportunity to try to get the *Blue Fire* operation turned off. I did just that, stressing to Rodríguez that sending the *Blue Fire* with all those people might push the situation over the brink. As Muskie had said in his letter, the two sides ought to keep open the possibility of some improvement in relations. If the *Blue Fire* reached Florida, that possibility might disappear altogether.

Rodríguez heard me out and read Muskie's letter carefully. "You can tell the secretary that I'll see what I can do. Come back tonight. I will try to have an answer for you."

Later that same day, I went to the Foreign Ministry to discuss a separate problem. As I was talking to Carlos Zamora, an officer on the North American Desk, there was a sharp explosion behind me. Thinking that a bomb had gone off in the building next door and that the window behind me would be turned into thousands of pieces of flying glass, I threw myself to my hands and knees in the shelter of the sofa.

Zamora had another reaction. He jumped up shouting, "It's an overflight! It's an overflight!"

After a few seconds had passed and the window remained intact, I got to my feet laughing. "Overflights are an obsession with you, Zamora," I said. "I don't know what that was, but it wasn't an overflight. More likely the boiler next door blew up."

"The building next door doesn't have a boiler," Zamora shot back. "It was an overflight."

He was right. Everyone in the western part of the city felt the shock. An explosion in a single building couldn't have been the cause. It had to be an SR-71 reconnaissance plane breaking the sound barrier over the city. I sent a flash cable to the department asking for confirmation. The answer was affirmative. I shouldn't have been surprised, but I was. To send me in to ask the Cubans not to load the *Blue Fire*—in effect, to ask for a concession—and at the same time do something that was bound to provoke them, struck me as utterly stupid. At the very least, they could have waited until I had Carlos Rafael Rodríguez's answer.

When I went back to see Rodríguez that evening, he too was puzzled. "I don't understand what your government intended," he said. "The *Blue Fire* isn't going to load, but I don't mind telling you that the overflight today almost ruined everything. A few people in the meeting this afternoon wanted to retaliate by loading not only the *Blue Fire* but several other vessels as well. Fortunately, cooler heads prevailed—this time."

So a confrontation was avoided. Rodríguez was also instrumental in defusing the problem at the interests section. While urging him and other Cuban officials to end the Mariel sealift, I had also been insisting that we get our four hundred refugees on their way to the U.S. Rodríguez eventually responded that although there could be no guarantees, I could assure those inside that the government did not intend to prosecute; rather, once they had returned to their homes, it would facilitate their departure to the U.S.

I reported Rodríguez's assurance to our four hundred refugees, but did not urge them to leave. Assurances were not guarantees. Leaving carried some risk, so I felt the decision should be entirely up to them. They were somewhat more receptive to the idea in July than they had been in May. For one thing, the atmosphere in the streets was changing. People were no longer being beaten up. A few decided to take their chances. They were not harmed in any way, and they and their immediate families found themselves quickly on the way to the U.S. Their experience encouraged more of the refugees to leave the building. By the end of July we were down to just over two hundred.

By then, also, Castro's political gyroscope seemed to be working again. He had at last realized that by embarrassing Jimmy Carter, he had increased the chances that Ronald Reagan would become president of the United States on January 20, 1981. That, he did not want. In his July 26 speech, he described the choice between Reagan and Carter as one between war and peace.

It was not surprising, then, that by late August, Castro was signaling his readiness to make amends. In early September, President Carter, in response, sent Peter Tarnoff back to Havana. This time Peter came alone, and so made immediate progress. We made no promises of any kind. We only stated that the Carter administration wanted to get back to discussing the problems between our two countries on an issue-by-issue basis. The Mariel sealift made that impossible. It had to be closed down before anything else could be done.

Castro replied without hesitation that he was ready to close it down. He would discuss the matter with the rest of the leadership and would let us know shortly. Turning to me, he said he wanted to get the problem of the interests section out of the way also. I could tell the fifty or so people who remained that Castro himself had said they had nothing to fear. They ought to come out quickly so as to be on their way to the U.S.

He planned to take a number of other steps which ought to be useful, he told us, but did not specify what they might be.

Before Peter returned to the U.S., Castro sent word that the Mariel sealift would indeed be terminated, and on September 26, it was. Shortly thereafter, he took the other steps, which turned out to be the release of all American prisoners (mostly drug smugglers) and a tough new decree to discourage aerial hijacking. Eventually, he returned two hijackers to the U.S. for prosecution.

Meanwhile, on September 23, the last of the house guests walked out our front door. As they left, I felt the same satisfaction as when I had watched the last American political prisoners being driven off to the airport. Looking back to that bloody day in May when the refugees had flooded into the building, I found it almost too good to be true that all four hundred were safe. Not a single one had been arrested or harmed in any way. With the exception of a handful who for personal reasons could not emigrate, all of them, plus their immediate families—almost 1,500 people—made it safely to the U.S.

A few days after their departure, Harold Vickers reminded me of our May 3 bet, and to the laughter and applause of the rest of the staff, returned the peso to me in a glass case, with the following inscription:

On May 3 (that historical morning after), "Bet-a-Peso Smith" stoutly wagered that within 24 hours, all Cuban migratory birds of freedom roosting within his sanctuary would fly the coop, and become American birds of passage. Three thousand four hundred eighty-three and one-half hours later, when the flock was finally airborne, "Bet-a-Peso" conceded to a slight slippage in his original flight plan.

In commemoration of that momentous takeoff, however, the entire birdwatchers of the Mission, pooling their nest eggs, retrieved the original financial obligation, which is hereby gratefully presented with a gentle reminder of that ancient adage from the back streets of old Havana, a bird in the hand is safer than one overhead.

With the crisis over, I wrote an assessment cable, pointing out again that the problem prior to the Mariel sealift was not that we had talked to the Cubans (and thereby, as some believed, shown weakness), but precisely the opposite, that we *had not talked to them at all* about the key issues of maritime hijacking and a normal system of immigration. Had we addressed the maritime-hijacking issue and discussed Cuba's other complaints in a sensible, straightforward manner, the situation might have evolved in a very different kind of atmosphere. There might have been no Mariel sealift at all. Hence, I concluded, while our inaction on important issues did not justify the sealift, the fact remained that our own inexplicable failure to deal with those issues had helped to provoke it. What Mariel pointed up more than anything else, I noted, was the need for an effective dialogue with the Cuban government. For the interests section to talk to the Cubans was not enough. Some answers out of Washington were also needed.

The Department of State's only response to this cable was hurriedly to reclassify it "not for distribution." That is one way to handle mistakes: to refuse to admit that you made them and refuse to let others read about them. That isn't, however, a very likely way to get the errors corrected.

The Aftermath of Mariel: A Stab at Negotiations

Foolishly, perhaps, I hoped some good might come of Mariel. I thought it might cause both sides to see that they had something to gain from a more normal relationship—and something to lose from the absence of one—so that now we might initiate the kind of constructive and continuing dialogue we had never had. President Carter, through Peter Tarnoff, had suggested that he wanted one, and the fact that Carter had excluded the NSC from our September meeting with Castro boded well for the usefulness of such a dialogue.

Had Carter won, U.S.-Cuban relations might have taken a turn for the better. One can speculate endlessly about what might have been. But Reagan, not Carter, was elected. His victory seemed to spell the end of any dialogue. The Reagan transition team may have wanted to bomb the Cubans; they certainly did not want to talk to them. I was surprised, therefore, when after the elections, the Cubans themselves suggested that we discuss the return to Cuba of the criminals and other excludables transported to the U.S. during the sealift. Prior to the elections, I had insisted that we had to get this issue out of the way before we could go on to the discussion of other problems. Once Reagan was elected, however, I assumed they would not be interested, since settlement of this matter clearly would not be part of, or lead to, the sort of dialogue suggested by Carter. The Cubans understood that but wanted to negotiate anyway. Perhaps they calculated that their doing so would take some of the confrontational winds out of the new administration's sails. They may even have hoped that they could begin the negotiations with Carter, then finish them with the incoming Reagan administration, thus getting off on a better footing.

Their conduct of the negotiations pointed to the latter explanation. Meetings were held in December 1980 and in January 1981, only days before the inauguration. By the end of the second meeting, only two small points remained to be resolved. Both were essentially matters of clarification. Had the Cubans wanted to conclude and sign agreements with Carter, they could have clarified their position then and there. Instead, they waited until after Reagan's inauguration. Then they signaled that they were ready for the third meeting. They were certain that once they had explained their position more clearly, we could reach agreement. There were no takers. The Reagan administration did not wish to discuss the return of the excludables, or anything else, with the Cubans.

More difficult to understand than the new administration's refusal to negotiate was its refusal to honor our commitment to process the former political prisoners registered with the interests section. As the last of our four hundred refugees left the building in September, that had been my first priority. I wanted to begin interviewing the ex-prisoners immediately. The Department of State, however, insisted that we wait until a secure access system had been installed at the interests section—bulletproof doors and windows in the visa office and a wall between consular personnel and visa applicants. By the time all that had been completed, Ronald Reagan had won the presidential election back home. The department then decided we should wait to see whether the new administration wanted to go ahead with our commitment to take the ex-prisoners.

The delay was irritating, and, I thought, a waste of time. I did not doubt that once Reagan was in office, the administration would instruct us to begin interviewing the ex-prisoners. They were, after all, long-suffering victims of Communism, exactly the kind of people President Reagan professed his eagerness to help. But as will be seen in the next chapter, no authorization was ever forthcoming.

9

Enter the Reagan
Administration

January 1981 marked the twentieth anniversary of the severance of U.S.-Cuban diplomatic relations, and brought back memories of arriving in Washington in a driving snowstorm. Few of us who got off the train that morning in 1961 would have guessed that even two decades later relations would not be restored.

We had returned to Washington that year in time to see the inauguration of John F. Kennedy. Now, in January 1981, Ronald Reagan was to be inaugurated as the fortieth president of the United States. Over the years, most Washington pundits had regarded his chances of ever becoming president as virtually nonexistent. But they had reckoned without the Carter administration, whose failure opened the way to Reagan's election. I had often disagreed with Carter's lieutenants in the National Security Council, but I regarded the failure of his presidency as a profound American tragedy. After the trauma of Vietnam and the embarrassment of Watergate, the American people wanted to believe in their president again. Jimmy Carter's promise never to lie to them touched a responsive chord. Like so many other Americans, I was impressed by Carter's obvious sincerity and decency. And his policies as initially articulated were eminently cogent. His emphasis on human rights, for example, helped to revive faith at home and abroad in the moral foundations of U.S. foreign policy. His conviction that Third World problems should not always be analyzed in an East-West context was exactly right. The important Panama Canal treaties were among the most notable results of this new approach. Without those treaties, we might long ago have had chaos in Panama, and have lost use of the canal.

But by saying he wanted one kind of foreign policy and then appointing a national security adviser who wanted the exact opposite, Carter sowed the seeds of incoherence that proved his undoing. Instead of following a clear policy line, his administration marched to discordant drums, which often directed us in several directions at the same time. This, together with his administration's inept handling of the Mariel episode and the Soviet-brigade issue, and the president's guileless expression of surprise over the Soviet invasion of Afghanistan, created an impression of drift and naiveté.

Worst of all, Carter presided over the death of idealism. He wrapped himself in the banners of good causes—human rights, sympathy with the democrats more than with the dictators in the Third World, promotion of peace in the Middle East, and a serious effort at arms control. His failure as president raised doubts about the causes themselves. In effect, Carter took the banners down with him. That was his legacy to the nation.

I had always considered myself a pragmatist rather than a liberal or a conservative. As a professional diplomat for more than twenty years, moreover, I had served both Republican and Democratic administrations. Indeed, one of my most satisfying assignments had been in Argentina under a conservative Republican ambassador, Robert C. Hill. But serving under Reagan would be different. His campaign rhetoric had suggested a foreign policy that I could only see as dangerous, unworkable, counterproductive, and inconsistent with basic U.S. values. The Reagan transition team that swept through Central America in November and December 1980 fueled my misgivings. They courted figures on the far right, such as the infamous Roberto D'Aubuisson in El Salvador. They downplayed U.S. interest in human rights and economic development, emphasizing military solutions instead. They talked of launching a "war of national liberation" against Castro. I had lived through one Bay of Pigs; I wanted nothing to do with a second.

I began to consider resigning, or at least requesting an out-of-the-way assignment unrelated to policy until August 1982, when I would turn fifty and could retire. Roxanna and I discussed the pros and cons evening after evening before inauguration day, and finally decided that I should stay on. I was, after all, a career officer. The campaign rhetoric of the incoming administration was disturbing, but who could say how much the rhetoric meant? Once faced with the realities of the world and with the hard responsibility for governing, perhaps the administration would ease into a more sensible approach. It might turn out to be far more pragmatic than suggested by past bombast. Further, we concluded, I should not take the initiative. My position on U.S.-Cuban relations was clear. If the administration wished to get rid of me, it certainly would. If, on the other hand, it left me in Havana, that might mean that despite all indications to the contrary, it did intend to carry on a dialogue with the Cubans. If so, I might be of some use.

I therefore stayed on, but I did not do so under false pretenses. My assessments and recommendations changed not at all, nor did I hesitate to articulate them. In lengthy policy-recommendation cables in March and April 1981, I continued to urge cautious engagement, and to stress that pure hostility would avail us nothing.[1] In a letter in May to the newly appointed assistant secretary of state for American republics affairs, Thomas O. Enders, I set forth two options: I would continue to serve in Havana if he thought I could be useful there; or I would cheerfully depart if he did not believe I would fit into the new scheme of things. I made it clear that my attitude would not change if I stayed. I told Enders:

The Cubans can be worked with, though after so many years of hostility, that is not easy. As we saw during the Mariel episode, they can be ornery and costly adversaries. But as we have also seen in other instances during the past year, they can also be quite cooperative. We do have something to gain from reasoned discussion of the problems between us. Certainly the new Administration does not wish to be perceived as being "soft" on Cuba. I think there is little danger of that. Having now put down clear markers to the Cubans, if the latter respect those markers, then the Administration can be perceived as having laid the groundwork for a more rational and productive relationship on terms acceptable to us. As I have said elsewhere and as I firmly believe, in the final analysis, we are likely to gain more from the Cubans through cautious engagement than through confrontation (though some of that may be necessary also from time to time). Over the years, we have tried invasion, sabotage, and name-calling. None of it has really worked. As I noted in a cable almost two years ago, if we wish our approach to Cuba to be perceived as more imaginative than was that of Sir Douglas Haig to barbed wire, we really should try something new.

Enders replied that he wanted me to stay. I took that to mean there might be hope for the policy I had recommended.

Meanwhile, however, the administration was moving toward confrontation. In February, it issued its famous white paper asserting that the turmoil in Central America was a textbook case of external Communist aggression, of Soviet expansionism articulated through its Caribbean surrogate, Cuba. On February 14, the Department of State's spokesman went so far as to suggest that there was "no native insurgency in El Salvador."

Amusement and dismay were equally valid as a reaction to this canard.

Secretary of State Alexander Haig publicly vowed to stop this "aggression" in its tracks and promised the president political and military victories in the near future.

To portray the problem as one of external aggression was to take it out of context. The turmoil in Central America was essentially internal in nature, the result of centuries of poverty, social injustice, and repressive governments. The Soviets and Cubans had not caused the turmoil. They were of course trying to take advantage of it, but their role was secondary, a problem we could have handled rather easily through diplomacy.

Cuban and Nicaraguan Interest in Negotiations

By opting for confrontation, the administration passed up diplomatic opportunities. Cuba and Nicaragua had indeed provided large-scale support to the January 1981 offensive of the Salvadoran guerrillas, apparently hoping that the guerrillas could defeat the government there and present the new U.S. administration elected in November 1980 with a *fait accompli* upon its inauguration. But the offensive failed, and when the Cubans and Nicaraguans reassessed the situation in February, they concluded that the guerrillas had no chance of winning soon, and that as the situation heated up in Central America, the risks of intervention might come to outweigh the gains. Cuba and Nicaragua therefore decided to seek political solutions in Central America. Both began to signal an interest in negotiations.

In Havana, I detected a clear shift in the Cuban position. All during 1980, my demarches regarding El Salvador had been parried with the argument that Cuba had no control over the situation in El Salvador and that if we wanted to talk about a solution there, we would have to talk to the guerrillas themselves. But as the guerrilla offensive palled, the Cubans suddenly began to speak of an end to the violence in El Salvador. Conditions now favored a cease-fire, they said. Both sides ought to seek political rather than military solutions. Further, they stressed, while neither Cuba nor the U.S. was directly involved in the conflict, both were interested parties and might contribute to a solution. With that in mind, Cuba would sit down with the U.S. to discuss ways of helping to end the violence. Cuba was prepared to urge the guerrillas to negotiate, but forbearance must be mutual. Cuba did not wish to urge its friends to the negotiating table only to see them gunned down—as a number of Salvadoran opposition leaders had been only a few weeks before.[2]

On the basis of these conversations, I sent two cables to the Department of State in February 1981 urging that we open talks with the Cubans. If we remained concerned over Cuban arms shipments to El Salvador, I noted, why not state those concerns face to face? It made little sense to pillory Cuba as the source of the problem in El Salvador, I concluded, but then refuse to discuss the issue with them.

The Department of State did not even respond to these cables. In March, I referred to them by number in a telephone conversation with Myles Frechette, the director of Cuban affairs. Was I to receive a reply?

After looking up the cables, Myles replied that no one was interested in that sort of approach. I would not receive a reply. His advice was to stop sending such recommendations.

In Managua, Ambassador Larry Pezzullo ran into the same stone wall. The Nicaraguans showed interest in regional peace talks. Pezzullo reported their willingness to negotiate and recommended that a dialogue begin, possibly sponsored by the U.S. The department was as unresponsive to him as to me.

At about this time, the Nicaraguans and Cubans also cut back drastically on their material support for the Salvadoran guerrillas. By March, the Cubans claimed they were sending no arms at all to El Salvador. The Nicaraguans had also suspended shipments.

The fact that the Nicaraguans had suspended these shipments should be emphasized. In recent years the Reagan administration has claimed that the Nicaraguans refused to heed our warnings and that this refusal pointed up Carter's naive and fruitless policy of trying to work with the Sandinistas. In fact, however, that policy had not been fruitless. The Sandinistas *did* heed our warnings. U.S. aid to Nicaragua had been suspended in early January 1981 because of recent Sandinista arms shipments to the guerrillas. Ambassador Pezzullo, in informing the Nicaraguans of the suspension, laid it on the line to them. We were willing to work with them, he said, but not if they continued to supply arms to guerrillas in neighboring countries. We had suspended aid. They now had the opportunity to terminate the arms flow. We would review the situation in a couple of months; if the shipment of arms had stopped, we would consider resumption of our assistance.

When the guerrilla offensive faltered in January, the Sandinistas did indeed halt, or at least drastically reduce, their support to the guerrillas, a fact confirmed by U.S. intelligence. Concomitantly, while Daniel Ortega, one of the ruling *comandantes,* did not admit to Ambassador Pezzullo that any arms had been shipped, he emphasized that Nicaragua understood the U.S. position, valued its relationship with us, and would attempt to accommodate our concerns. Since the Sandinistas were acceding to our demands, Ambassador Pezzullo and others in the Department of State felt we should at least resume food aid. Our assistance had obviously provided effective leverage in this instance; it might again be useful in the future.

But senior officials in the Reagan administration, including the secretary of state, had no wish to work with the Sandinistas. Their idea from the beginning had been to get rid of them, not to restrain them or point them in a more positive direction. Hence, even though Managua had acceded to our demands, we cut off aid anyway. With surprising candor (which the administration later regretted), the statement of April 2, 1981, which announced the cutoff, acknowledged that the U.S. had "had no hard evidence of arms trafficking within the last few weeks, and propaganda and other support activities have been curtailed." But, the statement went on, such support *might* be continuing through unknown channels. In other words, we had no evidence that it was continuing but since we had decided to cut off aid anyway, we would simply assume that it was.

Haig's Contradictory Assessments

Though in his public statements back in 1981 Alexander Haig insisted that the turmoil in Central America was orchestrated from Moscow and that Nicaragua and Cuba refused to heed our warnings, in his book *Caveat* (published in 1984), Haig contradicted these allegations. "The flow of arms into Nicaragua and thence into El Salvador slackened," he wrote, "a signal from Havana and Moscow that they had received and understood the American message." Moreover, Haig wrote, his conversations with Ambassador Dobrynin in Washington had convinced him that the Soviets were not particularly interested in Central America; rather, "Cuban activities in the Western Hemisphere were a matter between the United States and Cuba."[3]

Haig's subsequent assessment, then, was not far from my own, or from Ambassador Pezzullo's: that is, this was principally a regional rather than an East-West problem. The Cubans and Nicaraguans had respected our markers and indicated they wished to discuss ways of achieving peace. But while Pezzullo and I concluded that the U.S. was therefore in a good position to negotiate, Haig concluded the exact opposite. Seeing Cuban and Nicaraguan concessions as a sign of weakness, he decided that if the Soviets were not really interested in Central America, we had a free hand to resolve the problem through *military* means, without fear of Soviet retaliation. As Haig put it: "The way was open to solve the problem in Central America, and solve it quickly, through the unequivocal application of pressure."[4]

In fact, however, we did neither the one nor the other. Haig ruled out negotiations, but could not get others in the administration to go along with direct military measures, so he was left without an effective policy. He continued to huff and puff and to threaten to "take it to the source"—i.e., to attack Cuba—but this threat paid declining dividends.

Consultations in Washington

In June 1981, I returned to Washington for consultations. While there, I was offered a bit of advice by a friend in the front office: stop suggesting talks with the Cubans. Such recommendations angered the secretary of state, he said, and were out of step with what the new administration wanted.

I replied that I wasn't interested in being in step. I wanted to encourage a sensible policy. The administration could take it or leave it, but I would continue to urge the kind of policy I thought would best advance U.S. interests. That was what I was supposed to do as a career Foreign Service officer.

Worse was to come. The principal purpose in calling me back to Washington was to have me read over the policy recommendations of an interagency task force on Cuba. Normally, one would expect the views of the embassy, or other diplomatic mission abroad, to be sought at every step of the way. In this case, we had not even been informed that the process had begun. I suppose that knowing I would disagree, the task force simply waited until the recommendations were in final form before showing them to me—so that I would have less opportunity to cavil.

They were right about my disagreement. As I read, my heart sank. It was difficult to imagine a set of recommendations more divorced from reality and less likely to advance U.S. objectives. The basic assumption of the policy paper was that Castro could be intimidated. It therefore recommended a policy of steadily escalating tensions and uncertainties. The establishment of a new broadcasting service to Cuba, Radio Martí, was seen as a key element in this effort. Normalization was ruled out even as a distant possibility, no matter what Cuba did.

This approach would not work. Laying down markers to the Cubans was one thing. Trying to force them to accede to all our demands with threats and harassment was something else.

When I saw Assistant Secretary of State Enders for a few minutes, I indicated my opposition. The meeting was hurried, however, and I did not have an opportunity to present my case in any detail. Upon my return to Havana, therefore, I wrote a letter expressing grave misgivings. As formulated by the administration, I noted to Enders, the question was simply whether we could force the Cubans to change their behavior by adopting an increasingly hostile and threatening posture. I went on to say:

There is not the slightest doubt in my mind that the answer to that question is "absolutely not." The Cubans have a deeply ingrained conviction that the survival of their Revolution is due to their implacable refusal over the past 20 years to knuckle under to U.S. pressure. Hence, they react to sheer pressure in a predictable way, either by digging their heels in, or by adopting an even more aggressive posture toward us. No matter to what levels we escalate tensions and uncertainty, the Cubans will *not*, as a result of our threats, moderate their behavior. On the contrary, tensions and uncertainty will beget only more tensions and uncertainty. Certainly the steps we are contemplating short of invasion, i.e., establishment of Radio Free Cuba [Radio Martí], tightening the embargo, etc., will of course make the Cubans mad, and will cause them some inconvenience. They will not, however, have the slightest effect in terms of moderating Cuba's policy actions abroad. The contrary is more likely to be the case. That Radio Free Cuba will be counterproductive I have not the slightest doubt. . . .

You say this approach hasn't been fully explored. I can only say I have an

245

overwhelming sense of *déjà vu*, having been around for the Bay of Pigs, the CIA/exile raids and sabotage efforts of the 60's, the assassination attempts, the fully implemented embargo, the Swan-Island radio station, and so on *ad infinitum*. That approach did not produce any change in Cuban behavior then, when Cuba was in a weak position. Still less will it work now, when Cuba's position is much stronger. Sooner or later we really should try something new. This isn't.

Cuban Responses to Haig

Predictably, the Cubans responded to Haig's threats to "take it to the source" by organizing a People's Militia some 500,000 strong and bringing in enough rifles, machine guns, and mortars to arm it. Cuba, Castro said, was now ready to defend itself against anything the U.S. wished to throw at it.

On July 29, Haig pointed to the arrival of this unprecedented quantity of arms as new evidence of Cuba's aggressive designs. But as a Cuban friend put it at the time: "What did he think we were going to do? Disarm?"

On August 28, Haig asserted that some of these arms were being transshipped to Central America, and that there were Cuban advisers in El Salvador.

On September 3, the Cuban government issued a statement denying both charges and calling on Haig to back them up with evidence. He of course ignored the Cuban rebuttal.

I asked in a series of cables if we really had evidence for what we were saying. I received no reply, and took the silence to mean we had no credible evidence. Otherwise, why not cite it to me?

The Inter-Parliamentary Union Meeting

The Inter-Parliamentary Union (IPU) was scheduled to hold its annual meeting in Havana in September 1981. The U.S. Congress belonged to this UN-sponsored body and had sent delegations to all previous meetings. When it was announced, however, that Sen. Robert T. Stafford, a Vermont Republican, would head the U.S. delegation to Havana, the Reagan administration first tried to persuade the senator not to go, and, failing that, refused to provide his delegation with the usual Air Force plane. Undaunted, the U.S. congressional delegation arrived in a chartered Lear jet.

Of course, no one had asked what I thought about it, but I said so anyway. On balance, I had cabled, it would be better to have an American delegation at the meeting so that it could give the U.S. side of things and answer any verbal attacks. Privately, I had hoped the Cubans would so appreciate the courage and independence shown by the U.S. delegation in coming to the meeting that they might mute any verbal broadsides.

Faint hope! The night before Castro was to give the opening speech, I was called in by an officer of the Foreign Ministry and warned that the speech would contain several remarks strongly critical of the Reagan administration. President Castro had asked him to inform me of this and to request that I inform Senator Stafford. Castro hoped the senator would not take his remarks as reflecting a lack of courtesy or hospitality on his part, the officer noted. Castro had the greatest respect for the senator and for the U.S. delegation. Unfortunately, the Reagan administration had recently made a series of charges against Cuba which Castro did not believe he should let pass. Hence, he was going to answer in kind. He had felt, however, that he ought to forewarn us so that we could decide for ourselves whether to attend the opening session.

"There is nothing to decide," I told the Foreign Ministry officer. "We have to attend; it would look craven if we did not. And if the remarks are offensive to my government, I will walk out. Senator Stafford will respond in his own way. That's all there is to it. We appreciate the forewarning, but it changes nothing. And may I add on a personal basis that I think this is a serious mistake on the Cuban side. Name calling is out of place, whether practiced by one side or the other. Castro would show himself to be more of a statesman by concentrating on IPU matters and leaving his quarrel with the United States out of it."

The officer shrugged his shoulders. Obviously, the speech was written and anyway quite beyond his control.

I then went over to inform Senator Stafford. We agreed that if Castro was indeed offensive, I would walk out, while the senator would remain to speak in reply.

Diplomatic courtesies sometimes take strange forms. The same officer who had delivered the message from Castro was on hand the next day to make certain I had a seat on the aisle—so that it would be easier for me to walk out. Two other Foreign Ministry officials were requested to move over so that I could have that seat. "Wayne may have to walk out," he explained, "and we want him to have a straight shot at the door."

The speech was indeed a tough one and I did walk out—followed immediately by David Thomas, the British ambassador, who was offended by references to British imperialism in Northern Ireland. Senator Stafford remained, and shortly after Castro's speech delivered his own, a rousing defense of American democracy which received a standing ovation. Many delegates came down to congratulate the senator for his effective response to what they had seen as "Castro's discourtesy."

That Stafford had the opportunity to answer Castro, refuting several of his arguments, in my judgment confirmed the value of having a delegation at the meeting. Before I could send a cable to the department making that point, however, I was recalled "on consultations" as a signal of Washington's displeasure with the tone of Castro's speech. The trip back was certainly the most comfortable I had ever made. I flew nonstop from Havana to Washington in the American delegation's Lear jet.

The Interests-Section Cable on Radio Martí

I stayed in Washington only a week. While there, I discovered that the Radio Martí project had run into trouble. A number of congressmen and a strong group in the United States Information Agency (USIA) were arguing that it might be counterproductive and establish a bad precedent. I discussed the situation with the interests-section staff upon my return to Havana. All felt strongly that the project was unsound and that we should say so in a joint message. I had expressed my own reservations in letters to Enders, they noted, but the post itself had not weighed in. Perhaps the views of the entire staff would have some impact in the debate then raging in Washington. Accordingly, we drafted a cable for distribution to the USIA as well as to the Department of State. The thrust of our dissent was that a new and separate radio station for Cuba was unnecessary. The Voice of America (VOA) was already heard in Spanish and on medium wave in most parts of the island. It had a wide audience and established credibility. If we wanted to get more information to the Cuban people, the obvious way would be to expand VOA broadcasting. That could be done immediately, at very low cost and without the need for congressional authorization. Also, if the added broadcasts were handled by VOA, we could be sure that they would be accurate and responsible. If, on the other hand, we created an independent station, as was the administration's intent, we could have no assurance that it would avoid the kind of strident propaganda that had characterized earlier Cuban exile stations and that had proved decidedly counterproductive.

Unfortunately, someone in Washington leaked our cable to the press. I was criticized for having marked it for distribution to the USIA, thus, some seemed to believe, making certain it would be leaked. I regretted that the cable had appeared in the press, but not that it had been sent to the USIA. The whole purpose was to have some impact in the debate going on within the government. The USIA had a key role to play in that debate. If it was to be aware of the views of the interests section, I had to send it the cable. Enders was certainly not going to call our views to the agency's attention.

Enders, of course, was furious and lectured me in a letter on the need for team play—which in his mind seemed to work in only one direction. He had not consulted the interests section, for example, *before* the decision within the executive branch to go ahead with Radio Martí. Was the interests section not part of the team?

New Cuban Overtures

In October 1981 came the wildest kinds of U.S. press speculation that regular Cuban troops were fighting in El Salvador. Not even the Salvadoran government took these reports seriously. The U.S. government, however, gave the impression that it did. Secretary of State Haig, I was told later, even mentioned the matter to the Soviet ambassador.

On October 28, the Cubans flatly denied these allegations and again challenged Haig to produce any shred of evidence to back them up. Once again, having no evidence to present, Haig ignored the Cuban challenge.

Meanwhile, on October 22, the Mexican ambassador in Havana had informed me of a conversation which convinced him that Castro strongly favored immediate negotiations leading to elections in El Salvador. The guerrillas, Castro had said, were ready to negotiate without preconditions. First, Castro had suggested, agreement would have to be reached on the conditions for a cease-fire; then guidelines for elections could be considered. Castro had noted that without some kind of guarantees, the guerrillas could not lay down their arms, lest they end up—like so many others—as headless corpses.

That the Cuban government held this view was confirmed by

Vice-Minister of Foreign Relations Ricardo Alarcón in a conversation with me at lunch the same day. Alarcón emphasized that the time was ripe to begin talks and end the bloodshed.

The U.S. Rebuff and Its Effects

I reported these feelers to the Department of State, once again urging that we explore the possibility of opening talks. Once again, I received no reply. Instead, Haig on October 29 reiterated his earlier accusations, charging that Castro had expanded his "interventionist activities." In view of this, he went on, he had forwarded the appropriate recommendations to the president. The U.S., he concluded, was definitely going to act. This statement galvanized the Cubans. Haig was known to have been pressing for military action since the previous spring (when he had recommended the "unequivocal application of pressure"). The Cubans therefore decided the balloon was about to go up. On October 31, they mobilized and defied the U.S. to do its worst.

Policy makers in Washington were surprised. They had rattled the sabers, but they did not understand why the Cubans were mobilizing. At first, nonetheless, they thought this reaction not a bad thing. If the Cubans were worried, good. As tensions increased, however, Washington quickly sheathed its sword. During his November 10 news conference, Reagan stated categorically that the U.S. had no plans to put Americans in combat anywhere in the world. As the full implication of Castro's mobilization sank in, moreover, reaction in Washington became more somber. Clearly, if Castro was willing to defy what he had seen as an imminent invasion, the U.S. campaign of escalating threats was doomed to failure. Castro had carried the game to its last move and refused to back down. He had called Washington's bluff. At that point the steam went out of the campaign of steadily escalating threats. The Cubans seemed to sense the change, and anyway had seen by then that the U.S. was not in fact gearing up to attack them. They demobilized.

The administration, for its part, began to emphasize long-term pressures, particularly Radio Martí. From that point forward nothing more was said about taking it "to the source."

Just as the crisis was ending, I arrived in Washington on leave, and I asked to see Bud McFarlane, the department's counselor and Haig's right-hand man for dealing with Cuba and the Caribbean. I emphasized to McFarlane, as I had earlier emphasized to Enders, that pure threats would not work with the Cubans, as the outcome of the just-ended crisis ought well to have illustrated. I urged that we not ignore the chances of advancing our objectives through diplomacy.

McFarlane replied that the Cubans had blown U.S. intentions out of all proportion. We had never intended to attack. We were, however, going to make them pay a higher price for their adventurism. On the other hand, he said, we were always open to diplomatic solutions if those were possible.

My Decision to Retire

Moderately encouraged by what McFarlane had said, I returned to Havana in December thinking that perhaps the administration could still be induced to deal more sensibly with Cuba. I was surprised to learn from press accounts in early December that Haig had met with Vice-President Carlos Rafael Rodríguez in Mexico on November 23. No one had mentioned to me in Washington that this meeting was about to take place. From that omission, and from the fact that Enders had avoided receiving me during the week I was in Washington, I concluded that I no longer had even the minimal trust of the Administration. This did not surprise me. I never expected to be its fair-haired boy. To cut me out of the picture altogether, however, struck me as pettish and unprofessional. I had not hidden the fact that I disagreed with the administration's approach, but all my reservations and out-of-step recommendations had been expressed (as they should have been) privately and through official channels. The cable on Radio Martí had been leaked by someone in Washington, not by me. I had conveyed the administration's policy to the Cubans faithfully and in appropriately strong terms. In short, although I was not of the same mind as my superiors and had not hesitated to say so, I had obeyed orders, kept my mouth shut in public, not leaked any embarrassing information to the press, and generally tried to be a good soldier, as I thought I should be so long as I was in government service.

Still, I *did* disagree with the policy, and I would have understood perfectly if the administration had replaced me with someone more sympathetic to it. But leaving me in Havana while cutting me out of the policy process made no sense. For the secretary of state to meet with the Cuban vice-president without even informing his own representative in Havana not only undercut that representative's position with the local government, it was also an unsound way to conduct foreign relations.

Angry and frustrated, I considered asking to be removed from the post immediately. As I thought the matter over, however, I concluded that to do so might make me appear petty and might harm a process I myself had recommended. I had urged negotiations with the Cubans. Perhaps the Haig-Rodríguez meeting indicated that the administration was about to begin such a process. Should I quit just because I hadn't been included in it? And if I did quit, might not that somehow sidetrack the process? Accordingly, I decided not to ask to leave just yet. I would remain in Havana until August 1982. But no longer. I had stayed on to test Reagan's policies. It was now clear that my views and those of the administration were so irreconcilable that I could not remain indefinitely in the Foreign Service. The only honest course was to leave as soon as I was eligible for early retirement. That would be in August 1982, now only a few months away.

To my surprise, a week or two after I had decided to take early retirement, I received a cable from the Department of State saying I was to be put on a candidate list for the ambassadorship in a small African country. Were there, the department asked, personal or professional reasons that would prevent my accepting this post should I be selected for it?

Yes, I replied, there were. For one thing, I was thinking of taking early retirement. I therefore could not accept, and asked that my name be withdrawn. Subsequently, I confirmed that I would retire in August 1982, and asked that I not be considered for any other ambassadorial lists. "I regret leaving the Service earlier than I had planned," I concluded, "but I believe it is the only decision I can take in good conscience."

"The department works in wondrous ways," I commented to Roxanna that evening. "Enders won't even see me. I'm cut out of the policy process entirely and treated like a leper. Yet they've offered me a crack at an ambassadorial appointment—not much of an ambassadorship, I grant you, but even so, I'm surprised."

Roxanna was not. "No," she said, "it was a smart move on their part. They probably calculate that if you quit fresh out of Havana, you'll come back to Washington with all guns blazing. And people might listen to you. You'd be a credible witness. Far better for the administration to keep you far away from Washington and *in* the

Service, so you'd keep your mouth shut, which is the only reason the department has left you in Havana in the first place. After a year or so in Africa, they'd drop you like a hot stone. By then, you couldn't do them much damage on the Cuban issue. Your information would be dated and you'd be compromised by having accepted an ambassadorship from the very administration with which you so strongly disagree. You did the best thing by telling them that you don't want that ambassadorship or any other, that you are fed up, are leaving the Service, and that's the end of it!"

"Good God," I said after a moment, "I really must leave—if for no other reason than to save my wife from total cynicism. You've begun to think like the director of personnel!"

Cuban Suspension of Military Shipments to Nicaragua

From friends in the department, and eventually from the Cubans, I found out how the Haig-Rodríguez conversation had gone. Haig had run through the list of U.S. charges against Cuba. Rodríguez had said that Haig's information was in many cases incorrect, and that in any event, Cuba was prepared to discuss any differences between our two countries. Haig replied that what the U.S. wanted was action, not words. He did indicate, however, that he might send Gen. Vernon Walters, his roving trouble shooter, to hold further talks with the Cubans.

Against this background, in December 1981 I received a new overture from the Cubans. Since March 1981, they had insisted that they were not shipping arms to El Salvador. The words in which they did so were carefully chosen. The Cuban government does not like to tell outright lies, but like most governments is perfectly willing to mislead or to hide the truth in carefully crafted phrases. That seemed to be the case here. I would respond to the Cuban assurances by saying that of course they were not shipping arms *to El Salvador*. Indeed, they could not be, for El Salvador has no Caribbean coastline. But they were, I would remind them, shipping arms, ammunition, and other military supplies to Nicaragua, and some of that materiel might then be finding its way to El Salvador.

The Cubans would dance around the issue, saying that they had no evidence of this happening, that if any Cuban arms reached El Salvador, it was not by their design. Certainly the Nicaraguan government was not involved.

My response was always that be all that as it might, if arms originating in Cuba turned up in El Salvador, no one could be expected to believe the Cuban government blameless.

Then, in late December, the Cubans changed their position. Over lunch, Carlos Martínez Salsamendi, the senior foreign-policy adviser to Rodríguez, after listening to my usual spiel about Cuban shipments of military equipment to Nicaragua, shook his head and said very deliberately and carefully, in a manner that suggested this was a major policy pronouncement: "No, you are wrong. We are not making any military shipments to Nicaragua."

I was taken aback. "What do you mean, you aren't?" I asked. "The Cuban government has never before denied that such shipments were being made."

"I didn't say that they had not been made," Martínez Salsamendi went on; "I said they are not *being made.*"

"Well, then, when were they stopped?" I asked.

"I'm not going to get into that. What I can say is that all shipments of military equipment from Cuba to Nicaragua have been suspended and that we hope this improves the atmosphere for negotiations. Don't misunderstand me. Cuba reserves the right to provide Nicaragua anything it needs for its defense. But the fact is that we are in a position to suspend such assistance at this time. We hope this can lead to something positive," Martínez Salsamendi concluded.

These remarks were reported directly to Secretary of State Haig. At the time, I was unaware of Haig's November 23 admonition to Rodríguez asking for action rather than words. When I found out about it in January, it struck me that the suspension of arms shipments was intended by the Cubans to be the "action" Haig had asked for. If it was on the level, it represented a major concession.

Nothing of course should ever be taken at face value in international politics. I therefore reminded the Department of State of Martínez Salsamendi's assurances in December and asked if we had any evidence to the contrary. If U.S. intelligence had hard evidence of continuing Cuban shipments to Nicaragua, I wanted to know it so that I could go back to the Cubans and tell them I did not appreciate being misled. If, on the other hand, we had no evidence of continuing shipments, if it seemed the flow of materiel from Cuba to Nicaragua had indeed been suspended, we might take this as a serious gesture and consider opening substantive discussions with the Cubans.

Administration Adherence to a Hard Line

Meanwhile, despite the Haig-Rodríguez talks, all other signals from the administration indicated it intended to hold to a confrontational course. On December 14, for example, Enders presented to the Senate Subcommittee on Western Hemisphere Affairs a white paper charging that Castro had returned to the export-of-revolution policies of the 1960s. The paper implied that only tough measures would deter Castro's aggression. It did not mention Cuban offers to negotiate or even acknowledge that some reduction in arms shipments to Central America might have occurred.

In February and March 1982, the administration rebuffed a Mexican peace effort. Presented by Foreign Minister Jorge Castañeda, the Mexican plan called for a negotiated settlement in El Salvador, a nonaggression pact between the U.S. and Nicaragua, and U.S.-Cuban talks to reduce tensions. Mexico offered to mediate any disputes between the U.S. and Cuba or between the U.S. and Nicaragua.

Cuba and Nicaragua immediately endorsed the Mexican proposal and offered to cooperate. The U.S. at first zigzagged, and then in mid-March flatly turned down the Mexican offer. In a news conference, Haig said that the U.S. would be happy to see Mexico involved in the search for peace, but would do its own negotiating.[5] He might more accurately have said that the U.S. would "avoid negotiations" on its own.

Despite these continuing signs that the administration had not the slightest interest in negotiating anything, I kept pressing for a reply to my cable asking if we had evidence to contradict Cuban claims to have halted military shipments to Nicaragua. I sent follow-up cables in February. No reply. In early March, I demanded a response, and on March 10 I finally got one. No, the department acknowledged in its cable, we had no hard evidence that the movement of arms from Cuba to Nicaragua was continuing, though some reports indicated that it might be. The cable then cited some of these "reports," which were so insubstantial as to be almost laughable.

Anyway, the cable went on, it made no difference whether the flow from Cuba had been suspended; enough arms were stockpiled in Nicaragua so that shipments could continue to El Salvador even if none arrived from Cuba for a while.

Such a response of course conveniently ignored the fact that the

U.S. had said Cuban assistance in the military buildup in Nicaragua was itself a matter of concern. Cuba had apparently stopped that assistance, and the department's attitude was that this action didn't make any difference. The bottom line, clearly, was that even if Cuba had indeed stopped its military assistance to Nicaragua, we weren't interested in talks and weren't going to accept this as a gesture.

I found the department's reply profoundly disturbing. It was, first of all, intellectually dishonest. The administration cared not a whit about the facts or the objective evidence. It had dictated a policy in Central America—and toward Cuba—on the basis of ideological pre-conceptions and would not be budged from that policy no matter what the Cubans and Nicaraguans might do. The administration, further, had no interest in practical solutions which advanced U.S. interests; rather, it was intent on proving an ideological point. That is a dangerous, and usually self-defeating, approach in international politics.

Knowing that my effort was utterly futile, that no one on the other end was listening, I nevertheless commented that the department's cable had been most disappointing. Senior U.S. officials (including President Reagan) had recently stated publicly and categorically that Soviet arms shipments to Central America, through Cuba, were increasing. Yet, I pointed out, the department's March 10 cable indicated that we did not even have evidence that the flow was *continuing*, let alone increasing.

The Walters-Castro Conversation

As I learned later, Gen. Vernon Walters came to Havana in March 1982 to talk with Fidel Castro. I was not informed by the Department of State that Walters was coming and of course did not participate in the conversation. I could later see why: the administration wanted no witnesses. Once it became publicly known that Walters had been there, the Cubans themselves gave me a rundown on the meeting with Castro. Subsequently, I was able to verify the thrust of their account with a friend in the department who knew the details of the report Walters had made to Haig. Clearly, Walters had not gone to Cuba to negotiate anything. He had ticked off a list of problems to be resolved before there could be any significant improvement in relations between the two countries—problems such as Cuban involvement in Central America and Africa, the return of the criminals and other excludables, and compensation for nationalized American properties.

Castro had said that he perfectly understood that these would have to be addressed. The bilateral problems could be negotiated, he said, and several of those might be solved rather quickly. The foreign-policy issues could be discussed, rather than negotiated—obviously the U.S. and Cuba could not negotiate, say, the fate of El Salvador. Solutions there would be more difficult. Castro in no way *refused* to address our agenda. Quite the contrary, he made it clear that Cuba was ready to discuss all issues in disagreement. Walters departed, and the Cubans were left to wonder when we would begin to discuss the issues he had listed.

To make certain the U.S. understood their readiness to talk, the Cubans actively publicized it. In early April 1982, a senior Cuban official told a group of U.S. scholars and journalists in Havana that Cuba wished to play a positive role in bringing about a comprehensive settlement in Central America, provided the U.S. would also show restraint and work toward mutually satisfactory solutions. The offer's package was as noteworthy as its substance. There were no preconditions; rather, the Cubans said they were ready to sit down at the bargaining table immediately.

In a conversation with me a few days after this proposal was made, Carlos Rafael Rodríguez confirmed Cuba's seriousness of purpose: "We want a peaceful solution in Central America," he said. "We understand your security concerns and are willing to address them. If you are willing to meet us halfway and to deal with us on the basis of mutual respect, there is no reason we cannot at long last begin to put aside this unproductive animosity between us. We are as weary of it as you are."

Again, nothing had to be accepted on faith; rather, it was a matter of exploring and testing the other side's seriousness of purpose, at no risk to the U.S. Even so, I knew what the response would be: the administration would ignore the offer. Why then had it sent General Walters to Havana? Simple. That visit was a charade aimed at giving the impression of a willingness to talk where in fact no such willingness existed. The administration sent Walters to Havana secretly, but then carefully leaked word through diplomatic circles that he had been there. By April, his visit had been reported in the press. This was all in preparation for the new measures the administration intended to mpose against Cuba, measures more likely to be condoned by world public opinion if we could at least claim to have tried discussions first. Enders set the stage by telling Congress on March 25, 1982, that while the U.S. did not in principle reject discussions with the Cubans, the "record is daunting." The Cubans, he implied, simply would not negotiate seriously with us.

New Sanctions against Cuba

On April 19, the administration announced the new measures against Cuba. The 1977 fishing agreement (yes, the one I had helped to negotiate) was allowed to lapse. American citizens were effectively blocked from traveling to Cuba for tourism. The U.S. courts had earlier ruled that denying an American the right to travel where he or she wished was unconstitutional. The Reagan administration got around that by saying in effect that while it could not forbid American citizens to travel to Cuba, it *could* forbid them to spend even a dime in the process. Travel controls might be unconstitutional, but currency controls were not, and the latter were as effective in blocking travel as the former would have been. From a narrow legal point of view, the administration's position may have been correct. That did not alter the fact that the administration was curtailing a constitutional right, and doing so for no clear cause.

And the administration's explanation for the new measures? They were needed, said its April 19 announcement, because "Cuba . . . is increasing its support for armed violence in this hemisphere."

Yet as we have seen, only a month before, the Department of State had acknowledged that it did not have evidence even of *continuing* arms shipments to Nicaragua, let alone of *increasing* support. During the intervening month, moreover, I had seen U.S. intelligence reports which confirmed a drastic fall off in arms deliveries to the Salvadoran guerrillas. How then could we be talking of increased flows?

As was my habit, I asked the Department of State for an explanation. On what evidence had the April 19 statement been made?

The response came in a cable on May 1, subsequently released to me under the Freedom of Information Act. It presented no evidence at all; rather, it resorted to the most hackneyed kind of reverse logic. "We have no evidence Cuba and Nicaragua have stopped arms flows to Central America," the cable asserted, thus side-stepping the fact that the department had no evidence either that it was continuing.

A Pattern of Deception

The administration also claimed to have no choice but to impose these new sanctions because Cuba refused to negotiate our foreign-policy disagreements. This was where the Walters mission to Cuba came in handy. The administration could point to it and say, "You see, we tried to talk to them; but they wouldn't be sensible, so we had to resort to other tactics." In testimony before Congress, Assistant Secretary of State Enders put the matter in almost precisely those terms. Referring to reports of Cuba's willingness to negotiate brought back by the group of American academics who were in Cuba in early April, he said:

I have been asked why didn't the United States respond to those signals? Couldn't it have been an opportunity to seek a new direction in Cuban-American affairs? The answer is this: We had indeed taken the initiative to sound out Cuba's interests and intentions at a very high level, first in November of 1981 and again in March, 1982. But in each case we were told that what could be talked about was our bilateral agenda—migration, Guantanamo. Puerto Rico and the third-country agenda—Cuba's aggressive actions in Central America and Africa—were not negotiable.[6]

But Enders's testimony was a gross misrepresentation of the facts. Indeed, it directly reversed them. As we have already seen, Rodríguez had *not* told Haig that Central America or any other foreign-policy issue could not be discussed. In his own account given after he had quit as secretary of state, Haig says nothing of any refusal by Rodríguez to address all the issues.[7] Nor does Haig report any such refusal by Castro during his conversation with General Walters in March 1982. Rather, Castro is reported by Haig to have said only that a number of our bilateral problems could be solved rather quickly, while Nicaragua and El Salvador would be "more difficult."[8]

Unwittingly perhaps, General Walters himself has also contradicted Enders's assertions. In a November 1984 interview with Mike Wallace on the CBS program "60 Minutes," he stated that based on his March 1982 conversation with Castro, his judgment had been that the prospects for successful discussions of the Central American problem were not promising enough to warrant holding them.[9]

But again, this statement does not describe a refusal by Castro to hold talks; rather it suggests a demurral on our side, stemming from

Walters's judgment that the talks probably wouldn't achieve much (a judgment whose basis Walters has never explained).

In short, the administration simply lied. It had no evidence that Cuban support for armed violence in Latin America was increasing, nor had the Cubans refused to discuss anything with us. Quite the contrary: the Cubans were seeking to hold talks, and the U.S. was refusing. But even before Reagan took office, this administration had said new sanctions ought to be imposed against Cuba. It was determined to impose them, even if they accomplished nothing and even if it had to fabricate the justification for imposing them.

I found the whole episode deeply offensive. It confirmed something I had already come to suspect: this administration considered truth to be wholly malleable. All administrations construe things in ways most favorable to them and stretch the truth a bit in the process. This one, however, went beyond any limits of decency. It had no qualms at all about misrepresenting the facts altogether. I suddenly felt that I had reached the end of the line; I had experienced one disillusionment too many.

Nor could I any longer delude myself that there was any chance of a reasoned dialogue between Washington and Havana. The cynical and deceitful way in which the administration had used Walters's visit was conclusive evidence, in my view, that not the slightest chance remained. His visit had been used not to prepare for substantive discussions, but to provide an explanation for *not* holding such discussions.

I had remained in Havana in hopes of encouraging a process of dialogue, or at least so that my departure would not in any way be misinterpreted and impede such a process. But as it was now clear that no dialogue would take place, no matter what I might say or do, I saw no point in staying on. Too, I felt I should underscore my disagreement by asking to leave the post early. I cabled the director general of the Foreign Service and requested just that. It was pointless to remain at post, I said; I so strongly disagreed with the administration's policies and my analysis of the situation was so different from the department's that it would be best for all concerned if I was removed from the post as soon as possible and given a job unrelated to policy until my retirement, now only weeks away.

A couple of days later, the director general replied that orders would be cut for my transfer just as soon as the department could get another officer to take over in Havana.

Last Weeks in Havana

"Can we never leave this place under normal circumstances?" Roxanna asked. "The first time we were forced out by the Cuban government and this time by disagreements with our own."

Certainly the circumstances of our departure lent a poignancy to our farewells. It is one thing to say good-bye to diplomatic colleagues when one is being transferred to another post. The chances are that paths will cross again at some future assignment. At least, one always feels that to be possible, and farewells therefore seem less final. But when one is leaving the diplomatic service, the chances of seeing the others again seem more remote, and one also knows that if a meeting should occur, something in the relationship will have changed. Roxanna and I had many close friends in the Havana diplomatic corps —the Belgian ambassador and his wife, the Swiss, the British, the Guyanese, the Argentines, and many others. Certainly we enjoyed one another's company and did together the things that friends everywhere do: played tennis, partied, went to the beach. But the depth of our camaraderie also had to do with a common devotion to our profession. After enough time abroad, a diplomat often has more in common with other diplomats than with his own countrymen back home. Practitioners of the same art, they face common problems, follow the same rules of protocol, lead the same gypsy existence, and, if they are good diplomats, share at least one overriding objective: better understanding among their respective countries.

Diplomats, in short, form something of a club—a club I was now leaving. As I put it in a farewell toast to a group of friends just before departure: "Saying good-bye to you is painful, but the pain of that is dulled by the warm memories of you we will carry with us always. Even should we never see one another again, we will always be friends. But there is nothing to ease another pain, a pain I feel deep within me at the thought that should our paths cross again years from now, I will no longer be one of you. I will no longer be a diplomat. For that, there is no solace."

There were, however, a few light moments among the somber during those last weeks. Knowing of our departure, Fidel Castro made a point of inviting us to a small reception one evening so that he could say good-bye. Roxanna had been packing all day and was too tired to go; she sent in her place our daughter, Melinda, then a statuesque nineteen-year-old just home from college. Melinda caught

Castro's eye as we went through the receiving line, and when he heard she was just back from school in the U.S., he said he wanted to talk to her after the receiving line broke up. Half an hour later, as I talked to Raúl Castro on the other side of the room, I watched the Melinda-Fidel conversation in pantomime. It ended with a laughing Castro bowing low and saying something to Melinda that caused her to blush and giggle.

In the car going home I asked her what the bow had meant.

"Well," she said, "Castro asked me what American young people thought of the Argentine-British war over the Falklands/Malvinas?"

"And you said?"

"I told him I thought American young people, like young people everywhere, believed that when men came to armed conflict, they behaved irrationally. There are always ways of solving problems if there is any will to do so. And no one ever really gains anything from a war. Men know that, and yet they fight anyway."

"And Castro said?"

"He agreed with me, but he said that, unfortunately, in their innermost souls, men are still warriors; they respond to a primitive urge to fight, even though it gains them nothing. It will take generations of education to overcome these irrational impulses—if they can be overcome at all."

"How did you answer that?"

"I said he might be right, but that there were ways of handling mankind's aggressive tendencies so that the results would be less destructive. I told him Mom and I had been talking about it only a few days before and had agreed that if it ever came to the point of armed conflict between the U.S. and Cuba, rather than sending marine divisions to invade Cuba, the United States ought to send twenty thousand American girls in string bikinis and have them land right on Santa María beach."

"Was that when Castro bowed?"

"Yes, he seemed to like the idea. He bowed and said that if I would lead the invasion, he would meet me on the beach and personally surrender the island to me."

My conversation with Raúl Castro had also been about peacemaking—though of a kind less imaginative than that suggested by Melinda. "Why," Raúl had asked me, "can't we get some discussions started? We are ready and willing to talk about Central America, for example. We have told you that over and over again, but you never answer. Why is that?"

Raúl Castro's insistence on the need for negotiations was particularly interesting. A pet theory among analysts back in Washington was that Raúl was a hardliner who strongly opposed any effort to improve relations with the U.S. A hardliner he might be, but the analysts obviously had the rest of it wrong.

I had no satisfactory answer for him, of course. "I can only tell you," I had replied, "that I have faithfully reported all your government's overtures to my own. I will report this one as well. More than that, I cannot do."

The next day, I did report it. The usual cable went to Washington. As usual, there was no reply.

The Abandonment of Ex-prisoners and Divided Families

As I prepared to leave Havana, one piece of unfinished business distressed and puzzled me deeply. I disagreed with the administration's determination not to sit down with the Cubans, but at least that determination was consistent with the administration's own ideological preconceptions. But its flat refusal to honor our commitment to take some 1,500 former political prisoners I found totally incomprehensible.

These were the same former political prisoners who had been left in limbo by the riot of May 2, 1980, and its aftermath. Up until inauguration day in 1981 we had begged the outgoing Carter administration for the authorization to begin processing them, but the decision had been left to the incoming president. I had expected the Reagan administration to give us permission right after inauguration day. After all, the new president talked all the time about how much he sympathized with those suffering under Castro's rule, and he certainly gave the impression of wanting to help them. Here were anti-Communist dissidents—people who had opposed Castro and languished in his prisons because of it—and the previous administration had already said we would bring them to the U.S. Surely the Reagan administration would not welsh on that promise.

But it did. I sent cable after cable explaining the desperate plight of these people and asking urgently for authorization to begin documenting them for entry into the U.S. No reply. Finally, near the end of the year, an answer came back. We would not take them. There was no explanation, simply a flat and callous refusal. By that refusal, the Reagan administration condemned people who had had faith in us to more years in limbo.

I was deeply ashamed of my government. All during 1981, I had received heart-rending letters from these ex-prisoners. At first, the letters expressed hope that we would soon honor our word to them, but as the year passed their tone turned bitter. In December 1981, one ex-prisoner said he was writing for the last time. He had trusted in the good faith of the U.S. government, he said; he would trust no more. "The U.S. has not only abandoned us," he concluded, "it has dishonored its word." He was right.

The Reagan administration's indifference to the fate of these ex-prisoners was consistent with its whole approach to human rights in Cuba. While talking incessantly of human-rights violations, it made not the slightest effort to alleviate suffering. Whatever the faults of the Carter administration, it had brought about the release of thousands of political prisoners and reunited thousands of families. The Reagan administration, by contrast, brought about the release of not a single political prisoner; it refused to reunite divided families by providing immigrant visas to the spouses and children of Cubans already legally resident in the U.S.; and, worst of all, it turned its back on the former political prisoners. This shameful record was justly criticized by the OAS Human Rights Commission in its 1984 report.

Farewell

One of my last acts before leaving was to place a small plaque under the eagle's head which hung in the interests-section lounge. The head had a fascinating history. That it was still there as I departed symbolized, to me at least, my failure to achieve the goal I had set for myself upon arrival three years earlier.

Before the Cuban Revolution, the columns of the monument to the battleship *Maine* just down the street from our building had been topped by a large cast-iron eagle with outstretched wings. But on the evening of May 1, 1961, after the failure of the Bay of Pigs invasion, a rally had been held at the monument and a wrecking ball had sent the eagle crashing to the ground. Its body and crumpled wings were on display in the Museum of the City of Havana, in a room with other "relics of the imperialist past."

We had the head, however, for on the night of the rally, at great personal risk, four Cubans brought it to the door of the old embassy building and left it with the Swiss.

The eagle's head was in the basement when I took charge of the interests section in 1979. I'd had it brought up and mounted on the wall of the lounge, but I'd thought of that as only a temporary move. It had struck me as a fitting gesture, if U.S.-Cuban relations ever became normal enough to permit it, to rejoin the head with the body and wings. Indeed, this might have been seen as a symbol of our renewed relationship. We of course would not want the head amongst the other "relics of the imperialist past"; the Cubans probably would not wish to see the head and body together again atop the monument. But another resting place could have been agreed upon. I had discussed this with Dr. Eusebio Leal Spengler, the director of the museum, who agreed that it was a good idea "when our relations had improved enough to make it possible." But as I left in July 1982, that possibility seemed further away than ever. The best I could do was to leave a plaque in the lounge noting that if the head was ever joined to the body, we would know there could be peace in the Caribbean. It was, I'm afraid, the sort of histrionics to which one resorts when one has been unable to accomplish anything of substance.

Roxanna, Melinda, and Sanford returned to Washington ahead of me, leaving me to pack the last suitcase and say the final farewells. In 1961 we had left so quickly that the blinking of lights had been the only farewell for many of the Cuban employees, but this time I had the opportunity to say good-bye to each of the Cuban employees I had come to know so well over the years. As I looked over the faces of those assembled in the lounge to give me a parting *abrazo*, I felt a catch in my throat. Gabriel, Ambassador Bonsal's driver, was no longer there. He had died in 1980. Only two of the staff from 1961 remained, the others all having died or retired. As we exchanged *abrazos*, one of them said to me, "Don't wait sixteen years this time to come back; if you do, the two of us will no longer be here to see you."

"*Hombre,*" I said, "you needn't worry. I like the *mohitos* too much not to come back, and anyway, you'll always be here; it's your destiny to live forever."

The next day I flew back to the United States. Things had come full circle. As the plane banked north and I watched the rolling hills of Cuba drop behind, I remembered my first sight of them almost a quarter of a century before. Yes, I thought, this was a fitting end to my life in the Foreign Service. It had begun with those hills; it ended as they disappeared below the horizon.

IO

Epilogue

M y last few weeks in the Foreign Service were passed in a little
cubbyhole on the seventh floor of the Department of State
working on Polish political-asylum cases. It was the sort of routine
task that could have been done by the most junior clerk. I had no
complaints on that score, however; the job was unrelated to policy
and that was what I had wanted. I did my allotted number of cases
each day, left the building at five thirty, and spent my off-duty hours
working on an article for *Foreign Policy* magazine, an article critical
of the administration's policies in Cuba and Central America.[1]

Most of my friends in the Foreign Service understood why I had
opted for early retirement, but assumed I would leave quietly. Several
were shocked when I told them that, on the contrary, I intended to
speak out. They seemed to believe that an unspoken club rule prevented Foreign Service officers from expressing disagreement with
policy—even after leaving the Service.

I had never heard of such a rule. In any case, I heartily disagreed
with the concept, which, to my mind, reflected a sadly distorted
understanding of "duty."

Shortly after I left the Service, the department's *Open Forum Journal,* a classified in-house publication, asked me to explain my reasons
for going. I was grateful for the opportunity to go on record, and
stated my case as follows:

I came in . . . with the idea that if one had irreconcilable views, one left. One did not carp, one did not attack the administration, so long as one was in. And I did not. All my views and analysis were within channels until I left the Service. But I left the Service precisely because I so strongly disagreed with the policies of the Reagan Administration in Central America, with respect to Cuba, and with many of its policies elsewhere. I not only disagreed but was very concerned over the direction in which I believed and still believe those policies to be taking us. I wanted to have the opportunity as a private citizen to express my concerns and my deep reservations with respect to those policies. I certainly do not accept the idea that, once having been in the Foreign Service, one is supposed to keep one's mouth shut for all time. . . . I don't think such a view can be reconciled with the participatory obligations of the citizen of a free country. So long as you are in the Service, you must submit to its discipline, but if you are so concerned that you leave, then I submit that it is your duty as a citizen—not just your right, but your *obligation*—to express those concerns. I have exercised that right, that duty. I have violated no trust in doing so. Far from it.[2]

Radio Martí Again

On August 16, 1982, I became a private citizen. The debate over Radio Martí was in full cry, so I joined in on the side of the opponents.[3] Actually, "debate" is the wrong word. Proponents of Radio Martí never listened to the arguments of the opposition. Their central point was always that we had to establish Radio Martí in order to break Castro's monopoly on the news. As Sen. Paula Hawkins of Florida frequently put it: "When Radio Martí goes on the air, the Cuban people will for the first time be able to hear the truth."

This was utter nonsense, as interests-section cables had pointed out the previous fall. The Voice of America and various other stations from the U.S. had long been heard in Cuba. Time after time, this was pointed out to congressional committees, with the suggestion that we simply expand VOA broadcasting. It was as though we had not spoken. The next witness for the administration would begin his or her testimony by declaring that "in order to break Castro's monopoly on the news, we must establish Radio Martí."

It soon became apparent that we could not defeat Radio Martí outright. The administration was determined to have its way, and the issue was not sufficiently compelling to galvanize strong opposition. Most members of Congress reacted phlegmatically. They would say: "Well, you may be right. Probably we could accomplish the same thing by increasing VOA broadcasting, but on the other hand, where's the real harm in establishing Radio Martí? My constituents aren't much concerned one way or the other, and if I don't have to oppose the administration on this one, why should I, especially since if I do, someone may accuse me of being soft on Communism?"

Running hard up against this kind of mind-set, we fell back to a damage-limitation tactic: we insisted that if Radio Martí was established, it should be placed under the VOA. That was the best way, we argued, of being certain it followed the same high standards as did the VOA for accuracy and responsibility, and the best way of taking advantage of VOA's established audience.

Administration spokesmen at first fought tooth and tong against this compromise. They wanted nothing less than an independent station which they could turn over to the Cuban exiles. But they could muster no persuasive arguments against putting the station under the VOA, and in the end, in September 1983, Congress approved this version of the Radio Martí bill. We had not won outright, but had at least prevented the administration from setting up the kind of station that inevitably would have broadcast strident propaganda and done tremendous harm.

Return to Cuba

In March 1983, I returned to Havana with Sen. Lowell P. Weicker of Connecticut. Long convinced that there should be a more normal relationship between Cuba and the United States, Weicker went to sound out Castro's willingness to meet us halfway.

We spent many hours with Castro over a period of two days. During that time, he reviewed with us the agenda of contentious issues standing between our two countries—everything from inadvertent interference in one another's radio channels to the civil war in El Salvador. Castro reiterated his willingness to discuss all these issues with the U.S.—and to do so with a constructive attitude and a will to contribute to solutions. *No* issue was excluded.

Upon our return to Washington, we reported Castro's offer to Assistant Secretary of State Enders. Senator Weicker added that he thought Castro was in earnest. "I don't know how the negotiations might turn out," Weicker said, "but I'm at least convinced that Castro is prepared to begin them and that he would negotiate seriously."

Enders heard us out and thanked us for our report. His only comment, however, was that there was really nothing new in what

Castro had said and certainly nothing the administration would want to follow up on.

By then I would have expected no other reply. Even so, this dismissal of Castro's offer was rather extraordinary. Only three months before, Enders had told Congress under oath that Cuba would not address our agenda of third-country issues. Our report authentically contradicted that, yet Enders said there was nothing new in it!

Subsequent Cuban Overtures

As I write in 1986, the administration's attitude has changed not at all. It has continued to side-step every overture made by the Cubans (the single exception, after a delay of three years, being the immigration talks, discussed later in this chapter). On July 28, 1983, for example, Castro told American newsmen that he would be willing to bring all Cuban military personnel home from Nicaragua and to observe an arms embargo on the whole Central American area, provided the U.S. would follow suit. Perhaps this particular formula would not have been acceptable to the U.S. Certainly Washington would have wished to pin Castro down to a more specific commitment. But since he was in effect offering to resolve what we had said was one of our principal concerns—the Cuban military presence in Nicaragua—one would have expected the U.S. at least to be willing to discuss the matter with him. President Reagan at first suggested that we might. He called Castro's offer encouraging. We would give Castro the full benefit of the doubt in negotiations. Secretary of State George P. Shultz followed up with a letter to congressional leaders assuring them that we would thoroughly explore Castro's offer. Only a few days later, however, and without any explorations, President Reagan was saying we would not discuss this offer or anything else with Castro because we didn't think he was serious.[4] Then why had the president said we would give Castro the benefit of the doubt in negotiations? And how did we know Castro wasn't serious without testing him?

We never did test him. John Ferch, my successor as chief of the interests section, did ask the Cubans to define some of the terms of Castro's proposal. The Cubans answered that they were prepared to respond to such questions if the U.S. really wished to open talks, but since President Reagan had already ruled them out, there was no point in an abstract exercise. Vice-Minister of Foreign Relations Ricardo Alarcón emphasized, however, that the door remained open, should the U.S. change its mind.

The U.S. did not change its mind. When I visited Havana again in May 1984, Castro voiced his disappointment that the U.S. had ignored his offer, which, nonetheless, remained on the table. "The grounds for an accommodation acceptable to all are there," he said. "Negotiations, however, can only succeed if the will exists on both sides to make them work. And, frankly, our experience with the present U.S. administration has been such as to make us very skeptical."[5]

Castro was still holding the door open in January 1985 when Congressmen Bill Alexander of Arkansas, Jim Leach of Iowa, and Mickey Leland of Texas visited Cuba. He told them he fully supported the Contadora process launched by Mexico, Venezuela, Colombia, and Panama to find a peaceful solution in Central America; he was prepared to cooperate actively. As part of an agreement, he would withdraw Cuban military personnel from Nicaragua, stop shipments of military equipment from Cuba to Nicaragua, scrupulously honor any limitations on the size of the Nicaraguan armed forces, and accept procedures to verify compliance in all cases.

Department of State spokesmen pooh-poohed the proposals brought back by the congressmen. Privately, various members of the administration suggested that Castro had been frightened into feigning a conciliatory attitude by our invasion of Grenada in 1983. But they ignored the fact that Castro had made many other overtures *before* the invasion.

Grenada

In February 1980, the Grenadian ambassador in Havana, Richard Jacobs, had approached me with the idea of having lunch periodically in order to exchange views. Rarely did anyone from the American embassy in Barbados visit Grenada, he noted, and Grenada had diplomatic representation in only a few capitals. In most of those capitals, the American embassies had little idea of what was going on in the Caribbean and anyway seemed to have a hostile attitude toward their Grenadian colleagues. The U.S. interests section had a better appreciation of the situation in this area. He therefore had instructions from his government to begin a dialogue with me, in the hope that it might lead to talks at a higher level. Grenada wanted badly to improve its relationship with the U.S., which had gotten off to a bad start; perhaps the two of us could help put it together again.

I had told Jacobs that first day that while I would be happy to listen to what he had to say, all I could do was report it to the Department of State and to the American embassy in Barbados. Any decision would be up to them. I also pointed out that if his government really wished to improve relations with the U.S., it might begin by muting its propaganda against us. We found it difficult to take professions of friendship seriously just after being called a bloodsucking imperialist leech by Grenadian radio.

All during 1980 and 1981, Jacobs and I had our little lunches, discussed problems between our two countries, and told tall stories, and we became good friends. A giant of a man with a booming laugh and an infectious sense of humor, Jacobs was impossible not to like. But while we warmed to one another, relations between our two countries remained as cold as ever. The fault lay on both sides. The Grenadians would for a time curb their rhetoric, but before that fact had been digested in Washington, they would lose patience and go over to the attack again.

From Washington came no encouragement at all. I had always believed that a mixture of diplomatic pressure and economic inducement might turn the Grenadian situation around. Prime Minister Maurice Bishop himself, while a Marxist, was genuinely popular, and was intelligent and open to persuasion. We could not have gotten him to break his ties with Cuba or proclaim himself a free-market capitalist, but we might have worked out a *modus vivendi* and in the process curbed his more radical tendencies. It was worth a try. We never tried at all. There were a few half-hearted expressions of interest during 1980, but with the inauguration of Reagan in January 1981, the door slammed shut. I received no further responses to my cabled reports of conversations with Richard Jacobs. Finally I was advised by the Department of State to stop meeting with him. U.S. rhetoric during 1982 and the first part of 1983 became increasingly threatening toward Grenada. Even so, I doubt that the U.S. would have invaded Grenada but for the upheaval in Grenada itself. The Grenadian people would have fought for Bishop. But in October 1983, Bernard Coard, the deputy prime minister, and Gen. Hudson Austin seized power, arresting and then murdering Bishop, to the outrage of the

Grenadian people. The Cubans too were outraged, and condemned the coup in strong terms.

The Reagan administration could not pass up such a good opportunity. A naval task force that had been headed for the Mediterranean was diverted toward Grenada. At Fort Bragg, North Carolina, the Eighty-second Airborne Division began to emplane. On October 25, the invasion was launched.

Thoughtful Americans can only have conflicting reactions to our invasion of Grenada. On the one hand, Coard and Austin were thugs. They had murdered Bishop and might have launched a reign of terror. The Grenadian people were probably better off without them. Certainly under the circumstances Grenadians were pleased enough to see the Americans come ashore. More than anything else, their smiling faces appearing on American TV convinced people here at home that President Reagan had been right to invade.

On the other hand, the U.S., unlike the Soviet Union, has never professed the thesis that the end justifies the means. As Prime Minister Margaret Thatcher pointed out at the time, the Western democracies should not march in and change other governments simply because those governments are bad. To do so, she said, would be to establish our own Brezhnev doctrine.

The U.S. had not the slightest juridical basis for its action, nor were our reasons for going in compelling. American citizens, as it turned out, were not in any immediate danger and in any event could have been evacuated.

President Reagan made much of the airfield the Bishop government had been building. The landing strip was too long for Grenada's needs, he suggested, and must therefore be meant for some sinister military purpose. But UN tourism experts had in fact recommended that length for the strip. A British firm was participating in its construction and tourists were allowed to roam freely over the site, something the Cubans and Grenadians would not have permitted if a "sinister" operation had been in the works.

The president also claimed that Grenada constituted a threat to the other states of the eastern Caribbean, and that their governments had asked us to intervene. It soon became clear, however, that we had stimulated that invitation. Furthermore, despite its enlarged army and the thousands of small arms stockpiled on the island, Grenada had no means of threatening its neighbors—at least not in any immediate sense. It had no navy, no air force, no amphibious or airlift capability. And if it had enjoyed some such limited capability, the U.S. could certainly have assured the security of the other states simply by interposing a naval squadron. It would not have had to land marines.

None of the captured documents released by the administration after the invasion supported the charge that Grenada was planning to commit aggression against its neighbors. Nor did the captured small arms indicate any such intention. For years, the Grenadian government under Bishop had been warning that the U.S. planned to invade Grenada. It had asked Cuba and the Soviet Union for arms with which to defend itself. And since the plan had been to create a people's militia, modeled after the force in Cuba, thousands of weapons were required. Nothing in the military agreements with Cuba and the Soviet Union suggested that Grenada was to be provided with amphibious or airlift capability. And if the rifles and machine guns were intended for terrorists on other islands, who was to wear the twelve thousand uniforms called for under the agreements? Terrorists rarely wear uniforms; militia units do.

In sum, the evidence is overwhelming that the military buildup on Grenada was defensive. Until the morning of October 25, one might have thought it also reflected a certain paranoia on the part of the Grenadian government. As the marines came ashore, however, the fears were seen to have had a foundation after all.

To my mind, our invasion of Grenada exposed again the Reagan administration's incomprehension of the uses of diplomacy. For three years the Bishop government had pleaded for talks and signaled its interest in reaching accommodation with the U.S. The administration rebuffed these overtures and instead seized the first opportunity to settle the matter through force.[6]

At the time of the American invasion, just over 700 Cubans were on the island. Only about 200 of them were military personnel. Most of the others were construction workers building the airfield. Cuban military personnel at first put up stiff resistance, but when they recognized that their situation was hopeless, they surrendered—an act which won their commander stiff disciplinary action upon his return to Cuba. The already demoralized Grenadian army resisted hardly at all. Nevertheless, the vastly superior American force took almost a week to secure the island. No matter. The Reagan administration was delighted with its military "victory." Much was said at the time about Cuba's humiliation and about Castro having been frightened out of his wits and at long last coming to the realization that the U.S. meant business.

I thought both lines of speculation greatly overdrawn. In a confrontation between a small country and a superpower, the small country is never humiliated, for the outcome is not in doubt. The Cubans had understood as soon as Bishop was murdered that they had an untenable situation on their hands. The invasion did not surprise them. They were prepared to accept its consequences— though Castro doubtless wished his small contingent on the island had given a better account of itself.

And rather than intimidating the Cubans, the invasion may have had the opposite effect. They had never doubted that the Reagan administration was prepared to use armed might if circumstances favored it. The poor showing of the American invasion force, however, probably suggested to the Cubans that the U.S. armed forces would have heavy going if they tried to invade Cuba or Nicaragua.

The Immigration Issue Again

Back in February 1981, the Cubans had suggested a resumption of talks on immigration matters, but the administration ignored this and subsequent offers. Concurrently, it refused visas for members of divided Cuban families, and refused to honor our commitment to the 1,500 former political prisoners. When asked by Congress to explain this refusal, the administration replied that it could not process visas because Castro refused to take back the criminals and other excludables. This argument was not persuasive, since the Cubans were offering to work out modalities for the return of those excludables, while the U.S. refused to discuss the matter.

Finally, in the spring of 1984, Washington asked Havana if it was still willing to talk. Three years had passed. A U.S. presidential election was near. Suspecting that this sudden interest was part of an electoral ploy, and not wanting to be used in the administration's internal political schemes, the Cubans responded that, yes, they would be happy to discuss the issue—*after* the elections.

The Reverend Jesse Jackson planned to visit Cuba at the end of June, and the Department of State asked him to assure the Cubans that this was a bipartisan issue, that Democrats as well as Republicans wanted the talks to go ahead. Jackson did so, and the Cubans relented; he brought back word that the talks could begin.

In July, American and Cuban delegations at long last sat down to work out the few differences that remained from the last round of talks, in January 1981. This proved not difficult, and in December an agreement was signed. Under its provisions, the Cubans were to take back the excludables, including the criminals being held in the Atlanta penitentiary. The U.S. was to authorize the issuance of immigrant visas by the interests section in Havana, so that a normal flow of immigration could begin; it was also to take the ex-prisoners we had left stranded since late 1980.

The fate of those ex-prisoners had weighed heavily on my mind. I sometimes dreamed I was standing before a group of them earnestly assuring them that we would not let them down, that they would soon be on the way to join their families in the U.S. The dream would fade as their faces came into focus and I realized that none of them believed me.

My relief was premature, for the agreement was not to endure. It did begin to operate. The first criminals were sent back to Cuba; Cuban immigrants began to join their families in the U.S., and the first planeload of ex-prisoners arrived in Miami. Then, on May 20, Radio Martí went on the air. The Cubans were outraged. Why, is difficult to understand. The administration, after all, had said all along that immigration was a discrete matter, that although we had discussed immigration with the Cubans, we did not intend to discuss anything else. The Cubans had nonetheless deluded themselves that the signing of the immigration agreement marked a turning point, that tensions would now subside, and that no matter what it was saying at the moment, the administration would in time discuss other issues. Many of them believed that the administration's failure to get Radio Martí on the air more than a year after its approval by Congress was in fact a subtle signal of a change of heart.

The activation of Radio Martí dashed all those hopes. The Cubans said it was a hostile act, incompatible with the atmosphere in which the immigration agreement had been signed. Hence, they immediately announced the suspension of the agreement. The divided families would remain divided, and the ex-prisoners in limbo. At the very least, however, the onus was now more on Castro than on the U.S.

Nicaragua

No discussion of events related to Cuba since 1982 would be complete without a few words about Nicaragua. We seem determined to repeat and compound there all the mistakes we made earlier in Cuba.

If we were unwilling to sit down at the negotiating table with the Cubans, we are equally opposed to sitting down with the Nicaraguans. If we launched a counterrevolutionary invasion force against Cuba at one point, and resorted to sabotage and assassination attempts against Cuban leaders, we have gone to the same lengths against the Sandinistas. As early as the summer of 1981, the CIA made contact with the ex-Somoza guardsmen who had established themselves along the Honduran border in 1979 and had begun conducting raids into Nicaragua. By 1982, the U.S. government had organized and armed an army around this Somocista nucleus. This force, the *contras,* quickly became the major instrument of U.S. policy in Nicaragua, and in 1986 still is, even though we have not, by supporting the *contras,* achieved a single one of our principal objectives in Nicaragua.

One can only be astounded by some of the inconsistencies in the administration's explanations of its Nicaragua policy. Assistant Secretary of State Elliott Abrams has insisted on several occasions that the U.S. supports the Contadora process, but in August 1985 he described the very idea of a negotiated agreement with the Sandinistas as "preposterous," even though a negotiated agreement is just what the Contadora process is supposed to produce.

President Reagan has also insisted that his administration is cooperating fully with the Contadora countries. Yet, when their foreign ministers, backed by those of Argentina, Brazil, Peru, and Uruguay, came to Washington in February 1986 to ask that the U.S. give substance to those claims by halting its aid to the *contras* and resuming talks with the Sandinista government, they were unceremoniously rebuffed. The administration went right on asking Congress to continue aid, and right on claiming that it was cooperating with the Contadora process. Few believed its claims anymore.

By 1986, indeed, the U.S. was as isolated in its Nicaragua policy as in its Cuba policy. This was no coincidence, for what the administration's handling of the Nicaraguan situation points up more than anything else is that even after twenty-seven years, the U.S. remains incapable of dealing sensibly with Cuba or with any problem related to Cuba, as the Nicaraguan problem certainly is.

II

Conclusions

The gulf between the United States and Castro's Cuba is not imaginary. Castro's early goals were nothing less than to extend revolution throughout Latin America and in the process to challenge U.S. influence. In response to this out-thrusting on Castro's part, we felt we had to "contain" Cuba. It was this mix of his goals and our reaction to them that led Castro to align with the Soviet Union. He was determined to turn Latin America into a revolutionary cauldron. We were just as determined to stop him, using force if need be. Hence, he turned to the Soviets for protection, eventually embracing Marxism-Leninism in an effort to assure that protection.

Over the years, however, Castro's revolutionary fervor has cooled, as has his compulsion to export revolution. Cuban leaders continue to endorse armed struggle as a valid tactic—in the abstract; in practice, however, they stress that the conditions for revolution exist in only two countries: El Salvador and Guatemala.[1] Only in these two countries would it be appropriate for Marxist-Leninist groups to assist revolutionary organizations. And even in these two cases, Cuban support has been sharply curtailed and Cuba has signaled its willingness to cooperate with diplomatic efforts to find peaceful solutions—something it would have been unlikely to do in the 1960s.

Cuba continues to play an active role in foreign affairs to the distress of the U.S.—but increasingly it implements its foreign policy

278

through traditional means. Cuban troops were sent to Ethiopia in 1978 to support the Ethiopian government, not to overthrow it. Cuban troops are in Angola to aid the recognized government of that country against South African incursions and against Savimbi's guerrilla army, which is supported by South Africa. The U.S. may take the other side in these conflicts, but the point is that Cuba has adopted a traditional form of international behavior. It is perfectly normal—and legal—for one government to assist another; it is the effort of one government to overthrow another that violates acceptable conduct.

If the form of Cuban foreign policy has become more traditional, its substance nonetheless remains of concern to the U.S. Cuba is the military ally of our principal global adversary. Inevitably, we must analyze Cuba's actions in terms of their benefit to its more powerful patron. A Cuban expeditionary force in Angola, while legal, may also serve to extend Soviet power and influence, and is therefore to be viewed with suspicion. The time has not come when such Metternichian calculations are irrelevant.

Finally, the perceptions the two countries have about themselves keep them at odds. Cuban policy is much less revolutionary than it was a quarter of a century ago, but Cuba continues to believe itself to be "revolutionary." The U.S., by contrast, has been involved in many a subversive effort abroad, but perceives itself as a seeker of stability and the rule of law. Thus, at least in our collective self-images, Cuba's revolutionary ethos clashes with the American quest for stability and world order.

In the beginning, a clash of wills may have been inevitable. Given Castro's initial surge, and his determination to breathe fire in all directions, the U.S. probably could not have worked out an early accommodation with him. Even today, conflicting world views make for an adversarial relationship. Cuba and the U.S. will not soon be friends. Even so, a significant improvement in relations is now possible—indeed, has been possible for some time. Anti-Americanism once fueled Castroism, but Castro realized years ago that working out a *modus vivendi* with the U.S. would better serve his interests. For one thing, even a limited commercial link between the two countries would benefit both, but especially Cuba.

A *modus vivendi* makes sense also from the U.S. side. If we deal with the Soviet Union, why can we not deal with Cuba? If there are problems whose solution would benefit us, why not sit down at the negotiating table to resolve them? Cuba is an actor in the Central

American drama. If we wish to restrain its activities, why do we refuse to discuss the matter with Cuba?

Emotion is the enemy of pragmatism in Cuban relations. Cuba excites American passions as do few other foreign-policy issues, if any. At least in part, this reaction flows from factors peculiar to our view of Cuba. Having a Soviet ally so close by makes us very uncomfortable. That this small island only ninety miles off our shores has successfully defied us for twenty-five years is an irritating reminder of the limitations of power.

I suspect, too, that when most Americans think of Cuba today, they have a sense—perhaps not always at a conscious level—of the rightful order of things violated. Our former relationship with Cuba was too intimate for us not to take this view. Since the days of Thomas Jefferson, Americans have felt that Cuba ought one day to be ours, and while we never acquired it outright, it was virtually an American protectorate from 1898 until 1959. In the minds of most Americans, Cuba was independent because we allowed it to be. Cuba did our bidding and was a fun place to visit for a few days. No longer.

But while the flowering of our emotionalism may be unique to Cuba, our mishandling of the problem is not. Our failure to fashion an effective Cuba policy over twenty-five years is symptomatic of a much broader weakness: for a country itself born of revolution, the U.S. has shown a striking inability to deal effectively with revolutionary situations in other former colonies. Its record is especially dismal with respect to the fall from power of those whom Jeane Kirkpatrick has called "moderate autocrats"—Batista, Somoza, the shah of Iran, Haile Selassie, and their ilk. In her now famous article "Dictatorships and Double Standards," she suggests that in the face of budding revolutions, the U.S. ought to defend the status quo and maintain the autocrat in power. Trading a friendly autocrat for an unfriendly totalitarian government, she argues, does not serve the interests of our nation.[2]

Kirkpatrick's point is obvious. But is the choice ours to the extent Kirkpatrick implies? Just as obviously not. As we have seen, the Cuban people had turned massively against Batista. His inefficient and corrupt regime was not capable of adjusting to the challenge. The U.S. arms embargo in 1958 (our single step away from Batista) had some small impact, but was by no means the crucial ingredient. Batista would have fallen with or without U.S. arms. Indeed, even landing U.S. troops to prop him up could have saved him only temporarily, and we certainly should not have done that.

In different contexts, the same was true of Somoza and of the shah. The U.S. was not responsible for their departures and could not have propped them up indefinitely even had it wished to do so. But other options were open to us.

Intellectually, we seem to understand what the wise course would be in these cases: encourage the moderate forces available to fill the power vacuum before the situation becomes so polarized that one extreme replaces another. In neither Nicaragua nor Iran did we do that. Rarely have we followed that prescription in other cases. More often than not, we have done the exact opposite. We have propped the autocrats, and on occasion we have even returned them to power after their removal by revolutionary forces—in Iran in 1953 when we saved the shah's throne, and in Guatemala in 1954 when we overthrew Arbenz.

U.S. policy makers spoke of encouraging a centrist solution in Cuba while there was still time for one to take shape, but in fact, this policy never went beyond talk. In Nicaragua the Carter Administration made an initial effort to bring in a moderate transitional government, but then vacillated until it was far too late for a moderate solution to hold.

According to William Sullivan, our ambassador in Tehran in 1978, an alternative between the two extremes—the shah and Ayatollah Khomeini—might have been possible in Iran as well. Sullivan recommended that we try to develop one,[3] but Jimmy Carter, who had called the shah a great democrat, refused, reasoning that since the shah was doomed, he, Carter, wished to do nothing which might be construed as hastening his fall.[4] Sullivan felt it imperative that opposition leaders be given a greater voice in Iran's affairs. Carter responded by continuing to give the shah our complete and unreserved backing.[5]

One can understand Carter's concern not to be perceived as undermining the shah. But to do nothing was a luxury which we, as a global power with interests in the area, could not afford. Within guidelines defined by acceptable costs and risks, we ought to have worked toward the best available alternative. Instead, we read from an enchanted script whose spell we had not the will to break.[6]

The 1986 replacement of Ferdinand Marcos by democratic forces in the Philippines has been touted as a major victory for American diplomacy. One would wish that were so and that the favorable outcome in the Philippines means the spell has been broken. The evidence, however, does not support so optimistic a view. President Reagan's initial reaction to the situation in the Philippines was obviously based on Jeane Kirkpatrick's advice: he supported the dictator. Vice-President Bush praised Marcos as a great democrat, just as Jimmy Carter had praised the shah. President Reagan asserted that our choice in the Philippines was between Marcos and the Communists, thus suggesting that Marcos would have our unswerving loyalty.

The happy outcome in the Philippines despite this hackneyed U.S. approach owed little to American diplomacy. Rather, the victory was won by the Filipino people *despite* the Reagan administration. It was apparent during the president's press conference on February 10, 1986, that he was prepared to accept Marcos's fraudulent electoral victory. Both sides had been guilty of fraud, the president said; the important thing was that the losers cooperate with the winners. Senior spokesmen in the White House chided Corazon Aquino for not getting on the bandwagon and supporting the "winner"—Marcos. Clearly, the Reagan administration was ready to leave Marcos to mismanage the Philippines for yet a few more years—or until the situation became so polarized, so hopeless, that the Communists might indeed have a shot at power.

Fortunately, Aquino and the Filipino people refused to play the game. They would not accept the fraudulent electoral result. Digging in their heels, they brought the Marcos regime crashing down with an impressive demonstration of passive resistance. At the eleventh hour, the Reagan administration bowed to the inevitable and told Marcos he ought to go. American diplomacy thus ended up doing the right thing in spite of itself. One might say that it was carried unwillingly to the finish line by the Filipino people. Perhaps we learned something in the process. Perhaps next time we will not reach so automatically for the enchanted script. Perhaps.

No simple mechanistic solution will apply in all cases. Revolutions are by nature volatile. We are, moreover, dealing with sovereign countries, in which the U.S. has no jurisdiction and sometimes little influence. But to the extent that we can do something—and the U.S. can always do *something*—we must encourage responsible leadership to replace authoritarian rule.

Having failed to do that in Cuba, we sought halfheartedly to come to terms with Castro. When that didn't work, we resorted to a poorly conceived and undermanned clandestine military operation. Containment made sense; the Bay of Pigs and some of our other extreme moves—such as efforts to assassinate Castro—did not. But they too were part of a pattern.

In the past, great powers held sway over smaller, less developed states with a modicum of force. The U.S. maintained its authority in the Caribbean basin for half a century by dispatching a gunboat or two and sometimes landing a few marines. As recently as 1954, a small CIA-organized invasion force toppled the Arbenz regime in Guatemala. We thought we could get rid of Castro just as easily in 1961. But times were changing. Nationalism was on the rise in the Third World, accompanied by a new sense of Third World unity. As charismatic leaders galvanized popular support, it became increasingly costly, and sometimes impossible, for great powers to control the course of events in the countries of the Third World. The French defeat in Indochina in 1954 and the British-French defeat at Suez two years later were stark evidence of that. Not even the more ruthless Soviet Union could always maintain hegemony. The People's Republic of China broke away from its control—as had Yugoslavia a decade earlier.

The U.S. was to learn the same lesson at the Bay of Pigs. It grossly underestimated the extent to which Castro had harnessed the force of Cuban nationalism. It launched its small exile invasion force as though Theodore Roosevelt were still president. Even before the men of Brigade 2506 stepped ashore, their enterprise was doomed. Its only effect was to destroy internal Cuban opposition and to lock Cuba into the Soviet orbit—the exact opposite of our intention.

We learn little from experience. We followed the same pattern in Angola in 1975. A negotiated settlement was in place (the Alvor agreement). Instead of supporting it, we opted for another clandestine military operation with almost no chance of success. It blew up in our faces.

We bombed Cambodia with small thought for the consequences. Far worse, but with the same insouciance, we made the fateful decision in 1956 to support Diem's hopeless regime in not complying with the Geneva accord's provision for a plebiscite which would have determined the future of South Vietnam. We made that decision because both we and Diem knew that the result of such a plebiscite would almost certainly have been to reunite North and South under a government headed by Ho Chi Minh. This was not an outcome we wanted, to be sure, but it was hardly an intolerable one. Indeed, North and South have now been reunited for over a decade without causing serious damage to our broader interests in Southeast Asia. And not a single other Southeast Asian country has fallen to Communism. The domino theory proved invalid. On the contrary, once under Communist governments, the Vietnamese and Cambodians began fighting among themselves.

More than twenty years after the Bay of Pigs, with the same blindered analysis and with exactly the same motivation, we are trying to solve the Nicaraguan problem with another clandestine military operation. Diplomatic options have been available to us in Nicaragua; we prefer to back the *contras*, even though they cannot win.

In our dealings with the Soviet Union, we understand the limits of power. The Soviet Union can destroy us, just as we can destroy it. Clearly defined parameters exist within which we must do business.

An established framework also exists for our relationships with the European nations and with Canada and Japan. We have dealt with most of these nations ever since we ourselves became a nation, and we respect them. They are economic powers in their own right. The U.S. may be more powerful, but it cannot take them lightly or ride roughshod over them. The rules of the game are clear, and there are penalties for violating them. But in dealing with developing countries, we often seem to believe that we are still in the period of gunboat diplomacy and our superior power gives us an infinite margin for error.

We need not fold our arms passively in the face of events that affect our interests. We *are* a global power. But we must learn to deal with ambiguity and to realize that we need not always insist on optimum solutions. In this complex world, moreover, there are sometimes better instruments than force, whether openly or clandestinely applied, to achieve our ends.

Since getting rid of the Castro regime is not a viable option, American policy makers should be asking themselves how best to deal with him so as to advance legitimate U.S. objectives. To do this would be simply a matter of facing facts. It would not imply that we have come to like Castro or to find him a compatible neighbor; rather, we would be approaching the problem realistically and pragmatically.

Since 1961, no American president has dealt sensibly and effectively with the Cuba problem. Most have refused to deal with the Cubans at all. In several cases, our failure to devise an effective Cuba policy has had consequences far beyond the context of U.S.-Cuban relations. The Bay of Pigs was Kennedy's saddest hour. He regained the confidence of the Western alliance—and of the American people—only as the world came to the brink of war with the 1962 Cuban missile crisis, which Kennedy handled brilliantly but which left us with a *status quo ante* in Cuba. The SALT II treaty had to be shelved in 1979 because of the Carter administration's inept handling of the Soviet-brigade issue. The treaty died, and with it the hope of détente, when we sought withdrawal of a Soviet unit which had been there for years, which posed no conceivable threat to the U.S., and which we had not the slightest possibility of evicting.

In the final analysis, indeed, the Carter administration's approach to the Cuba problem differed little from that of past administrations. It was not based on realistic expectations, was not geared to achievable objectives, and was not conducted on the basis of reciprocity. Had Secretary of State Vance had the upper hand, matters might have turned out differently. He genuinely wished for a new beginning in our Cuban relationship, and he also wished our actions to be carefully geared to clear and sensible U.S. objectives. But Brzezinski's National Security Council very quickly came to have the deciding voice in Cuba policy, and it was little interested in that sort of patient and low-keyed approach. Brzezinski, indeed, often seemed more interested in scoring propaganda points against the Cubans than in resolving discrepancies between us. As relations became strained anew, the Carter administration retreated to the time-worn tactic of threats and invective. Little thought was given to seeking through long-term engagement what we could not achieve in the short term through preemptory demands.

The problem was not that diplomacy availed us nothing; quite the contrary, it was that we made little use of diplomacy. This was true in the Angolan situation; it was true again in Ethiopia; and it was certainly true of our handling, or mishandling, of the Mariel crisis.

Under the Reagan administration, relations between Cuba and the U.S. have reached a new low. While Ford and Carter showed some initial, albeit short-lived, willingness to be more flexible toward Cuba, the Reagan administration's approach from the beginning has been one of unbending hostility and rigid refusal to negotiate any of the problems which stand between the two countries. More than with any previous administration, this refusal is based on an ideological mind-set. The Reagan administration sees the world in Manichean terms, and Castro represents the darkest of the forces of darkness. Its conviction, despite much evidence to the contrary, is that Castro has changed not at all in twenty-five years and that he remains as unwilling to accommodate our concerns now as he was in 1959.[7]

The administration has not tested this hypothesis. It has made no real effort to engage the Cubans in meaningful dialogue and see if they are in fact serious. Nor has the administration's hard line accomplished anything. Cuba is no less a problem to us today than it was five years ago. Soviet influence has not been reduced. No political prisoners have been released. Cuba's foreign policy has not become less assertive since 1981, and we have not succeeded in isolating Cuba. Quite the contrary, Cuba has greater respectability in Latin America today than when the Reagan administration came to office.

If our failure to deal effectively with Cuba were an isolated phenomenon, if the attitudes and miscalculations behind that failure had not been repeated elsewhere, we might dismiss it as of limited importance. But that is not the case. Neither the failure to devise an effective policy nor the factors behind that failure are unique to the Cuban case. They are part of a syndrome with general application, and hence all the more necessary to correct.

There is much else that we need to correct. If American foreign policy is to be true to the dreams of our forefathers, it must be guided by higher principles and hew to more rigorous standards than has been the case of late. Ours is a nation under law, dedicated to the proposition that the rule of law should prevail in the international community as well. That proposition is undermined by the clandestine military operations which have become a growing habit with us. These operations are not only illegal and unworthy of us but also ineffective. What did we accomplish by printing an assassination manual for the *contras* and illegally mining Nicaraguan harbors? How can we claim to further the rule of law by refusing to accept the jurisdiction of the World Court?

Further, our democratic system rests on the presumption that the people are informed. But how can they be informed, how can they know the facts, and how then can our system function as it should, when our government so consistently misrepresents the facts, and even lies outright? Misrepresentation became a habit during the Vietnam war, and it is one we have not broken; rather, with the Reagan administration it has been raised to an art. This willingness to mislead and misrepresent is intolerable. The American people have a right to expect more of their government.

There are those who believe that to find fault with our government's conduct is unpatriotic. Criticism of President Reagan's policies is enough to qualify one for inclusion in Jeane Kirkpatrick's "blame America first" crowd (though of course Kirkpatrick didn't hesitate to criticize President Carter's policies when he was in office). But those who put forward such concepts in fact demonstrate nothing more than their own ignorance of our system, which is firmly based on the free debate of ideas and on the citizen's right to criticize. Were it otherwise, were we expected to accept all our government's actions and assertions with bovine smiles, then indeed we would have entered an Orwellian world. But that, thank God, is not the case. America is still America. The chorus on the right notwithstanding, it is *not* unpatriotic to demand better of ourselves and our government—and thus of our country. It is when we do not do so that we traduce our heritage.

Notes

1. EARLY DAYS, 1957–1959

1. For an excellent glimpse of those differences, see John Dorschner and Roberto Fabricio, *The Winds of December* (New York: Coward, McCann and Geoghegan, 1980), pp. 48–59.

2. Quoted in Jules Dubois, *Fidel Castro* (New York: Bobbs-Merrill, 1959), p. 216.

3. Ibid., pp. 218–19.

4. *New York Times,* 3 March 1958, p. 11.

5. Earl E. T. Smith, *The Fourth Floor* (New York: Random House, 1962), p. 69.

6. *New York Times,* 23 March 1958, p. 12.

7. Smith, op. cit., p. 66.

8. Ibid., pp. 66–68.

9. Ibid., p. 71.

10. Ibid., p. 86.

11. Ibid., p. 87.

12. For a full discussion of de Velasco's account, see Dubois, op. cit., pp. 223–25.

13. Ibid., p. 229.

14. Smith's conversation with de Velasco and the subsequent issuance of the Joint Committee's March 18 statement were reported to the Department of State by Embassy Dispatch 739, 20 March 1958. As this would have been received in Washington several days after it was dated, the department was informed well after the fact. Smith threw cold water on the statement's significance by saying in the dispatch that it called for the Batista regime to commit suicide and that "it seemed unrealistic to expect the government to heed such a call."

15. Walter LaFeber, *Inevitable Revolutions* (New York: W. W. Norton, 1983), p. 137.

16. Smith, op. cit., p. 10.

17. Dorschner and Fabricio, op. cit., pp. 71–72.

18. Ibid., pp. 158–71.

19. As related to me by John Topping in a conversation in January 1959.

20. Ibid. See also Dorschner and Fabricio, op. cit., pp. 159–61.

21. See Smith, op. cit., pp. 170–75, for an account of his meeting with Batista.

22. Dorschner and Fabricio, op. cit., is an excellent account of the last days of the Batista regime.

2. EARLY DAYS, 1959–1961

1. *Communist Threat to the United States through the Caribbean.* Hearings before the Senate Subcommittee to Investigate the Administration of the Internal Security Act and Other Internal Security Laws, 86th Cong., 1st sess., 164–66. Testimony of Gen. C. P. Cabell, deputy director of the CIA, 5 November 1959.

2. An adjective I often heard applied to Guevara by Soviet officials during the time I was stationed in Moscow. Cuban-Soviet relations in 1967 and early 1968 had reached a near breaking point, and the Soviets did little to hide their disdain for the Cuban leadership, especially for Guevara—until his death in October 1967.

3. Dubois, op. cit., pp. 372–74.

4. *Revolucíon,* 20 April 1959.

5. *Revolucíon,* 18 April and 20 April 1959.

6. Quoted in Herbert S. Dinerstein, *The Making of the Missile Crisis* (Baltimore: Johns Hopkins University Press, 1976), p. 41.

7. As reported in Andrés Suarez, *Cuba, Castroism and Communism, 1959–1966* (Cambridge, Mass.: M.I.T. Press, 1967), p. 48.

8. For an eloquent statement of this view, see Maurice Zeitlin and Robert Scheer, *Cuba: Tragedy in Our Hemisphere* (New York: Grove Press, 1963).

9. As related to me by Robert A. Stevenson, who was Cuban Desk officer during Castro's visit in 1959.

10. As related to me by Juan "Pepín" Bosch, the head of the Bacardi rum company, who accompanied Castro to the U.S. as one of his economic advisers. Bosch was my neighbor in Recife, Brazil, in 1962. We had many conversations at that time about Cuba and Castro.

11. Philip W. Bonsal, *Cuba, Castro and the United States* (Pittsburgh: University of Pittsburgh Press, 1971), pp. 70–77.

12. For another discussion of this question, see my occasional paper *Castro's Cuba: Soviet Partner or Nonaligned?* (Washington, D.C.: Woodrow Wilson Center, 1984).

13. Herbert Matthews, *The Cuban Story* (New York: George Braziller, 1961), p. 191.

14. David Burks, *Cuba under Castro* (New York: Headline Series, Foreign Policy Association, 1964), p. 31.

15. *Bohemia* (Havana), 31 January 1960.

16. *Revolución,* 17 April 1961.

17. *Revolución,* 2 December 1961.

18. *Pravda,* 10 July 1960.

19. Burks, op. cit., p. 13.

20. For a more detailed discussion of this point, see my "Soviet Policy and Ideological Formulations for Latin America," *Orbis,* Winter 1972, pp. 1127–28.

Notes

21. For an excellent discussion of Castro's calculations, see Jacques Levesque, *The USSR and the Cuban Revolution* (New York: Praeger, 1978), p. 10.

22. *Pravda*, 2 May 1962.

23. Bonsal, op. cit., p. 128.

3. THE YEARS OF DIVORCE, 1961–1977

1. For an excellent account of the disaster, see Peter Wyden's *Bay of Pigs: The Untold Story* (New York: Simon and Schuster, 1979). See also Tad Szulc and Karl Meyer, *The Cuban Invasion: The Chronicle of Disaster* (New York: Ballantine Books, 1962).

2. For an independent account of the aid mess in the Northeast, see Joseph Page, *The Revolution That Never Was* (New York: Grossman, 1972).

3. For the best discussions of the crisis, see Robert F. Kennedy, *Thirteen Days: A Memoir of the Cuban Missile Crisis* (New York: W. W. Norton, 1969); Herbert S. Dinerstein, *The Making of a Missile Crisis: October 1962* (Baltimore: Johns Hopkins University Press, 1976); and Henry M. Pachter, *Collision Course: The Cuban Missile Crisis and Coexistence* (New York: Praeger, 1963).

4. Duplicates of the "Kennedy and Khrushchev messages are in my files.

5. See Dean Rusk, Robert McNamara, George Ball, Theodore Sorensen, and McGeorge Bundy, "The Lessons of the Missile Crisis," *Time*, September 27, 1982, pp. 85–86. See also Kennedy, op. cit.

6. Wayne S. Smith, "Clements Guilty of Revisionism on JFK's Cuba Understanding," *Dallas Times Herald*, 26 March 1984.

7. See Raymond L. Garthoff, "American Reaction to Soviet Aircraft in Cuba, 1962 and 1978," *Political Science Quarterly*, Fall 1980, pp. 438–39.

8. William Attwood, *The Reds and the Blacks* (New York: Harper and Row, 1967), pp. 142–44. I am grateful to Bill Attwood for taking the time to discuss this episode with me and give me his personal views on the matter. Attwood, like Kennedy, had the impression the Cubans were sincerely interested in easing tensions.

9. Maurice Halperin, *The Taming of Fidel Castro* (Berkeley: University of California Press, 1981), p. 110.

10. For example, in the Khrushchev-Castro communiqué issued at the end of Fidel's trip to Moscow in January 1964, the Cuban side stated that it was "ready to do whatever is necessary to establish good neighborly relations with the United States." A copy of this communiqué is in my possession.

11. *New York Times*, 6 July 1964, p. 1.

12. Halperin, op. cit., pp. 94–106.

13. For an excellent account of the Tri-Continent Congress, see D. Bruce Jackson, *Castro, the Kremlin and Communism in Latin America* (Baltimore: Johns Hopkins University Press, 1969).

14. For the text of Castro's July 19 speech, see *Granma*, 20 July 1969.

15. See my testimony of 5 April 1978 in *Impact of Cuban-Soviet Ties in the Western Hemisphere*. Hearings before the House Subcommittee on Inter-American Affairs, 95th Cong., 2d sess., 56–61.

16. *Toward Improved United States–Cuba Relations*, Report of a Special Study

Mission to Cuba, 10–15 February 1977 (Washington, D.C.: U.S. Government Printing Office, 1978).

17. Ibid., p. 71.

18. Ibid., p. 65.

19. Ibid., p. 57.

20. For revealing accounts, see John Stockwell, *In Search of Enemies: A CIA Story* (New York: W. W. Norton, 1978); Roger Morris, "The Proxy War in Angola: Pathology of a Blunder," *New Republic*, 31 January 1976, pp. 19–23; John A. Marcum, "Lessons of Angola," *Foreign Affairs*, April 1976, pp. 407–25; and, for one of the most thorough accounts, William M. Leogrande, "Cuban-Soviet Relations and Cuban Policy in Africa," in *Cuba in Africa*, edited by Carmelo Mesa-Lago and June S. Belkin (Pittsburgh: University of Pittsburgh Press, 1982).

21. *New York Times*, 19 December 1975, p. 1.

22. Stockwell, op. cit., p. 68.

23. Ibid., p. 67.

24. Ibid., p. 68.

25. Ibid., p. 188.

26. Leogrande, op. cit., p. 25.

27. Much of this account is drawn from my article "A Trap in Angola," *Foreign Policy*, Spring 1986, pp. 61–75.

28. *Toward Improved United States–Cuba Relations*, op. cit., pp. 49–50.

29. Ibid., p. 52.

4. The Carter Opening, 1977

1. *New York Times*, 11 January 1977, p. 1.

2. Secretary of state's press conference, 31 January 1977.

3. Statement at the Department of State's noon briefing, 3 February 1977.

4. Statement at a press conference in Plains, Georgia, 13 February 1977.

5. Press conference in Plains, Georgia, 11 March 1977.

6. *Toward Improved United States–Cuba Relations*, op. cit., p. 43.

7. Secretary of state's press conference, 4 March 1977.

8. Senator McGovern's press conference, 11 April 1977, after his return from Cuba.

9. See *Toward Improved United States–Cuba Relations*, op. cit., p. 37.

10. Ibid., p. 38.

11. Ibid., p. 36.

12. This certainly was the view of Secretary of State Vance. See Cyrus Vance, *Hard Choices* (New York: Simon and Schuster, 1983), p. 131.

13. *New York Times*, 13 November 1977, p. 1.

14. Guinea, Guinea-Bissau, Sierra Leone, Benin, Equatorial Guinea, Congo (Brazzaville), Angola, Mozambique, Malagasay Republic, Tanzania, Uganda, Ethiopia, and Libya.

15. *New York Times*, 17 November 1977, pp. 1, 11.

16. Vance, op. cit., p. 71.

Notes

5. Cuba, the United States, and Africa

1. Vance, op. cit., p. 73.
2. Stated to me by Fidel Castro in a conversation in June 1978.
3. *Afrique-Asie* (Paris), 13 June 1977.
4. *New York Times*, 12 June 1977, p. 1.
5. Vance, op. cit., p. 73.
6. Ibid.
7. Ibid.
8. Zbigniew Brzezinski, *Power and Principle* (New York: Farrar, Straus and Giroux, 1983), p. 179.
9. Stated in our conversation in June 1978.
10. Nelson Valdes, "Cuba's Involvement in the Horn of Africa: The Ethiopian-Somali War and the Eritrean Conflict," in *Cuba in Africa*, edited by Carmelo Mesa-Lago and June S. Belkin (Pittsburgh: University of Pittsburgh Press, 1982), p. 71.
11. Vance, op. cit., pp. 74–75.
12. Brzezinski, op. cit., pp. 181–84.
13. Ibid., p. 189.
14. Ibid., p. 184.
15. Ibid., p. 185.
16. Vance, op. cit., p. 88.
17. Ibid., p. 90.
18. *New York Times*, 10 June 1978, p. 1.
19. *New York Times*, 26 May 1978, p. 10.
20. *New York Times*, 15 June 1978, p. 18.
21. In a conversation with me in 1982, Carlos Rafael Rodríguez recalled his consternation at receiving two such mixed signals on the same day. Castro was quoted in the *New York Times* of 13 June 1978 as expressing puzzlement on having received a courteous reply to his offer to Lyle Lane (the cable Vance had instructed me to send) and then virtually the next day having been called a liar by the NSC.
22. *New York Times*, 13 June 1978, p. 8.

6. The Cubans Try to Revive the Process, 1978

1. A perception confirmed to me by Castro in a conversation in 1980.
2. This was confirmed to me by a mid-level Cuban official in 1980.
3. According to a friend in the Cuban government who related it to me in a conversation in 1979.
4. *New York Times*, 19 November 1978, p. 13.
5. *Washington Post*, 25 November 1978, p. 14.
6. Garthoff, op. cit., pp. 427–39.

7. Growing Problems, 1979

1. Quoted in Shirley Christian, *Nicaragua: Revolution in the Family* (New York: Random House, 1985), pp. 86–87.
2. Ibid., p. 99.
3. For one such statement, see the *New York Times*, 9 July 1980, A 10.

4. Senate Foreign Relations Committee statement of 17 July 1979, in Media Notice of that date.

5. Vance, op. cit., p. 361.

6. Ibid., p. 362. See also Jimmy Carter, *Keeping Faith* (New York: Bantam Books, 1983), p. 263.

7. The text of Castro's speech at the Sixth Non-Aligned Summit appears in the English-language version of *Addresses Delivered at the Sixth Conference of Heads of State and Governments of Non-Aligned Countries* (Havana: Editorial de Ciencias Sociales, 1979), pp. 3–16.

8. THE YEAR OF MARIEL, 1980

1. *Granma*, 10 March 1980.

2. *Granma*, 18 April 1980.

3. *New York Times*, 24 April 1980, p. 1.

4. *New York Times*, 6 May 1980, p. 1.

5. *New York Times*, 15 May 1980, p. 1.

9. ENTER THE REAGAN ADMINISTRATION

1. Havana telegram 2069, 25 March 1981, "Assessment of Internal Conditions in Cuba," and Havana telegram 2376, 10 April 1981, "Cuban Foreign Policy: Recapitulation and Assessment," have been released under the Freedom of Information Act and are available for examination by those interested in the sort of recommendations that were being made by the U.S. interests section in Havana at that time.

2. In November 1980, six leaders of the Revolutionary Democratic Front (FDR), who had met in a Jesuit school to discuss political openings to the government, were abducted by the army and murdered.

3. Alexander M. Haig, Jr., *Caveat: Realism, Reagan, and Foreign Policy* (New York: Macmillan, 1984), p. 131.

4. Ibid.

5. *Washington Post*, 27 March 1982.

6. *Dealing with the Reality of Cuba.* Hearings before the House Subcommittees on Inter-American Affairs and on International Economic Policies and Trade, 97th Cong., 2d sess. Testimony of Thomas O. Enders, 14 December 1982. Published subsequently by the Department of State as Current Policy Paper No. 443, p. 2.

7. Haig., op. cit., pp. 133–36.

8. Ibid.

9. "60 Minutes" program of 25 November 1984.

10. EPILOGUE

1. Published as "Dateline Havana: Myopic Diplomacy," *Foreign Policy*, Fall 1982, pp. 157–74.

2. Unclassified supplement to the *Open Forum Journal*, Summer 1984.

3. On 18 August 1982, only two days after I had left the Foreign Service, my article "Why Start a Radio War?" appeared on the op-ed page of the *Washington Post*.

4. See *New York Times*, 30 July 1983, p. 1, and *Washington Post*, 14 August 1983, p. 1.

Notes

5. See "Time for a Thaw," *New York Times Magazine*, 29 July 1984, p. 22.

6. See my discussion of these issues in "The Price to be Paid," on the Opinion and Commentary page of the *Baltimore Sun*, 11 November 1983.

11. CONCLUSIONS

1. For example, in Prensa Latina dispatches of 27 and 28 April 1982.

2. *Commentary*, November 1979, pp. 34–35.

3. See William H. Sullivan, *Obbligato, 1939–1979: Notes on a Foreign Service Career* (New York: W. W. Norton, 1984), pp. 261–79.

4. As stated by David Aaron in a public forum at the Department of State, 26 June 1984.

5. Jimmy Carter, op. cit., p. 44.

6. Gary Sick makes the argument that the ingredients for a moderate solution were really missing from the Iranian situation and that Ambassador Sullivan was simply misreading the signs if he thought otherwise. See *All Fall Down: America's Tragic Encounter with Iran* (New York: Random House, 1985), pp. 132–38.

7. See, for example, the statements in *The Soviet-Cuban Connection in Central America and the Caribbean*, a pamphlet jointly released by the Departments of State and Defense in March 1985. And at a round-table discussion in 1983, an administration spokesman asserted: "The fundamental goals of the Cuban leadership have not changed in nearly twenty-five years." See *Report on Cuba: Findings of the Study Group on U.S.-Cuban Relations* (A Westview Press/SAIS Foreign Policy Institute Edition, 1984), p. 14.

Index

Italicized page numbers refer to photographs

BOOKS ON LATIN AMERICA IN NORTON PAPERBACK

Five Letters, 1519-1526 by Hernando Cortes

Empire in Brazil: A New World Experiment with Monarchy
by C. H. Haring

*Journeys Toward Progress: Studies of Economic
Policy-Making in Latin America* by Albert O. Hirschman

Inevitable Revolutions: The United States in Central America
by Walter LaFeber

Puerto Rico: A Political and Cultural History
by Arturo Morales Carrión

*An Affair of Honor: Woodrow Wilson and the Occupation
of Veracruz* by Robert E. Quirk

Cuba: The Making of a Revolution by Ramón Eduardo Ruiz

The Great Rebellion: Mexico 1905-1924
by Ramón Eduardo Ruiz